Elvis Presley, Richard Nixon, and the American Dream

Elvis Presley, Richard Nixon, and the American Dream

by CONNIE KIRCHBERG *and* MARC HENDRICKX

McFarland & Company, Inc., Publishers
Jefferson, North Carolina

For Presley and Nixon,
whose determination inspires us all
to believe in ourselves.

Frontispiece and front cover: Richard Nixon and Elvis Presley in the Oval Office on December 21, 1970. (Photographs by Ollie Atkins. Courtesy Nixon Presidential Materials Project, National Archives.)

Lyrics from "Good Time Charlie's Got the Blues" by Danny O'Keefe ©1968 (renewed) Warner-Tamerlane Publishing Corp. and Road Canon Music, Inc. All Rights Reserved. Used by permission of Warner Bros. Publications U.S. Inc., Miami, FL 22014.

> *The present work is a reprint of the illustrated case bound edition of* Elvis Presley, Richard Nixon, and the American Dream, *first published in 1999 by McFarland.*

LIBRARY OF CONGRESS CATALOGUING-IN-PUBLICATION DATA

Kirchberg, Connie, 1956–
    Elvis Presley, Richard Nixon, and the American dream / by Connie Kirchberg and Marc Hendrickx.
        p.   cm.
    Includes bibliographical references and index.

    ISBN 978-1-4766-6399-9 (softcover : acid free paper) ∞
    ISBN 978-1-4766-2337-5 (ebook)

    1. Presley, Elvis, 1935–1977.   2. Rock musicians — United States — Biography.   3. Nixon, Richard M. (Richard Milhous), 1913–1994.   4. Presidents — United States — Biography. I. Hendrickx, Marc, 1969–   II. Title.
ML420.P96K57   2015
306'.0973 — dc21   99-41213

BRITISH LIBRARY CATALOGUING DATA ARE AVAILABLE

© 1999 Connie Kirchberg and Marc Hendrickx. All rights reserved

No part of this book may be reproduced or transmitted in any form or by any means, electronic or mechanical, including photocopying or recording, or by any information storage and retrieval system, without permission in writing from the publisher.

Printed in the United States of America

McFarland & Company, Inc., Publishers
    Box 611, Jefferson, North Carolina 28640
        www.mcfarlandpub.com

Table of Contents

Introduction   1

1. From a Jack to a King   3
2. Education Makes the Man   9
3. A Watchful Eye on the Future   12
4. Let the Games Begin   29
5. The Shaping of a Hero   43
6. The Survival of the Fittest   58
7. The New America: Hippies, Drugs, and Vietnam   80
8. The King Meets the President   89
9. No Man Is an Island   98
10. The Cancer Within   111
11. My Way: The Lonely Road to Recovery   141

Conclusion: Let the Record Show   169

Appendix: Documents and Photographs Pertaining to the Presley-Nixon Meeting   173
Notes   207
Select Bibliography   215
Index   219

Introduction

There is probably an element of malice in the readiness to overestimate people; we are laying up for ourselves the pleasure of later cutting them down to size.

— Eric Hoffer, American philosopher

Elvis Presley and Richard Nixon. At first glance, one cannot help wondering what these two men could possibly have in common. Yet close examination reveals amazing parallels, fateful circumstances that guided each through his rise from humble beginnings to the pinnacle of success. By the time their paths crossed at the height of their respective careers, Nixon and Presley had overcome numerous, similar hardships in their struggles to capture the elusive American Dream. How that dream slipped from each man's grasp — and why — provides the focus for this book.

History is rich with legends and heroes. Whether Presley and Nixon will share space with Beethoven and Lincoln depends on the criteria used in judgment. What, for example, defines a legend? "One that inspires legends or achieves legendary fame," according to the *American Heritage Dictionary*. An interesting supplement is found in the usage note: "The words legend and legendary have come to be used in recent years to refer to any person or achievement whose fame promises to be particularly enduring, even if its renown is created more by the media than by oral tradition." Few would argue that this type of "legend" has become common in modern times: rock stars who make headlines by punching fans, sports celebrities who break contracts when a teammate receives more money, criminal attorneys who handle high-profile cases. We come to know their names and faces from the covers of the tabloids, but does that notoriety qualify them as bona fide legends? Most are unlikely to be remembered five, let alone 50, years from now.

To understand the true meaning of a legend, we must go beyond the simple definition quoted above and trace the history of the word in its basic form.

"A legend is a long-told story or a group of related stories about a person or a place that is popularly believed to have some historical truth," reports *Grolier's Encyclopedia*. "Mythology, in contrast, frequently takes the divine or the supernatural as its primary subject. Myths and legends are often intermixed." Indeed. What person could stand alone as a legend without a little bit of myth thrown in? A rumor here, an exaggeration there, and an already bigger-than-life individual becomes superhuman, an example to look up to, an ideal toward which we strive.

When exploring the synonyms for legendary, we find renowned, celebrated, great, noble, glorious, unfading, immortal, eternal. Negative terms are noticeably absent. How, then, is it possible for a human to become a legend? People are not without faults, nor are they immortal. Although men and women might rise to legendary fame, it is their *reputations*, surviving in the wake of their mortality, that become legend.

"A person noted for special achievement in a particular field," states the *American Heritage Dictionary*, is a hero; "a person noted for feats of courage or nobility of purpose." A person. A mortal, not without faults. Before there were legends, there had to be heroes.

Although most synonyms for "hero" are positive (good person, sterling character, model of virtue), others are ambiguous (idealist) or afflicted or challenging (brick, diamond-in-the-rough, ugly duckling). Exhibiting the range of such qualities, Nixon and Presley strove for, and ultimately realized, the American Dream. Whether their reputations will become legendary, only time will tell. As Ralph Waldo Emerson aptly put it, "To be great is to be misunderstood."

Chapter 1

From a Jack to a King

Life is essentially a cheat and its conditions are those of defeat ... the redeeming things are not "happiness and pleasure" but the deeper satisfactions that come out of struggle.

— F. Scott Fitzgerald, American author

In fiction, memorable characters become real to the reader by seeming to live and breathe on the page. How does an author manage to create this fictive illusion? Every character is a combination of the writer who creates him, the people she knows, and the town in which she grew up. This is no less true of real people. By examining their histories, we can see how their characters and personalities evolved and gain a basic understanding of their behaviors in given situations. We begin our study, then, with a glimpse into the Presley and Nixon family albums.

No one who lived across the tracks in East Tupelo, Mississippi, ever referred to Vernon Presley as a stellar family provider; he drifted from one low paying job to the next, with substantial rest periods in between. But when the responsibility of fatherhood landed on his shoulders, Vernon proved up to the task. Despite his precarious history, he managed to secure a $180 mortgage to build a house for his wife, Gladys, and their child-to-be.

In this sturdy two-room shack, with no indoor plumbing or electricity, Gladys gave birth to twins in the early morning hours of January 8, 1935. The first child, Jesse Garon, emerged from the warmth of his mother's womb cold and still, unable to cope with the hardships of life. Elvis Aron burst onto the scene thirty minutes later, lungs breathing and heart pounding, ready to take on the world. Jesse was laid to rest in an unmarked grave at the local cemetery, a spot Elvis would return to many times.

The roots of his humble beginning remained deeply embedded in Elvis's character as he rose to heights far above even his own expectations or dreams. "The money, the financial end of it isn't the most important," he said during an interview amid the glitzy backdrop of Hollywood some 27 years later. "It can't be, because if it was, it would show, and I wouldn't care about other people."[1]

Life did not have quite so tragic a beginning for Richard Milhous Nixon although, economically, his family was not much better off than the Presleys. The senior Nixons ran a floundering lemon ranch in Yorba Linda, California, a small farming community about 30 miles east of Los Angeles. Richard, the second of five sons born to Francis and Hannah Nixon, entered the world on January 9, 1913, in a "poor, lower-middle-class family," as he would later describe it. "I suppose it could be said that we too were poor," he admitted, "but our parents left us a legacy far richer than anything money could buy."[2]

No more blessed with opportunity than Vernon, Francis had been only eight when his mother died of tuberculosis. Four years later, he was forced to quit school after completing the sixth grade; an able-bodied "man" at the ripe age of 12, he was expected to help support the family. Among his many jobs were farm hand, sheep shearer, and oil field roustabout. Like Vernon, his self-taught carpentry skills enabled him to build a modest home for his family when the time arrived.

Unlike the elder Presley, however, Francis Nixon was ambitious. Everyone who knew him gave him that. According to Richard, this was because he wanted only the best for his sons. "Above all, he wanted us to have the education he had been unable to have," Richard Nixon wrote in *In the Arena* (page 80). Francis was determined his boys would perform to the best of their abilities as far as their studies went and made it clear that he would accept no less.

Vernon, too, wanted his son to get an education. Referring to himself as a "common laborer,"[3] however, he obviously viewed the world through less-demanding eyes. Like Francis, he had dropped out of school well before graduating, most likely for similar reasons: he was capable of contributing to the family income. Because such attitudes continued to prevail in East Tupelo, one of the poorest communities in Mississippi, it stands to reason that Vernon, barely able to read himself, would have been happy if his son made it through high school. Expecting straight *A*s was beyond comprehension.

Speculation aside, one thing is certain: both Elvis and Richard grew up knowing what hard work meant. Times were rough. Their mothers had to find paying jobs to put food on the table. Although two-income families are in the majority today, such was not the case during Presley's or Nixon's childhood.

Gladys Presley did whatever necessary to make ends meet, even when it meant swallowing her pride. Head held high, she trekked off to the welfare office every week, Elvis in hand, to collect the family's allowance of butter, rice, and cheese. Most days were spent on a nearby farm, where she picked cotton for 50 cents per 100 pounds.[4] When Elvis was old enough to be left with a relative during the day, she went to work at the Mid-South Laundry.

During Richard's early years, Hannah Nixon worked side by side with her husband at the family lemon ranch her parents had helped them establish in their home town of Yorba Linda. Profits were not as generous as expected, however, forcing both Hannah and Francis to supplement their income with various odd jobs. When Richard was nine, the Nixons sold the property and moved to Whittier, where they ran a gas station and small grocery store. Hannah rose at four in the morning to bake the pies and cakes that were sold at the deli counter.

This self-sacrifice on their mothers' parts did not go unnoticed by Elvis or Richard and surely contributed to each boy's inner desire to make good, to be deserving of such unconditional love. Neither son would disappoint.

For Presley, the mission to prove himself worthy began when he was born. He lived, Jesse Garon died. As soon as he was old enough to comprehend his brother's death, Elvis must have asked himself why he had been the one to survive. There were no immediate answers, making it probable that young Presley felt terrible guilt simply for being alive.

As fate would have it, Elvis remained an only child; Gladys suffered a miscarriage when he was seven and was unable to conceive again. This, too, probably weighed on Presley's mind as he was growing up. He was the special one, the chosen one, the *only* one. Why?

The guilt came later for Richard Nixon. He was 12 when his younger brother Arthur became ill. What was thought to be a simple case of the flu turned serious overnight. Doctors were called in, none of whom was able to determine the exact cause of Arthur's deteriorating condition. The boy slipped into a coma and died three days later. The cause of death was listed as tubercular encephalitis.

Certainly Arthur's death was no more tragic than Jesse Garon's, though it stands to reason that Richard may have felt his brother's death more because he was older when it happened. Elvis could only wonder what his brother might have been like. Richard knew. For seven years, he had watched Arthur grow up beside him. Now he was gone. In his memoirs, Nixon wrote that memories of Arthur haunted him every day for weeks after the funeral, often bringing him to tears. One can only imagine the hours, the days, spent searching for answers that simply could not be found.

The questions did not end there. Another of Richard's brothers, Harold, contracted tuberculosis. During the traumatic period that followed Arthur's death, Hannah moved to Arizona with her sick child, hoping the dry climate would improve his condition. While caring for Harold, she rented a large house and took in three other patients to make ends meet. In addition to cooking and cleaning, she provided around-the-clock nursing care for all the residents.[5]

Despite Hannah's drastic efforts, Harold died in July 1933. Richard, by then on the verge of manhood at 20, was again faced with the question of how such tragedy could continue to befall his family, while he seemed exempt.

Such feelings would have naturally led to further guilt. It is logical to assume that Richard, a teenager at the time his mother went to Arizona, would have been jealous of his brother having their mother all to himself for three long years. Any child would, despite the awful circumstances.

In any event, Nixon weathered the emotional storms and became stronger for them. "With the death of Harold his determination to make us proud of him seemed greatly intensified," Hannah related in an interview years later. "Unconsciously, too, I think that Richard may have felt a kind of guilt that Harold and Arthur were dead and that he was alive."[6]

Indeed, there was plenty of guilt to go around. Gladys Presley surely asked herself if Jesse's death could have been attributed to something she had or had not done. What mother wouldn't? Living with such an after-the-fact perspective made her vow to take special care of the child who *had* survived, especially when she learned he would be her last.

Amid the dreary life of poverty-stricken Tupelo, Elvis became the one bright spot in his mother's life, and she treated him as such, but there is a notable difference between loving a child and smothering him. Naturally, Gladys was overprotective of her son at first, having lost Jesse Garon. But stories of her walking Elvis to school until he was in the tenth grade have been overblown and, for the most part, misunderstood.

Neither Gladys nor Vernon had finished elementary school, and what had been the result? One menial job after another, one run-down apartment after the next, barely enough money to put food on the table for a family of three. Gladys was determined that Elvis would not end up in the same dismal situation. She walked him to school to make sure he went every day and encouraged him to do well in his studies. When he was 13, she took him to the Tupelo library and proudly scribbled her name on the form so he could be issued his very own card, thus becoming part of the one percent of local children to make use of the facilities.[7]

In the well-researched *Elvis and Gladys*, author Elaine Dundy cites many examples of young Presley, between the ages of eight and ten, going off to town by himself on Saturday afternoons to listen to local musicians, attend radio shows, or hang out at theaters. Nowhere is there mention of Gladys standing on the sidelines, watching. She wanted for her son what all mothers want: a chance for her child to have a better life.

Stories of Elvis being forbidden to play football or participate in other rough activities because his mother was afraid he would get hurt have also been exaggerated. Presley did play football in high school. "I played end for two years," he related during an interview in Little Rock, Arkansas, in May 1956. Speaking on the same subject a few months later in Florida, he added, "I tried to play football, but...I was never very good."[8] He was not thrown off the team because of his long hair, as has been erroneously reported, usually in the context of the infamous bathroom scene, in which he was said to have been cornered by a couple of boys with scissors and then rescued by upperclassman Red West. He quit of his own accord.

While there was nothing obsessive about Gladys's love for her son, it is obvious the two formed a tight, emotional bond. At times Gladys might have been overprotective but no more so than Elvis was toward her. How many times did he watch her lay flowers on Jesse's grave? Being the son who had survived, he took great care not to endanger that life, to cause his mother any more grief. If that meant being ridiculed by some of the other boys, it seemed a small price to pay for his mother's peace of mind.

The pressure of being the "man" of the house also weighed heavily on young Presley's mind. His father made long-distance hauls for a local trucking company for a period of several years and, later, took work in Memphis, from which he was able to commute home to Tupelo only on weekends. In Vernon's absence, Gladys had to be breadwinner, housekeeper, and role model all in one. What boy would not feel guilt, knowing how hard his mother had to work just to keep a roof over his head?

Although Elvis was too young to remember his father serving jail time for forging a check (he had been less than two when Vernon was incarcerated), the embarrassment resulting from the incident followed the entire family for their remaining years in Tupelo. No doubt it contributed to Vernon's poor luck in finding a decent job locally, although, again, he had never been known as the most ambitious sort. Regardless, how could a lack of steady employment on his father's part have gone unnoticed by Elvis, even at an early age? Somewhere along the road, he came to realize that the only way his mother would ever have a more comfortable life was if *he* found a way to give it to her.

In contrast, Francis Nixon had rarely been without work when Richard was a child. His drive and determination had been enough to outweigh his lack of formal schooling.

A well-educated woman for her time, with two years of college, Hannah Milhous came from a fine Quaker family. Her quiet, soft-spoken personality was in sharp contrast to Francis's sometimes violent temper. Richard admitted the two seemed oddly matched. While it was his father's quick, Irish temper that he noticed most as a small boy, Hannah impressed him with her ability to hold her emotions in check, regardless of how harsh life became.

Together, the Nixons provided their sons with a "do as I do" example; it was one thing to fail, quite another to quit. The lemon ranch had been a bust, but Francis refused to give up on the idea of having his own business. He and Hannah took whatever odd jobs they could find until they had saved enough to try again. With every family member pitching in, the gas station Francis built proved successful enough that they were able to add on a small grocery/delicatessen. Each son was expected to pull his fair share, helping out at the store before and after school and on weekends. The Nixon boys learned early that there were no free rides in life.

Elvis may have learned a similar lesson, but Gladys softened the blow. While she did not hesitate to do whatever she thought necessary to teach her son the ways of the world, the harshness of reality was often eased by a physical warmth that Richard never knew.

In his philosophical autobiography, *In the Arena*, Nixon recalled, "For my mother, religion and love were sacred, and she never spoke of either in a familiar way.... In her whole life, I never heard her say to me or to anyone else, 'I love you.'" That was not to say that Hannah did not love her children. "Her eyes expressed the love and warmth no words could possibly convey," Nixon concluded. "She never questioned the customs of others to be more public in their professions of faith, but she insisted on doing it her way, and I followed her example."[9]

Gladys's no-holds-barred affection stayed with Elvis until the day he died. During his final television special, *Elvis in Concert*, he requested that security assist his father onto the stage. The doting son then put his arm around Vernon and told the audience how much he had missed his daddy. The elder Presley had been ill, unable to join Elvis on tour for some time.

Hannah loved quietly, more privately, from a distance. Nixon learned to do the same.

It is here, amid the realm of emotion, where we find the first major difference in our character studies of Presley and Nixon — and it proves to be the most significant one.

CHAPTER 2

Education Makes the Man

Every uneducated person is a caricature of himself.

—Friedrich von Schlegel,
German philosopher, critic, and writer

While both Presley's and Nixon's parents proved instrumental in stressing the value of a good education to their sons, they chose different means to convey the message.

Francis demanded that his boys push themselves beyond their limits—and when he talked, people listened. In his memoirs, Nixon recalled many an argument between his father and brothers Harold and Don, arguments that were carried on so loudly that they could be heard well down the street. "He was," Nixon admitted, "a strict and stern disciplinarian."[1]

If his father's hard-line approach affected young Nixon adversely, he made no mention of it in his later writings. On the contrary, there is every indication that the elder Nixon's tactics worked exactly as he had intended, at least in Richard's case. He related in *In the Arena*:

> One of the hardest things for parents is to resist the temptation to make life too easy for their children. It is contrary to human nature, but nonetheless true that not giving children something they want is often an indication not of how little you love them but how much.... I do not mean to suggest that it is good to make life hard for children. But if you make it too easy, their inevitable realization as adults that life is a continuing struggle may find them unprepared for it.[2]

Although Hannah shared in Richard's educational development—she taught him to read by the time he was six, providing him with such advanced skills that he skipped the second grade—she also realized how important it was that he develop interests *outside* of his studies. Relying heavily on her own Quaker upbringing, she made religion an important part of family activities.

The Nixons said grace at every meal, often reciting Bible verses, while on Sundays, Richard attended church four times: worship service in the morning and evening, Sunday school, and a youth meeting known as Christian Endeavor. The Nixons alternated their attendance between Methodist and Quaker churches to appease Francis, who remained a devout Methodist.

Music played an important role in Hannah's life, thus she was delighted when Richard picked up the basics of piano and violin from his Uncle Griffith. It was not long before her son was playing piano for his Sunday school class. "I thought he would be a musician, for he had a natural ear," she said in discussing Richard's childhood.[3] His talent so impressed her, in fact, that when he was 11, she sent him to live with her sister, Jane Beeson, so he could study music on a full-time basis. Jane, an accomplished performer and teacher, had studied at the Metropolitan School of Music in Indianapolis. For six months, Richard stayed with her family in Lindsay, another Quaker community in central California, receiving daily instruction.

Nixon soon had other plans for his future, but he never abandoned his musical training. Throughout his college years, he remained in the drama club, and after graduation he acted in local theater productions during his spare time. "Playing the piano is a way of expressing oneself that is perhaps even more fulfilling than writing or speaking," he wrote many years later. Musical talent, he went on to say, was one of the "highest aspirations."[4]

Elvis's introduction to music came Southern gospel–style at the First Assembly of God, where the Presleys enjoyed raising their voices in praise of the Lord. Sitting in the congregation on Sunday mornings, Gladys and Vernon watched in amazement as their two-year-old son rushed to the front of the church, determined to sing along with the choir. No matter that he was too young to pronounce the words. Imagine the sense of pride that must have filled Gladys's heart several years later when Elvis, discovering he had a natural ear for the piano, began to play for his Sunday school class.

Although Mrs. Presley continued to stress the importance of a good education throughout Elvis's childhood, as time wore on and his talent became more obvious, she saw the writing on the wall: her son would not need a college degree to become the next Jimmie Rogers. What he did need was encouragement, and this she dutifully provided: she allowed him to go into town alone on Saturday afternoons at the tender age of eight to sit in on the radio shows held at the courthouse; she talked him into accepting a guitar for his tenth birthday gift, rather than the rifle he had wanted; and, most important, she listened to him talk about his music and shared his dreams for a better tomorrow.

Unfortunately, the best of intentions aside, a parent's wishes can only go so far. When Elvis contemplated quitting school before his senior year, there was little Gladys could do to stop him. Whatever reservations Vernon had were quickly suppressed in favor of Elvis's argument: adding another full-time salary to the family income would make life easier for everyone.

Elvis was anxious to get out into the world, to find himself a full-time job and earn some money, especially when he had to watch his mother go off to her job at the hospital, where she worked as a nurse's aide. She had put on weight, her legs were swollen. If he could lighten her load with a job of his own, why waste time finishing school?

As convincing as this argument is, it would be misleading to suggest it was Elvis's sole reason for wanting to drop out of high school. So, too, are previous theories that link Presley's dilemma to academics. When questioned, former teachers and classmates described him as an "average" student; Elvis confirmed this in an interview, stating that he "got his share of B's and C's." (He remained an avid reader throughout his lifetime, with particular interest in studies of religion and philosophy.) Elvis was not on the verge of flunking out. He was itching to get a band together and start playing some of the local clubs, hoping he might be discovered.

In the end, Presley gave in to his mother's wishes and remained in school — not because he feared her wrath, but because he respected and loved her.

Likewise, Nixon remained in charge of his own destiny. While he may have credited his father for his relentless drive and determination, in the end, it was Richard who did the studying, Richard who won the debates, Richard who worked his way through law school. Clearly, a college education had been on his mind as early as age nine, when, upon reading of the Teapot Dome scandal, he proclaimed, "Mother, when I get big, I'm going to be a lawyer they can't bribe."[5]

Thus, sporting a varied foundation of love and support, Presley and Nixon began their respective journeys in search of the American Dream.

CHAPTER 3

A Watchful Eye on the Future

I have always thought that one man of tolerable abilities may work great changes, and accomplish great affairs among mankind, if he first forms a good plan, and, cutting off all amusements or other employments that would divert his attention, make the execution of that same plan his sole study and business.

— Benjamin Franklin

Battling the circumstances of their respective milieus, Presley and Nixon remained determined to achieve the education valued by their parents.

In Richard's case, he carried out his father's wishes far beyond a high school diploma. With college plans looming on the horizon at an early age, extracurricular activities — sports, drama, and the like — were incorporated into his schedule on a very limited basis. While most young men would have rebelled against such a restricted social life, Nixon embraced it as an opportunity to achieve his intermediate goal: to finish at the head of his class academically, so that his next focus point, a college scholarship, would fall within reach.

It was a plan that looked good on paper but, for Richard, achieving those grades was not simply a matter of gathering his books together and retreating to his bedroom to study. Harold's prolonged illness put a tremendous strain on the family's modest finances. Even Hannah's devout Quaker ideals could not keep Francis from operating the store seven days a week. While Richard may have credited his father's personality for fueling his early drive and determination, that same commanding authority produced an atmosphere of constant tension on the home front. Day and night, Francis Nixon was a time bomb ready to explode at the least provocation.

Richard saw his brothers repeatedly step on land mines. Learning from their mistakes, he managed to manipulate his way around the explosives; more important, he did so without creating distance between himself and his father. In discussing Richard's childhood, Hannah said she could not recall him ever being spanked, a fate not shared by any of the other Nixon boys. Richard confirmed as much in later writings, concluding that if he had not learned to abide by the rules, he probably would have "felt the touch of a ruler or the strap as [his] brothers did."[1] As a child, he must have done his fair share of raising his father's ire. Boys will be boys. But *this* boy escaped his brothers' fate of physical punishment by thinking before he acted. Not an easy thing for a child to do, but Richard was not one to search for the easy way out.

Watching from the sidelines when his father's passion for politics struck, Nixon also came to appreciate the positive aspects of emotion. On numerous occasions, he listened while his conservative father argued with Bill Ross, a liberal Democrat with whom Francis had about as much in common as do Senator Edward Kennedy and former Speaker Newt Gingrich today. Despite their strong differences of opinion as to the government's role in society, Francis and Ross remained the best of friends, a lesson that disagreement and tolerance could work hand in hand.

The parable went beyond its surface definition, of course. When all was said, Francis rarely came away with the short end of the stick. Richard took the lesson to heart: consider all sides of the issue but learn how to win.

The tactic proved successful as early as the sixth grade, when Richard was involved in his first debate. The question: whether it was more profitable to own or rent your home. Girls were to argue for owning, boys for renting. A discouraged Nixon was convinced the girls had the only winnable argument, but his father was unwilling to concede so easily. Francis explained to his anxious son that while home ownership might be more prestigious to the ego, the actual cost of renting was far less because repairs and upkeep were the responsibility of the landlord. Richard worked out the figures for a test case. The boys won the debate.

The next year, the topic was whether insects were more harmful than beneficial. Nixon had to argue in the bugs' favor. Francis's advice: when in doubt, consult an expert. He took Richard to visit his Uncle Philip, an entomologist for the State Inspectors Service, who pointed out that if it weren't for bees pollinating the plants, all foliage would die. Another winning argument.

Nixon came away from these early endeavors with yet another valuable lesson: "The best tactic in a debate is always to concentrate on one fundamentally strong argument rather than to scatter your fire over a broad area."[2]

Concentrating on one thing became a strategy he incorporated into other aspects of his life. Although his academic pursuits remained a top priority throughout high school, he also set time aside for social activities, because they were an essential part of his plan. If he expected to become a successful politician, Richard knew he would have to overcome his shy personality.

Today, television correspondents are on the scene with cameras to record every move; a candidate can speak to a small group and have her remarks reach millions of viewers. In the 1930s, congressional hopefuls became known to their constituencies only by interacting with them face to face. TV was still in its infancy 25 years later, when Elvis burst onto the music scene, yet the power of its impact at that time cannot be denied. Although Presley's early records did well in the South, national exposure was not forthcoming until he appeared on the *Dorsey Brothers Stage Show*.

Nixon made wise use of the forums available at the time. The debate team and drama club were natural extensions of his early interests (the latter a direct link to his early musical training), but neither group afforded him popularity among the greater student body. Sadly, not much has changed in the past 60 years. A young man determined to get noticed in high school does not excite his peers by securing the top spot on the honor role.

Who can argue that the star of Friday night's game is the hero in Monday morning's classroom? By Nixon's own admission, he was a poor athlete, yet he tried out for all the major sports: football, basketball, baseball, track. Clearly, he wanted his classmates and teachers to know who he was and, probably, at least early on, he wanted them to like him. Unfortunately, Nixon struggled with the same "poor boy" image that would dog Presley throughout his childhood. Kids can and will be cruel, picking on anyone who is different, whether or not it is of his own choice or doing.

Elvis seemed more willing than Richard to accept that he would never quite fit in. Rather than force the issue, he used his individuality to make a statement, from his sideburns to his flashy manner of dress. When he proved his taunters wrong, he was content to let his success speak for itself. Nowhere is Presley on record criticizing those who had ridiculed him when he was growing up.

Nixon was not as forgiving. He related to a friend in later years:

> What starts the process, really, are laughs and slights and snubs when you are a kid. Sometimes it's because you're poor or Irish or Jewish or Catholic or ugly or simply that you are skinny. But if you are reasonably intelligent and if your anger is deep enough and strong enough, you learn that you can change those attitudes by excellence, personal gut performance, while those who have everything are sitting on their fat butts.[3]

He was no less tolerant of himself. As a high school senior, he ran for class president and lost the election. While most kids would have chalked it up to experience, Richard referred to it as his first political defeat.

The loss proved one of many that lurked around the corner as young

3. A Watchful Eye on the Future

Nixon eyed his dream. Upon graduating, he was offered a partial scholarship at Yale, but the family's financial situation being what it was, he had to turn it down. Determined to make the best of things, he enrolled in Whittier College and applied himself as if he were at Yale, in the hopes of being accepted at a noteworthy school down the road. Richard Nixon was always looking ahead.

Grades remained his top priority at Whittier, though he still managed to involve himself in other aspects of campus life. His poor financial status was more of a factor now than it had ever been, but he refused to let it hold him back. During his freshman year, rather than apply to the Franklins, a well-established campus club for men known for its high social standing, he formed the Orthogonian Society and became its first president. According to Nixon, the name meant "Square Shooters," and the club was aimed at the common man, athletes and guys who were working their way through school.

"They were the haves, and we were the have-nots, see?" he explained in an interview on the subject years later.[4] A look at his class annual emphasizes the point clearly: the Franklins had their pictures taken in tuxedos; the Orthogonians wore open-necked shirts. So much for the complacent "if you can't beat 'em, join 'em." Nixon did not compromise. He invented his own way.

An important part of his way was learning how to extract the positive from the negative. Still as poor an athlete as ever, he insisted on being part of the college sports scene. Persistence and sheer determination finally won him a spot on the football team. While his performance on the field failed to earn him any letters, his coach's methods made a lasting impression. In his memoirs, Nixon said that riding the bench for Chief Wallace Newman taught him more about life than college courses ever could. Newman's philosophy: win by playing better than you think you can, and when you lose, go ahead and feel angry, just so long as that anger is expressed at the right target — yourself, for not playing well enough to win. Perhaps the most important lesson Nixon came away with from his endeavors on the playing field: never let any loss stop you from trying harder the next time around.

Richard took Newman's advice to heart. During his senior year at Whittier, he again ran for president of his class. This time he won. His defeated opponent took the loss well, calling Nixon a "smart politician."[5]

He was so smart, in fact, that he graduated second in his class. Thanks to hard work and tenacity, the elusive scholarship was not just a dream anymore. In the fall of 1934, less than six months before Elvis was born, Richard packed his bags and headed east to Duke University.

Life at the prestigious North Carolina law school was not easy, but by then Nixon had to come to expect as much. Again he found himself looked down on because he did not come from a wealthy family. His scholarship took care of the tuition, but he had to work for the clothes on his back and the roof over his head. "Bill Perdue, Lyman Brownfield, Fred Albrink, and I shared two double beds in one bedroom in a farmhouse in the middle of the Duke forest. We called it Whippoorwill Manor. We had no indoor plumbing, running water, or central heating. But it only cost five dollars a month, and as a result we were able to afford to go to law school."[6]

Despite the hard times, Nixon was not complaining. "I learned a lot from working my way through school. I was an assistant to the librarian, Miss Covington; did research for the dean, Claude Horack; and spent a summer mimeographing a new case book on constitutional law for Douglas Maggs. Sometimes the work was boring, but I never resented having to do it."[7]

That is not to say he had gotten over resenting those whose lives were made easier by virtue of their parents' financial status. In his first book, *Six Crises*, published in 1962, Nixon wrote of his early achievements: "I won my share of scholarships, and of speaking and debating prizes in school, not because I was smarter but because I worked longer and harder than some of my gifted colleagues" (page 295). Although it is possible Nixon was simply stating a fact here, it is hard not to imagine a touch of sarcasm in the choice of the word "gifted." Some are haves; some are have-nots.

In fairness, Nixon had many experiences from which to develop a grudge. Though he graduated from Duke third in his class, he was snubbed by the law firms he approached in New York and eventually had to return to Whittier, where he halfheartedly accepted a position with the local firm of Wingert & Bewley.

It was a setback that might have proven fatal. He had worked hard and long, and still it was not enough to propel him beyond his poor boy image. But Nixon did not allow it to end his dream. He had the law degree from Duke; no one could take that away. He would simply do as he had done all of his life: make the best of a less than desirable situation and see to it that he came out a stronger person because of it.

Nixon's new job was a far cry from the excitement of Wall Street. Mostly, the firm handled business matters: wills, estates, and the like. Perhaps because he was short on enthusiasm, his career got off to a rocky start; one of his first cases resulted in a malpractice suit against Wingert & Bewley. He learned from the experience and got past it, attaining full partnership in the firm during his second year.

Of course Nixon had far bigger things in mind than practicing business law in Whittier for the rest of his life. Though he remained at Wingert & Bewley for more than four years, much of his time was spent making local political connections. Continuing in the tradition of his academic years, he set about making a name for himself on the social scene.

His decision to become active in local theater productions wound up having a lasting impact on his life. During casting tryouts for the melodramatic mystery *The Dark Tower* on January 16, 1938, he met a striking, 26-year-old high school teacher named Pat Ryan. "It was a case of love at first sight," Nixon related in *RN* (23). Pat was not quite as taken with Richard. She rebuffed his invitation for a date after the audition and remained cool toward his advances for the next several months.

As it would turn out, the couple proved quite well matched.

The daughter of an Irish prospector and a widowed German immigrant, Pat — christened Thelma Catherine Ryan on March 16, 1912 — was the youngest of five children, two of them from her mother's first marriage. For years, the family struggled to make a living in the poor farming community of Artesia, California, some 20 miles southwest of Los Angeles. Thelma had been all of 13 when she took over the family household chores and, in addition, cared for her cancer-stricken mother, who died in January 1926.

Thelma held her family together while somehow managing to keep her grades high enough to achieve membership in her high school's honor society. At home, she became caretaker for her father, who had contracted tuberculosis. After his death in May 1930, Thelma changed her name to Patricia (it had been her father's favorite name) and enrolled in Fullerton Junior College. Her part-time job as a cosmetics salesperson at Bullocks led to work as a Hollywood extra, where she earned enough to finish her education at USC. She graduated with honors in June 1937. Three months later, she began her first teaching job at Whittier Union High School at the then-impressive salary of $1,800 a year.[8]

Nixon met Pat's rejection with the same determination that had kept him going thus far: by refusing to accept defeat. And once again, persistence paid off. The couple became Mr. and Mrs. Richard Nixon on June 21, 1940.

To broaden his business contacts, Nixon joined the Kiwanis and became a member of the chamber organization of nearby La Habra. The latter led to an unsuccessful bid for city attorney.

Nixon pressed on, now aided by Pat's support and the security of a happy marriage. Upon learning that his district representative in the California Assembly might not seek another term, he campaigned for support among regional groups and organizations. His efforts produced yet another dead end when the incumbent decided to run again.

Regardless of these early defeats, Nixon realized he was gaining valuable experience. Unfortunately, local connections only went so far. He needed broader appeal if he were to break out of the pack, national exposure that could only come from the nation's political hot seat. Pat fully agreed with his assessment, and with her blessing he gave notice at Wingert & Bewley in December 1941 to accept a position with the Office of Price Administration (OPA) in Washington, D.C. Granted, acting as attorney for the tire rationing division was probably not the most thrilling employment in the world, but what better way to learn the inner workings of government than by observing it firsthand?

In his memoirs, Nixon surmised that his mother was probably relieved when he took the position with OPA because she thought it would keep him from compromising his Quaker values by fighting in the war. He neglected to mention another obvious concern, which must have weighed on Hannah's mind: the possibility of losing yet another son.

Many young men employed in government jobs sought and secured draft deferments, but Nixon was not one of them. In the summer of 1942, he applied for, and was granted, an officer's commission with the navy.

Nixon's decision was probably based on a combination of factors. A stint in the navy would provide an insider's view of the military, while satisfying whatever moral or patriotic duty he felt toward his country. As an added bonus, he would escape his boring job at the OPA. When reviewing Nixon's history to this point, however, the most notable benefit the armed forces offered was yet another opportunity to get noticed. On campus, the star was the football player in the team jersey, pledging allegiance before the game, but in the real world, at that time, nothing captured the public's attention more reliably than an officer decked out in his dress uniform, saluting the American flag.

Regardless of motive, Nixon's navy years proved relatively uneventful. When his tour in the South Pacific was over, he served the remainder of his military career behind a desk, drawing on his legal skills to help terminate contracts for war supplies between the government and manufacturers.

During this winding-down period, Nixon's move east finally began to pay dividends. Associates and friends back in Whittier were impressed with the local boy who had refused to settle for a mediocre life at Wingert & Bewley, and in September 1945, they wondered if he might be interested in returning home to replace the district's Democratic representative in Congress.

At 32 years of age, Richard Nixon was finally on his way.

For young Presley, the road to success proved every bit as rough as Nixon's had been. The path led in a different direction, however, and the journey itself took far less time.

Elvis's studies were a necessary but secondary goal. He knew his mother was right, that there were no sure things in life and that he had best be prepared if his dreams and plans did not work out. But he did not allow the bitter realities to keep him from focusing on his dream. As early as the third grade, he was spending his Saturdays in the studio at WELO on Spring Street, watching his idol, Mississippi Slim, perform.

Slim, born Carvel Lee Ausborn, was no Hank Williams, but he was certainly a legitimate artist, having four tapes to his credit at the Country Music Hall of Fame in Nashville. He played guitar and harmonica, but it was his hillbilly singing that drew crowds in his home town of Tupelo.

To eight-year-old Elvis, Slim must have seemed a bona fide legend. The man sang on the radio. People knew his name, recognized him on the street. Most important, Slim actually made a living with his singing.

3. A Watchful Eye on the Future 19

As previous reports suggest, Elvis might well have preferred a bicycle or a rifle for his tenth birthday present on that crisp January day way back when. But deep inside, he knew the guitar was the better choice. Mississippi Slim played, and look what it had done for him. One can imagine the handsome, blue-eyed child nodding, that sultry look on his face, when Gladys smiled down at him and said, "Son, wouldn't you rather have the guitar? It would help you with your singing, and everyone does enjoy hearing you sing."[9]

While some beginners might be too shy or stubborn to ask for help, Elvis realized the best way to learn was by asking others who already knew. His Uncle Vester, Vernon's brother, was a music lover, occasionally playing at honky-tonks and dances around Tupelo. Vester showed his young nephew some chords. Elvis practiced. When he was ready for additional help, Presley sought out Frank Smith, the young preacher at the First Assembly of God. Frank, blessed with considerable musical ability, was delighted to help his young parishioner grasp the basics.

Without a doubt, the most influential teacher was none other than Mississippi Slim, who just happened to be the older brother of Presley's classmate James Ausborn. Although the hillbilly star was both irritated and impressed by Presley's attention, he never turned the boy away. Slim even went so far as to provide accompaniment for his young admirer's appearance during one of the amateur Saturday afternoon shows held at WELO. From Slim, Elvis learned the more difficult chords: sharps, flats, and minors. Eventually, he improved to the point where Slim invited him to appear on his weekly radio show.

Certainly each of Presley's guitar teachers played an important role but, as with Nixon's studies and other endeavors, determination and practice were the key to success. Once Elvis was proficient enough to accompany himself on the tearjerker "Old Shep," a song about the love between a boy and his dog, he sang it at every opportunity. It got so that his classmates would shake their heads and roll their eyes, some jokingly, others not, while pleading, "Oh no! Not another round of 'Old Shep' today!"[10]

If Elvis was discouraged by the negative reaction of his peers, he did not allow it to slow him down. Nor did he back off when several of his teachers took an interest in his singing, even though it added chants of "teacher's pet" to the already common "mama's boy" teasing he had endured since the first day of school, when Gladys walked him to the door.

Gradually, his efforts began to pay off. His fifth grade teacher, the dreaded Mrs. Grimes, as some of her former pupils described her, was moved to the point of tears when she heard him sing "Old Shep." She was so impressed that she marched him off to the principal, Mr. Cole, for a repeat performance. Agreeing that Elvis had obvious talent, Cole entered his young student in the children's talent contest at the upcoming Mississippi-Alabama Fair and Dairy Show.

Presley must have been thrilled by the very idea of *attending* the fair. His parents had never been able to afford the price of admission, let alone money for candy and rides. Finally, rather than prowl around the empty fairgrounds after the fact, trying to imagine the sights, smells, and sounds of the real thing, he would enjoy every moment firsthand. More than that, he would be center stage, performing for an unfamiliar audience, many of whom would be adults. This was not a makeshift stage in a tent that held 100 people; the grandstand had a seating capacity of 2,000. It was a day Elvis would remember forever.

From the mixed accounts, it is difficult to say whether or not Presley accompanied himself on his guitar that day as he wooed the crowd with a heart-wrenching version of "Old Shep." Claims that he had not yet acquired the instrument are inaccurate, however; classmates' teasing about another round of "Old Shep" came well before he played the song for Mrs. Grimes, who was not yet his teacher at that point.

Elvis's placement in the winner's circle, which was determined by audience applause, was also under dispute for many years. Only recently has research revealed that he did not win first, second, or third but rather a more modest fifth place: $5 and unlimited free rides for the day. Not bad for a few minutes' work for a boy his age, in that time and place.

Looking back, it seems odd there is no mention of Elvis having sung at the fair again until he returned to headline the event 11 years later, but given the Presleys' financial situation, it is understandable. Vernon was not earning enough to keep the little house on Berry Street that he had purchased the year before, so he sold it to get out from under the payments. The Presleys moved back to the poorer side of town, across the tracks near the city dump. Socially, Elvis went from "acceptable" to "poor white trash"—hardly the period in his life upon which he would want to focus.

In any event, this first result of practice shows that Elvis, like young Richard, realized at an early age that in order to reach his goal, he would have to prepare well in advance. The plan entailed countless hours of refining his skills alone in his room, after school and on weekends, searching for the right chords, memorizing them, playing a single tune again and again. This in addition to the necessary time spent practicing in front of an audience: entertaining his classmates, singing with his parents at church services and revivals. While such dedication produced impressive results, the cost was high for both Presley and Nixon. Neither boy had many friends as he was growing up. There simply wasn't time.

In Presley's case, the early years were made all the more difficult by Vernon's inability to hold a steady job. The family moved several times a year during their stay in Tupelo, scraping to pay their month-to-month rent. Elvis was 14 and living in Memphis before he could call the same place home for more than a year. Although the Nixons relocated when Richard was nine, once they opened the gas station, he remained in the same house until he left for Duke University some 12 years later.

3. A Watchful Eye on the Future 21

It is unlikely, of course, that either boy could have persevered through all the hardships unless he was reaping rewards from his efforts. Richard's early debating victories were sign enough he could get where he wanted if he kept at it. Likewise, the successful appearance at the fair provided Elvis with enough validation to continue his musical endeavors despite an unstable home life.

Having become skillful enough on the guitar to accompany himself, Presley took up the piano. Sources quoted in Dundy's work indicate he had a natural ear for music, thus the need to read the actual notes on paper never arose. He would listen to a song a number of times, then sit at the piano and play it. Elvis later confirmed that he had never learned how to read music.

Volunteering to play for his Sunday school class was a great way to gain the necessary experience, plus it provided a captive audience by which to judge his performance. No doubt he spent countless hours at the Assembly of God, perfecting his natural talent. Like Nixon, young Presley was constantly planning.

By the time he was in the sixth grade, Elvis was comfortable enough with his guitar playing to haul the instrument along with him to school every day. His teacher that year, Mrs. Camp, was as impressed with his talent as Mrs. Grimes had been. Interviewed in Dundy's book, she speaks of taking him to other teachers' classrooms to show him off.

The reaction of the pupils when Elvis sang was similar to Mrs. Camp's, but it was another story when the show was over. While the other children might have been impressed with Elvis's talent, even awed, such was not the case with Presley himself. He was just another poor kid in overalls, and once he was done singing, that was exactly how they treated him. Presley noticed. And he remembered.

Continuing to sing whenever anyone would listen, Elvis spent his lunch periods in the school basement, jamming with Mississippi Slim's little brother, James. On Saturdays, the boys would go down to the radio station where Slim was performing, and Elvis would continue to pick up occasional tips. "You're good to be as young as you are," Slim told him, "you just keep on working."[11]

All things considered, young Presley's life seemed to be moving in the direction he wanted. Such was not the case for his parents, however. Vernon got fired from his delivery job for using the truck after hours — and not for honorable purposes. Tupelo residents confirm that the elder Presley was using the vehicle to transport moonshine. This, combined with the memories of his conviction for the forged check, made the prospects of future employment in Tupelo unlikely at best. Wisely, Vernon decided it was time for a change.

In the fall of 1948, as Nixon basked in the victory of his second congressional term, the Presleys packed up their belongings and headed for Memphis. "We were broke, man, broke," Elvis often said when relating the event in later years.[12] But at least they were heading for a new city, a new start. No one would know about the mishaps in Tupelo. Life would be better.

The Presleys' newfound sense of hope faded quickly, especially for Elvis. Not only was he still a poor kid in overalls, he was a *new* kid, having arrived after the school year had already begun. A new kid whose mother walked him to the corner every morning for all to see. No matter that Gladys's real concern was that her boy get an education, for Elvis it was just one more shame to endure.

Ever so gradually, however, things did prove better in Memphis. By the time Elvis began the ninth grade at Humes High, his family was living at Lauderdale Courts, a housing project on Winchester Avenue. The two-bedroom apartment needed minor repairs, but for $35 a month, it was a pretty good deal. Vernon was working as a loader at United Paint. His wages were higher than those he had earned in Tupelo, though the family's annual income was still well under the project limit of $2,500.

The Presleys had much in common with the rest of Lauderdale's residents; they were common people, as the Nixons had been, good, honest folks struggling to keep their heads above water. Neighbors who remember them say Gladys was the friendly one. Vernon kept pretty much to himself, often displaying a gruff, solemn look. Elvis was just plain shy. His ninth grade homeroom teacher, Susie Johnson, described him as "a gentle, obedient boy," who "always went out of his way to try to do what you asked him to do."[13]

In comparing Presley's teenage years with Nixon's, it would seem as though Presley got the better of the deal. Nixon worked at his parents' store after school and then hit the books until bedtime, which was often two or three in the morning. Elvis, on the other hand, was, perhaps for the first time in his life, busy making friends. One of his neighbors at Lauderdale, an older boy named Buzzy Forbess, shared Presley's interest in collecting comics. The two quickly formed a friendship, which led to Elvis being accepted into Buzzy's group. They played football, rode their bikes, and went to the movies. "What we didn't do was crack the books and study a lot," Buzzy recalled.[14]

While Nixon's goals clearly required a college education, Presley's did not. The people who could help him were not sitting on the board of trustees at some university, they were handing out advice a few blocks away, making music in the nightclubs on Beale Street.

Young Presley knew where he wanted to go and had a pretty good idea how to get there, but the move to Memphis had put a damper on his plans. In the midst of adolescence, life had suddenly become overwhelming. More than 1,600 students attended Humes, and Elvis hardly knew any of them. His voice was changing, his body maturing. Like most other boys his age, he worried about everything from cars to girls to acne. It comes as no surprise, then, that during his first two years at Humes, no one recalls him breaking into a chorus of "Old Shep."

Presley knew he would have to prove himself all over again — start from ground zero and work his way up. Mississippi Slim could not help him any-

3. A Watchful Eye on the Future 23

more. He was in a strange city full of thriving, successful musicians. Which one should he approach for help, and how?

Just as he had learned in Tupelo, contacts were the name of the game.

Presley's early friendship with Mississippi Slim's younger brother James may very well have been a coincidence. Likewise, it might have been only a touch of luck that one of Elvis's first friends at the Lauderdale Courts was Johnny Black, whose older brother, Bill, made a living as a professional musician. Kids are naturally drawn to others who have similar interests. But, like Nixon, Presley was no ordinary kid. He was a young man with a dream, determined to do everything possible to make it come true.

It is probable that the Presleys' dismal financial situation, while an obstacle of sorts, served as further incentive. Vernon worked more steadily in Memphis, but his back was giving him trouble, or so he claimed. Gladys picked up the slack, toiling at various odd jobs, as a seamstress at Fashion Curtains, later as a waitress in a cafeteria, and finally as a nurse's aide at the hospital. Elvis pitched in when he could, working after school as an usher at Loew's State Theater and later at Precision Tool and M.A.R.L. Metal Products.

In spite of their team effort, it was not until midway through Elvis's senior year that the Presleys' income had finally risen enough to put them over the limit at Lauderdale Courts. They moved out on January 7, 1953. After a short stay at a boardinghouse across town, they rented a place in their old Lauderdale neighborhood. Be it sheer coincidence, or thanks to a tip from Johnny, the Presleys' new home at 462 Alabama just happened to be right across the street from the home of Bill Black.

It must be noted here that the difference in Presley's and Nixon's ages proved an important factor in how they approached their respective goals. Although both men's dreams involved years of preparation, Nixon continued to prepare years *after* he had left the security of his parents' home. Presley, on the other hand, was not looking to become a singer six or eight years down the road. He wanted it as soon as possible. Whereas Nixon was a grown man who made his own decisions, Presley was still a boy, living at home with his parents. The close relationship he had with them played an undeniable role in determining how he pursued his future plans.

Since early childhood, Elvis had vowed to take care of his mother. As a high school student, the most educated member of the family, he was slowly becoming the decision maker; his parents valued his opinion, trusted his judgment. Soon he would be on equal footing with his father in financial contribution, working a full-time job after graduation. The Presleys looked to their son for advice and support more often than he looked to them.

Due at least in part to his adult responsibilities, Elvis was a senior at Humes before he had firmly established himself as an entertainer to classmates and teachers. He had introduced his music quietly the first couple of years, playing and singing with his new friends at Lauderdale. "He wasn't shy about it," said his pal Buzzy, "but he wasn't the kind of kid you just turn him around and put him on stage, either. He got used to it right there, with us."[15]

The change at Humes began with a different image at the start of his junior year. Gone was the shy boy who would do anything not to be noticed and picked on. He grew sideburns and slapped on hair tonic to keep his locks in place. He wore loud clothes, bright-colored shirts that demanded attention. He even tried out for the football team. To the teachers and students at Humes, he was a new Elvis; in truth, he was the old one from Tupelo who had finally found the courage to show himself again.

He sang at the Humes Annual Minstrel Show in April of his senior year, accompanying himself with his guitar on the then-popular Teresa Brewer song "Till I Waltz Again." He won, and his classmates were impressed. "It was amazing how popular I became after that," Elvis recalled in an interview several years later.[16] Cashing in on this newfound admiration, he took his guitar to the class picnic at Overton Park and became the main attraction of the event.

Paralleling the days of Tupelo and Mississippi Slim, Presley spent countless hours at local radio station WMPS watching his new idols, the Blackwood Brothers Quartet, perform on *High Noon Round-up*. The emcee of the show, disc jockey Bob Neal, would soon prove an invaluable contact.

Meanwhile, Elvis continued to make music with his friends, among them Johnny Black, who had turned into a decent bass player. The boys sang at the Lauderdale Courts, in the park, on street corners, wherever people might stop to listen. They went out to Overton Park and listened to the orchestra concerts. On evenings and weekends, Elvis hung out at Charlie's, a record shop downtown, and at Lansky's, his favorite clothing store, on Beale. He attended all-night gospel sing-alongs at Ellis Auditorium with whomever he could drag along.

With music an everyday part of his life, Elvis's confidence soared. Was it possible his dream could become reality? A week before graduation, he entered a talent contest at the Father of Country Music Festival, hoping to build on his growing momentum. Details of this event are not part of the basic Elvis story, perhaps because they present a different side of the normally mild-mannered young man, a side that displays an interesting parallel to Richard Nixon. Elvis had read about the contest in the newspaper but had neither the money nor transportation to make the 240-mile trip to Meridian, Mississippi. Nor did he meet the requirement of state resident. Presley went anyway, covering the distance by hitching a ride. Once there, he wandered around the grounds with his guitar until Curtis Robinson, a reporter for the *Meridian Star*, inquired what he was doing. When Presley said he had come all the way from Tupelo to enter the contest but only had a dime in his pocket, Robinson gave him enough money for room and board so he could return the next day to be in the show.

3. A Watchful Eye on the Future

Elvis won second place. His prize, a brand-new guitar, beat the heck out of $5 and free carnival rides. Why was it that he never spoke of the event after he became famous?

A footnote from Robinson provides a compelling, believable explanation. Three years after the contest, Presley returned to Meridian for the annual Jimmie Rogers Memorial, where he was on the main bill with Hank Snow and Roy Acuff. Elvis performed "I'm Left, You're Right, She's Gone" and "Baby, Let's Play House" and was promptly booed off the stage. The audience, tried and true hillbilly fans, wanted nothing to do with the jumpy kid in sideburns and his modernized style. A furious Elvis swore that he would never mention the festival or Meridian again.

Like Nixon and his politics, Elvis took his lifeblood seriously. He might not have held a grudge against those more fortunate than himself, as Nixon did, but let people start messing with his music, telling him he couldn't sing, well, he'd show them a thing or two, and when it was over, he'd be the one who was laughing.

Vindication arrived much sooner than anyone could have imagined.

Elvis graduated on June 3, 1953, and began work the very next day at M. B. Parker Machinists at a salary of $33 per week. The exact date he left Parker's and began working side by side with his cousin Gene Smith at Precision Tool is unknown; estimates range from a few weeks to a couple of months. From there he moved on to Crown Electric, where he drove a truck.

Early biographical accounts had Presley working at Crown when he dropped by 706 Union Avenue to make his first recording. More recent works contend he was still employed at M. B. Parker when the historic event took place. Regardless, sometime during July or August 1953, Presley made the most important decision of his young life: he determined he was ready to proceed with the next phase of his plan.

Marion Keisker, somewhat of a celebrity from her radio talk show days, was behind the front desk at Sun when Elvis strode in with his guitar. He "wanted to make a record for his mother," so the story goes. Certainly the tale fits the mold of Presley's personality: a shy, polite young man who loved his mama. Wouldn't it have been just like him to spend some of his hard-earned money — $3.98 plus tax, to be exact — on a recording of his voice that she could play over and over?

It might have been just like him, but that is not the way it happened. In keeping with everything we have seen to this point, it is obvious this was no spur-of-the-moment decision but, rather, another step in the master plan. Presley walked into the studio that day with one thing on his mind: to be heard by the owner, Sam Phillips, in hopes of being signed to a recording contract.

Living in Memphis, Elvis would have been well versed on Sam Phillips and his up-and-coming label, Sun Records. Rufus Thomas's "Bear Cat" had recently climbed the charts. "Walkin' in the Rain" by the Prisonaires — an actual group of inmates from the state penitentiary in Nashville — was on its way to becoming a hit. An article about the latter had appeared in the *Memphis Press Scimitar* in mid–July. Word around Memphis said Phillips was open to talent of any kind, proven or unproven, black or white. The point was emphasized by his business card: "We record anything–anywhere–anytime."[17]

Phillips was especially interested in the rhythm-and-blues sound of the black musicians playing on Beale Street, which explains why he recorded mainly black artists for the first few years. These records were not selling as well as they might have due to the racial factor, thus Marion Keisker's claim that Sam was on the lookout for a white boy who could sound black. It is doubtful Elvis saw himself in that light when he walked into the Memphis Recording Studio on that muggy Saturday afternoon. He was there to sell his style for what it was: his own.

What type of music did he sing? Marion wanted to know. Who did he sound like?

Actually, he sang "all" types of music, and he "didn't sound like nobody," thank you very much.

A dispute regarding whether it was Sam or Marion who had the foresight to turn on the tape machine while Presley made his record has never been fully resolved. What we do know is that part of the first song, "My Happiness," and all of the flip, "That's When Your Heartaches Begin," were captured on studio tape. Although Presley's audition did not end the way he had hoped, the trip had not been a waste of time either. His demo was filed away, stamped with the notation "Good ballad singer. Hold."

And hold it Phillips did.

When Elvis left the studio that day, his dream must have seemed within reach, but he coasted back to reality when the phone did not ring. He had refined his skills as much as he could on his own. He needed a helping hand like the one Nixon had been offered when the Whittier businessmen called, but no one was offering one, least of all Sam.

Life on the home front remained stagnant as well. Vernon was earning no more than Elvis, and, with his lack of education, it was a pretty sure bet he never would. Meanwhile, Gladys' health had begun to deteriorate. Increasing weight made it difficult for her to continue as a nurse's aide, which called for heavy lifting and many hours on her feet.

Compared with his parents, Elvis had a world of opportunity waiting. He was a healthy young man with a high school diploma. Chances were he could find a job just about anywhere: Nashville, New York, or Los Angeles. Wherever he would have the best shot at getting discovered. If he pounded the streets, auditioned for all the record labels, *someone* would be willing to take a chance.

In all likelihood, someone probably would have — but Elvis never left

3. A Watchful Eye on the Future

Memphis to find out. His parents were counting on his 40-some dollars a week to help pay the bills. They were counting on *him*. For 18 years they had struggled to keep a roof over his head. It was his turn now. His dream remained as important as ever, but his sense of responsibility had to come first.

He hung around Memphis for the rest of the summer, through the fall, and into the winter. Every so often he stopped by Sam's studio to inquire if they had come across a band that might be looking for a singer. Every time, the answer was no. But they had his number, Marion would say with a smile. If something came up, they would be sure to give him a call.

Several accounts contend that during this time Presley was performing in and around Memphis at various functions, some going as far as to dub him semiprofessional. "No way," said Memphis DJ George Klein, a classmate of Presley's who remained a close friend in later years. "Elvis never sang in public at all for money, or for performance, before his record came out."[18]

Presley agreed, insisting that he never performed in public prior to touring with Scotty and Bill. Of course, ten- or fifteen-dollar engagements at corner honky-tonks is not something young stars like to look back upon when being interviewed, let alone playing for free at sock hops and school dances.

In any case, it is clear that Presley developed a backup plan during this period, if for no other reason than to soothe Gladys's mind. If his singing did not work out, he hoped to elevate his position at Crown from truck driver to electrician. "I was driving a truck," he explained to an interviewer in Wichita Falls, Texas, while on tour there in 1956. "And I was studying to be an electrician, too, see."[19]

In reviewing Elvis's life to this point, it seems unlikely he considered this as anything but a last resort, although looking at it from a realistic standpoint, his goal of becoming an entertainer must have seemed impossible to him at times, especially when his efforts to secure a contract with Sun had not yet worked out. Still, Presley had no intention of giving up until he had exhausted every possibility. "When I was driving a truck, every time a big shiny car would go by it started me daydreaming," he would later reminisce. "I always felt that someday, somehow, something would happen to change everything for me."[20]

"Someday" must have seemed a long time off as 1954 began. He was still driving a truck. Sam Phillips had yet to call.

Just as Nixon could have used the stack of New York rejections as an excuse to give up rather than accept a lesser position at Wingert & Bewley, Elvis might have accepted Sam's no-call as the end to his dream.

Instead, sometime in early January, Presley returned to 706 Union to cut another record. This time, Phillips was definitely working the controls as Elvis sang "I'll Never Stand in Your Way" and "It Wouldn't Be the Same without You." Phillips was sufficiently impressed to praise the young lad when it was over, something which, by his own admission, he rarely did.

Sam noticed something special in Elvis's performance that day, something he could not quite put his finger on, but whatever it was, he knew he wanted to see it again. Unfortunately for Presley, that day was still a few steps down the road; he left the studio with only his acetate in hand.

Meanwhile, another would-be star, guitarist Scotty Moore, was making a similar bid for Sam's attention. Scotty was older than Elvis, probably a little more secure. Moreover, he already had a band: a hillbilly group called the Wranglers. Moore was either convincing or persistent enough that Sam eventually gave the Wranglers a shot. A record was cut in May. Around that same time, Phillips mentioned he had a new ballad singer who Scotty might want to give a listen to. Scotty agreed. Phillips finally made the long-awaited call.

Nineteen-year-old Presley was on his way.

Chapter 4

Let the Games Begin

We should not glorify struggle or reckless risks as ends in themselves. But we should recognize that the most important achievements in life involve at least some risk, struggle, and adversity.

— Richard Nixon

As had been the case since their dreams began, Presley and Nixon continued their journeys at far different paces.

Realizing his pilgrimage to the mountaintop would entail a number of small, progressive steps, Nixon was prepared to take them one at a time. The first, and perhaps most difficult, required that he leave the political hot seat of Washington, D.C., to accept the Whittier businessmen's offer to run for congressman in California's Twelfth District.

While at first glance a return to his home town may have seemed a step backward, it was in no way similar to his accepting the job at Wingert & Bewley some eight years earlier. This time, he was not returning home for lack of a better offer. He was, however, still fighting to prove himself worthy. Upon confirming his interest in the Whittier group's offer, Nixon was informed that he was only one of six being considered for the nomination. The candidates were to appear at a dinner meeting on November 2, at which time each would be given the chance to explain why he was the right man for the job.

The participants drew lots to determine their speaking order. Nixon came up with the short straw. Speaking last was a clear disadvantage; the audience would be tired, some might have already made their choice.

Nixon knew he would have to strike quickly and leave a lasting impression. He had already made some headway on the latter, having worn his navy uniform to the dinner. Drawing on his early debating experience, he concentrated on one strong point rather than attempting to summarize each separate aspect of his political convictions.

He began by explaining how he viewed the nature of the American system as having two conflicting strains: the New Deal, which he viewed as governmental regulation of peoples' lives, and the more "individual" capitalistic approach, where a person's initiative supposedly controlled his success or failure. Not surprisingly, Nixon sided with the latter. He reported having spoken with returning veterans, whom he claimed did not want government handouts; rather, they wanted jobs in private industries where their efforts would be recognized and appreciated by others. If Nixon were chosen as the candidate, he vowed to center his campaign on a platform of "practical liberalism," which he felt would give Republicans the best chance of unseating the Democratic incumbent.

The committee members liked what they heard. Nixon won the nomination with a total of 63 votes. His closest competitor finished with 12.

The excitement of this first political victory was tempered with restraint on Nixon's part, as it meant taking a sizable gamble. He was a virtual unknown beyond the city limits of Whittier. Running an effective campaign against Jerry Voorhis, the Democratic incumbent, would not be easy or cheap. If Nixon won the primary in June, he could expect contributions from state Republican supporters, but in order to reach that point, he would have to campaign full time for the next six months.

Nixon had come a long way from his Whippoorwill Manor days at Duke, but his have-not image continued to haunt him. Despite his accomplishments, he and Pat were living a modest life. During Richard's absence overseas, Pat had worked as a price analyst for the OPA. Nixon, bored from the daily routine aboard the supply ship, had taken up poker and, to his surprise, found he had quite a knack for the game. His winnings, in addition to his navy income and Pat's salary, had enabled them to put aside $10,000 — money they had expected to use as a down payment on a house when Nixon reentered the private sector. Accepting the committee's nomination would require that the Nixons move back to Whittier and use their savings for living expenses during the campaign. Should he lose, the couple would be back to square one: no money in the bank and a less-than-rosy outlook in a tight postwar job market. The scenario was all the more chancy given that Pat was expecting their first child in February.

It is the element of risk, of course, that limits the number of heroes. If Elvis had played it safe, he would have gone on to become an electrician, settling for weekend gigs at the clubs on Beale, waiting to be discovered. Nixon, who had already done more than his fair share of waiting, certainly had not come this far only to be discouraged by the possibility of failure. Following his discharge from the service in January 1946, Nixon and his wife packed their bags and headed west.

Drawing on his well-practiced study habits, Nixon familiarized himself with every aspect of Voorhis's political career. When he learned that the incumbent had once been a registered member of the Socialist party, he used the connection to portray the Democrat as soft on Communism. He backed up his accusation by citing Voorhis's voting record and his endorsement by the National Citizens Political Action Committee (NCPAC), an organized labor group suspected of being associated with Communists.

The social skills he had struggled to perfect throughout his high school and college years were put to good use. Several heated debates with Voorhis and relentless one-on-one contact with the public in the form of "house meetings," in which constituents opened up their homes to neighborhood gatherings, produced a primary win for Nixon in June. Election Day in November tallied 65,586 votes for Nixon, 49,994 for Voorhis. Much bigger and better things lay ahead, but, as Nixon later confided in his memoirs, none would equal the excitement or the happiness of winning his first congressional seat.

In later accounts, Nixon's victory was attributed solely to having fueled the American fear of Communism at Voorhis's expense. His defeated opponent did not see it that way. In his autobiography, *Confessions of a Congressman*, Voorhis blamed the general state of the nation as the cause of his defeat. All the workingman's troubles, he theorized, were seen by voters as the fault of the incumbents, thus challengers like Nixon were welcomed with open arms. Bottom line, the blue-collar work force wanted candidates who understood the circumstances surrounding their everyday lives.

Nixon had gotten elected not only because he understood those experiences but because he had witnessed them firsthand. Like Presley, his upbringing provided a decisive advantage in connecting with the average American: clerking in his parents' store, sitting on the bench during college football games, acting in the drama club. Middlebrow voters supported Richard Nixon because he was one of them.

In January 1947, the Nixons returned to Washington, eager to put their proletarian experience to work. His first congressional assignment was to the Education and Labor Committee, where he was joined by another freshman whom he described as a "good-looking, good-humored young Democrat from Massachusetts." His name was John Fitzgerald Kennedy. Nixon admitted the vast differences in their backgrounds kept them from becoming close friends, but he insisted they never had less than an "amicable" relationship.

Kennedy certainly fit the stereotypical "have." Why didn't Nixon discard him as such? Perhaps because he saw in the debonair young JFK a refined version of himself. While he admitted that Kennedy's shyness at times made him appear cool and distant, it was the type of shyness "born of an instinct that guarded privacy and concealed emotions. I understood these qualities," Nixon admitted, "because I shared them."[1]

While it is obvious from this statement that Nixon never overcame his introverted personality, he was able to project a much more gregarious image when the opportunity for advancement arose. The national publicity that had been generated by his anti-Communist campaign against Voorhis netted him another committee assignment during his freshman year, and he wasted no time using the appointment as a major stepping-stone toward advancing his political career.

In *RN*, Nixon said he accepted the position on the House Un-American Activities Committee (HUAC) with reservations, due to its questionable reputation. The committee had been established in 1938 as a result of the growing labor movement, which many government officials feared was infiltrated with Communists. The committee had fallen out of favor with the Truman administration, however, which viewed its activities as nothing short of aggravated witch-hunts.

Nixon may have been reluctant to lend his name to the group, but, as would hold true in later years, once he made his decision, he stood behind it. During his first speech in front of the House on February 18, 1947, he bypassed the usual freshman "support the party policy" approach in favor of attacking Gerhart Eisler, a known Communist agent who had refused to appear before the HUAC. Nixon called for a contempt of Congress citation against Eisler for refusing to testify. When a final count was taken, only one congressman voted against the citation. Eisler was eventually indicted for passport fraud, jumped bail, and fled to East Germany where, according to Nixon, he became director of propaganda for the Communist regime.

Nixon's colleagues were impressed. In July, the Speaker of the House, Joe Martin, chose him to be one of a 19-member committee that would travel to Europe and prepare a report in conjunction with the administration's postwar foreign aid package, known as the Marshall Plan.

Opposed to the policy at first, Nixon was stunned by the scene that greeted him across the waters. Stepping off the fancy ocean liner in Southampton, England, he saw the results of starvation and chaos up close and personal. Every country the committee visited displayed similar signs of pending disaster. By the time the trip was over, Nixon was more than convinced that U.S. financial aid was the only thing that would save Europe from revolution, a revolution he felt certain would lead to Communist rule. Nixon's view that the spread of Communism threatened the future of world peace would continue to escalate from this point onward, as would his belief that it was his destiny to prevent it from happening.

By the time he returned to the United States, Nixon had made up his mind to support the plan, but he knew persuading his constituents in the Twelfth District to support his decision would be an uphill battle: a poll revealed 75 percent were opposed to the idea of any foreign aid. He managed to turn the tide through a series of newspaper articles and local speeches, during which he described the scenes he had witnessed in Europe. That December, his public's backing in hand, Nixon voted with a majority of the House, 313–82, in favor of the Marshall Plan.

Nixon's active freshman year proved instrumental in laying the ground-

4. Let the Games Begin

work for his early rise to national recognition. The HUAC gained headlines in the fall of 1947 with the case brought against the "Hollywood Ten," a group of screenwriters who, like Gerhart Eisler, had refused to testify in front of the committee. Each writer was cited with contempt and eventually sentenced to time behind bars.

While conservatives reveled in the wake of exposing Hollywood as a hotbed of Communist activity, Nixon was busy chasing a much bigger rabbit. Alexander Hiss, a retired State Department official, had been accused of being a spy. The man behind the allegation, Whittaker Chambers, was a senior editor at *Time* magazine — and a former member of the Communist party. Chambers claimed he had known and worked with Hiss ten years earlier, stealing classified documents and passing them on to the Soviets.

Hiss vehemently denied ever having known Chambers, but a thorough investigation by Nixon and several other members of the HUAC proved otherwise. Once the connection was established and Hiss admitted it, claiming he had known Chambers by another name and had simply forgotten, he lost credibility even among his most outspoken supporters. The investigation climaxed with the discovery of the "Pumpkin Papers," three rolls of microfilm hidden in a hollowed-out pumpkin on Chambers's property. On the film were documents ranging from, as Nixon put it, "inconsequential bureaucratic trivia to top-secret ambassadorial cables."[2] Reportedly, many were in Hiss's own handwriting.

Because of the time frame involved (the statute of limitations had run out), Hiss could not be prosecuted for espionage. Instead, he was indicted on two counts of perjury. His first trial ended in a hung jury. The second netted him a five-year prison term.

Richard Nixon was dubbed a national hero for his efforts, though, as would be the case for Presley when he rose to the top of the charts several years later, not everyone joined in the celebration. Charges surfaced that Nixon had used unscrupulous methods in proving Hiss's guilt, some going so far as to suggest that the evidence found on Chambers's property had been planted. The accusations of misconduct were unfounded, according to Foster Dulles, foreign policy advisor to Tom Dewey, the Republican presidential nominee in 1948. "I formed a very high judgment of the sense of responsibility under which Nixon operated," Dulles said about the case. "He wanted to be careful about hurting reputations and sought the opinions of people who knew Hiss as to the weight of the evidence."[3]

In later years, Nixon blamed the publicity surrounding the Hiss case for having permanently blacklisted him in the eyes of what he referred to as the liberal East Coast press. While there may be some truth to his theory, there is no question that the good outweighed the bad. As he admitted in his memoirs, the Hiss case had given him publicity most congressmen could only dream of.

All of his life, Nixon had made the most of the few opportunities granted him, and the Hiss case was no exception. Into his second term by now (he had won reelection easily in 1948), he was ready for a new and bigger challenge. Harry Truman's unexpected victory over Dewey in November had turned the capital into a Democrat's paradise — and a Republican's nightmare. Despite the strides he had made as congressman, Nixon viewed the changing of the guard as a major roadblock to his political future. Overnight, he had gone from an enthusiastic up-and-coming representative of the favored majority to a junior member of the minority. A "comer," as he put it, "with no place to go" (*RN*, 72).

If Nixon had waited to be dealt a winning hand, he might have remained at Wingert & Bewley forever. The time had come to take yet another risk, and this time, it was a big one. Against the advice of most his colleagues, who suggested he was committing political suicide, Nixon decided to challenge Sheridan Downey, California's Democratic senator, for his spot in the 1950 election. Downey eventually pulled out of the race due to health problems, throwing the Democratic nomination to Congresswoman Helen Gahagan Douglas, wife of the popular actor Melvin Douglas.

It was a dream come true for Nixon, who wasted no time in branding the liberal Douglas a left-wing extremist. As he had done with Voorhis four years earlier, he cited her voting record as proof of the charges. Douglas fought back, suggesting that Nixon was a Communist in disguise. "The Big Lie!" read one of her campaign flyers. "Hitler invented it. Stalin perfected it. Nixon uses it.... You pick the Congressman the Kremlin loves!" The voters complied, electing "Tricky Dick," as Douglas had branded him, by a margin of 680,000 votes.[4]

As Nixon began his Senate term in January 1951, names were already being considered for the party's presidential nominee for the 1952 election. The two front-runners were General Dwight Eisenhower and Senator Robert Taft of Ohio. Taft, son of the former president and a veteran of the Senate since 1939, was the favorite among party leaders. Eisenhower was viewed as a nonpolitician, a Washington outsider. As a result, his popularity among the general public was overwhelming. The general's personal appeal, combined with the nation's growing discomfort with the Truman administration, made an Eisenhower ticket look like an easy winner. The only problem was Ike's lack of political experience, a gap that Richard Nixon, up-and-coming young senator and friend of the blue-collar working class, would fill perfectly.

In May 1952, Nixon was asked by Tom Dewey, still a major force in the party and an outspoken Eisenhower supporter, to be the main speaker at the New York State Republican party's annual fundraiser. Nixon's speech, which was broadcast live on radio, was so well received by the audience that they gave him a standing ovation. When the applause died down, Dewey grasped Nixon's hand, congratulated him on a great speech, and told him if he retained his enthusiasm and good health, he could rise to president someday. He was chosen as Eisenhower's running mate two months later.

It had been an amazing climb, from political unknown to vice presidential nominee in six years' time. Unfortunately for Nixon, he was still a have-not in the eyes of his party's leaders, a distant face behind Ike's polished handshake and ingratiating smile. If the seasoned politicians had had their way, he would have been a ghost by the November election.

As the campaign kicked off in mid–September, headlines about a secret fund began appearing in newspapers. The rumors concerned a $20,000 expense account that Nixon was supposedly using to supplement his personal income. The money had been solicited through a public fundraiser by Dana Smith, Nixon's finance chair during his Senate campaign, and was used strictly for political expenses: travel back and forth between Washington and California, business mailings, and the like. All payments had been made by check and were completely documented, thus there was nothing "secret" about them. No one person had contributed more than $500 and most less than $200. "The fund was not illegal or even unethical," concluded Nixon biographer Tom Wicker, "although the latter word has little meaning, anyway, in the jungle world of political money."[5]

How true. Smart politicians know voters are much more likely to remember headlines than the truth behind the story. After examining the facts, Eisenhower's people were convinced Nixon had done nothing wrong, but they feared the Democrats would ride the question of his integrity all the way to the election, and they asked him to resign from the ticket.

The official request arrived via a phone call from Dewey a mere hour before Nixon was scheduled to go on national television to explain the fund. When asked whether he would agree to resign from the ticket at the end of his speech, Nixon responded that the only way Ike's advisors would find out what he was going to do was if they listened to his speech. His final message for the candidate's troops: "Tell them I know something about politics too!"[6]

Indeed, he would soon prove he knew a lot more than something. Nixon took his case directly to the American people, in what would become known as the "Checkers Speech," one of the most famous of his career.

Still reeling from his conversation with Dewey, Nixon went in front of the cameras without cue cards. A few pages of loosely organized notes sat off to his side, though he would rarely refer to them. Speaking directly to the viewers, he began: "My fellow Americans, I come before you tonight as a candidate for the vice presidency and as a man whose honesty and integrity have been questioned."[7]

Considering Nixon's background, it is understandable why he felt the need to get personal with his audience rather than reel off a prepared speech. Quakers value morals and character above all else. It was not only Nixon's reputation that was at stake, or even that of his family. He represented an entire social class: the common worker striving to compete against the privileged haves.

Nixon proved up to the challenge. With the cameras rolling and Pat at his side, he proceeded to divulge the Nixons' entire financial net worth in front of a national television audience, a practice unheard-of in the political arena at the time. His figures were backed by an audit that had been prepared by Price Waterhouse. Every dollar of the "secret fund" could be accounted for and had been used exactly as Nixon had said — for political expenses. Contrary to recent headlines, the Nixons were still a long way from joining society's haves. Their assets included a 1950 Oldsmobile, $20,000 equity in their Washington residence, $3,000 in the California house Richard's parents were living in, and a $4,000 life insurance policy. Their personal debt totaled $38,500, including the homes.[8]

After convincing the grassroots voters he was still deserving of their trust, Nixon sought to strengthen the kinship.

> One other thing I probably should tell you because if I don't they'll probably be saying this about me too, we did get something — a gift — after the election. A man down in Texas heard Pat on the radio mention the fact that our two youngsters would like to have a dog. And believe it or not, the day before we left on this campaign trip we got a message from Union Station in Baltimore saying that they had a package for us. We went down to get it. You know what it was? It was a little cocker spaniel dog in a crate that they sent all the way from Texas. Black and white spotted. And our little girl — Tricia, the six-year-old — named it Checkers. And you know the kids love that dog and I just want to say this right now, that regardless of what they say about it, we're going to keep it.[9]

Whether sharing the story was a calculated political tactic or a genuine attempt on Nixon's part to reach out to the people, it was a brilliant move. Not only did it pull at the heartstrings of American families, it clearly distanced him from the Washington coalition the Eisenhower ticket hoped to unseat. Most politicians would have quit while they were ahead, but Nixon sensed he was on a roll. With Ike's camp watching, most likely through clenched teeth, Nixon closed by taking the biggest gamble yet of his political career.

Ignoring Dewey's request, Nixon said he thought it should be up to the public to decide whether he remained on the ticket, and he asked that viewers send their opinions via telegram to the Republican National Committee after the broadcast. Those of Eisenhower's supporters who questioned Nixon's political savvy were quickly put in their place. Within a matter of minutes, the committee was flooded with messages demanding that Nixon remain on the ticket. Among the many telegrams sent straight to Eisenhower was one from Nixon's mother, assuring the general that she had the utmost confidence in his ability to make the right decision regarding her son's integrity.

4. Let the Games Begin

The Checkers Speech was one of the rare times Nixon used the powerful medium of television to his advantage. Historians contend it was his emotional manner throughout the broadcast, in which he sometimes appeared on the verge of tears, that swayed voters. Perhaps so, but as Presley's appearances on the *Ed Sullivan Show* would do a few years later, it also provided critics with a clip of fresh ammunition. Liberal analysts denounced the speech as a cheap attempt to evoke sympathy from the public at the expense of the issues; a valid argument had Nixon tried to whitewash details of the fund. As it was, the accusation only strengthened his bond with his "fellow Americans."

The fund scandal was Nixon's first real lesson in political loyalty: friends would come and go, depending solely on whether their support would benefit their own interests. It was a lesson he remembered as the years wore on.

Come November, Eisenhower beat his Democratic challenger, Adlai Stevenson, by more than 6.5 million votes. Richard Nixon, 39-year-old son of a lemon farmer, was a heartbeat away from the presidency of the United States.

Nixon's rise, though swift by political standards, took an eternity when compared with Presley's.

Elvis had always viewed his future in terms of tomorrow, and rightly so, as few thirty-something men become teenage heartthrobs. Age and experience were a plus for Nixon but would have hindered the young singer's chance of success, as it was his fresh, spontaneous style that was the key to his appeal. Still, it is doubtful that even Elvis could have imagined how quickly the sun would rise in the aftermath of Phillips's call.

Per Sam's request, Scotty invited Bill Black, who was then working as a studio musician for Phillips, over to his house for a warm-up session with young Presley. While the result was nothing special in Scotty's or Bill's opinion, Sam decided to judge for himself and arranged session time for the trio a couple of nights later. They worked on the ballads "Harbor Lights" and "I Love You Because," doing more than a dozen takes on each. The hours passed. Nothing clicked. Sam suggested they call it a night and wandered into the control room to shut things down.

With the pressure off, Elvis began fiddling with an old blues song, "That's All Right," a tune he had played often with Johnny Black at Lauderdale Courts. For the first time all evening, he had fun with his music — clowning around, jumping up and down as he plunked out the chords on his tinny guitar. Scotty picked up on the mood, Bill joined in, and Sam stopped worrying that his faith in Elvis had been a mistake.

Phillips captured the magic and played it back for the boys. "We couldn't believe it was us," Bill Black said, reminiscing about the historical event.[10] It mattered little that a follow-up session the next evening was, for the most part, a bust. Phillips had his confirmation. He had been right about Elvis. Barely able to contain himself, Sam called his old buddy Dewey Phillips (no relation), the disc jockey at WHBQ in Memphis. After hearing the song, Dewey agreed to play it on his show the next night and see what happened.

It took only one spin, and calls to WHBQ came flooding in. Gladys later admitted she had been so caught up in hearing Phillips announce her son's name over the air that she hadn't even heard the record the first time through. No matter. At one point, it was repeated an astonishing seven times in a row. The audience response was so strong that Dewey requested Elvis come by the studio to do an interview. When it was over, Presley sauntered off into the hot Memphis night, his lifelong dream flirting with a touch of reality.

The moment was similar to when Nixon had won the Whittier businessmen's support for the nomination, but it differed drastically in that Nixon had control of how he would market himself to his public. It had been his campaign, his money at risk. Elvis was a 19-year-old kid struggling to help support his parents, and, like most of the hopefuls who showed up at Sun Records, he had neither the means nor the experience necessary to promote himself.

Sam, of course, was in the business of doing just that. He knew he had a hit on his hands in "That's All Right," but a flip side would be needed before he could release the record. It took several more evenings of studio work, but the magic was re-created in an upbeat version of Bill Monroe's "Blue Moon of Kentucky." Per Sam's suggestion, Scotty became the trio's manager on July 12, exactly one week after their first recording session together. Live appearances quickly followed, the first major one on July 30 at Overton Park, where, a little over a year earlier, Elvis had spent countless hours listening to some of his favorite artists.

He was an instant hit at Overton and just about everywhere else around town, from the Elk's Club to the Eagle's Nest. At the same time, "That's All Right" was climbing the charts — and not just in Memphis. *Billboard* reviewed it in early August, dubbing Presley "a strong new talent."[11] By the end of the month, the record had entered *Billboard*'s regional charts, and Elvis was jiggling his hips all around Memphis to crowds of hysterical teenage girls.

Not everyone raced to jump on the Presley bandwagon. Conservative DJs, including those from his home town of Tupelo, refused to play the record. Critics blasted the new sound, calling it an insult to popular music. Community leaders were appalled at the idea of a white boy sounding black.

Amid the backlash — and perhaps in part because of it — Presley's longtime dream of playing the Grand Ole Opry materialized on October 2. Afterward, he would consider it more of a nightmare. The mostly adult hillbilly audience, used to standard country fare from performers like Chet Atkins and Hank Snow, reacted to Elvis's performance with curious stares and mild applause. Some reports went as far as to say he was booed off the stage.

The experience could have been a major setback, but Presley was able to put it behind him and move on. He still believed in himself, and, thanks to Sam, he was no longer alone in that belief.

4. Let the Games Begin

Phillips had released Elvis's second record, "Good Rockin' Tonight," a day before the Opry broadcast. Folks behind the production of the famous *Louisiana Hayride* radio program were impressed enough to request that Elvis perform on their show. Though not as prestigious as the Opry, the *Hayride* had a CBS hookup, allowing it to reach stations in 28 states. Elvis and the boys made their first appearance on October 16, 1954. Audience response was so favorable that the trio was signed to a one-year contract just a few weeks later.

Presley's growing popularity soon proved too much for Scotty to handle as manager, given that he was also in the group. Following the first *Hayride* appearance, Memphis DJ Bob Neal, whom Elvis had first met during the *Saturday Night Roundup* show a few years earlier, took over as manager, although a formal contract was not signed until January 1955.

"That's All Right" surpassed everyone's expectations, but the world is full of one-hit wonders. Like Nixon, Presley realized how important it was to strike while his name was in the headlines. On Neal's advice, he quit his job at Crown so he could take his show on the road full time with Scotty and Bill.

Certainly this could not have been an easy decision to make. Nixon had labored over whether he should enter the race for congressman, and he had had only his own and Pat's welfare to consider. Elvis knew his parents depended on his income to pay the bills. He loved his mother more than anyone else in the world; the idea of intentionally causing her worry must have broken his heart. In addition to losing his salary, whatever hope she still had that her son might become an electrician would vanish for good.

Presley wanted his dream to materialize so badly — as much for his parents as himself — that he was willing to take the risk. While Nixon continued to gamble until the very end, increasing the stakes with every toss of the dice, Elvis grew progressively more cautious as he moved up the ladder. "I don't like to take chances," he said in an interview years later." As long as I'm doing okay, why change it?"[12] As 1954 wound down, however, things were hardly okay for Elvis or his parents. He saw the chance to better their situation, and he went for it.

Countless pages would be needed to detail Presley's on-stage performances in the months that followed. What is important to this study is the reaction to his near-instant success. While Nixon's climb from unknown to vice president evolved at an impressive pace, he still had time to consider the consequences of every step he took. Presley was thrust into the fast lane overnight; he had little chance to sleep, let alone reflect on what was happening.

Nixon covered his fair share of ground on the campaign trail, racking up more than 46,000 miles on his vice presidential run alone, but the "whistle stops" were done by train, affording time to rest from one city to the next. Presley was cramped behind the wheel of a car, dodging potholes on winding country roads. From October 1954 to March 1955, Elvis, Scotty, and Bill logged more than 300,000 cross-country miles, playing one night stands.

Elvis coped as best he could for a 19-year-old boy. To this day, many Presley fans blame Uncle Sam for the entertainer's introduction to amphetamines, claiming he was given pills to help him stay awake on watch during his tour in the army. This theory is a comfortable way of passing the buck. More likely, his habit began on his first extended road trip, after he relinquished his job at Crown.

"If you ask me, Elvis was taking amphetamines for a number of years already," said Rex Mansfield, one of Presley's buddies from the army days. "He brought me into contact with it in January/February 1959, and I was also present one time when he filled up his stock at the local drugstore. Four beakers, filled to the brim."[13]

Uppers were nothing new to traveling musicians in the fifties. Air travel was too expensive for all but the biggest stars, and trains didn't stop in every little corner of the country. Most entertainers had no choice but to pack up their equipment, haul it in the back of their vehicles, and drive to the next stop on the tour. "We slept in the back of the car," Elvis recalled in a 1972 interview. "We'd do a show and get offstage and get in the car and drive to the next town and sometimes just get there in time to wash up and do the show."[14]

A hectic road life was not the only price Presley paid for realizing his dream. Whereas an exuberant Pat Nixon worked side by side with her husband, cheering him on, Dixie Locke, whom Elvis had dated steadily since graduating from Humes, reacted to his success with mixed emotion.

Dixie was thrilled that Elvis's dream had come true, but she also realized what it meant as far as their future together was concerned. Evening strolls and picnics in the park had been replaced by long-distance phone calls and rumors of one-night stands with other women. Even when the couple did spend time together, music overshadowed the romance. "I felt like all of a sudden I was not a part of what he was doing," Dixie said years later. "And he loved it."[15]

Times were changing for Vernon and Gladys as well. While Nixon's political career had certainly affected his parents' lives to some extent, there had been no immediate change in their social or financial status when he was elected from California's Twelfth District. The Presleys' universe was turned upside down in a matter of several months. Following the success of "That's All Right," they left their old neighborhood behind, moving first to a small four-bedroom house on Lamar Avenue, later to a brick house on Getwell Street. Although both homes were located in modest, middle-class areas of Memphis, they were a world away from the familiar Lauderdale Courts.

Vernon adjusted well to his new lifestyle, which was not surprising, as it relieved the pressure of having to maintain outside employment. His son's

4. Let the Games Begin

income was already far above what he ever could have imagined. For Gladys, however, financial independence did not equal a stress-free life. While it was true that she no longer had to empty bedpans at the hospital, she felt nervous and uncomfortable in her new surroundings. Neighbors looked at her curiously, fans gathered on the lawn at all hours. Meanwhile, her cherished son was hardly ever at home. In the midst of his continual absence, she had to deal with what was being said and written about him. The harshest criticism came from religious organizations, dubbing Elvis' hip shaking as sinful, a threat to the morality of America's youth.

Considering the importance religion played in Gladys' life, these comments must have been particularly upsetting. She knew Elvis was a good, decent boy who loved God and country. While she conceded that he might look a little strange, wiggling around on stage, he was not doing anything wrong. He just felt the music and let it carry him away.

Critics were not interested in a doting mother's explanation, of course. They wanted stories that sold copy. Predictably, the more successful Elvis became, the harder they hit. The *Americana*, a weekly Catholic magazine, warned parents that Presley's movements while singing "were not only suggestive but downright obscene."[16]

No doubt Nixon's parents had suffered a few sleepless nights when rumors of the fund scandal topped the headlines, but they were mature, experienced businesspeople with lives of their own. They knew the strength of their son's character and believed in his ability to pull through.

Vernon, having experienced his share of rumors after his prison term, took the attacks on Elvis with a grain of salt, but Gladys seemed to dwell on them. She was losing her son to the cruel, outside world, and there was nothing she could do about it. As he drifted further away, she struggled to cope with her lonely home life. Occasionally, she would enjoy a few beers in the afternoon, sometimes with a friend or relative, sometimes alone. On her son's urging, she spent money on herself for things she neither needed nor wanted. She bought clothes and jewelry, most of which she never wore. She went to the beauty parlor and the movies. But mostly she worried about her boy.

Elvis was concerned with the effect his fame was having on his mother, but he had no intention of allowing criticism from mean-spirited strangers to alter his future plans. He had gotten this far by remaining true to himself and his style. Why tamper with success?

Bob Neal concurred, assuring Elvis there was no end to how far they could go together — especially if they made the right connections along the way. Neal, acquainted with several national promoters working the country circuit, knew the value of marketing his product. One of his contacts, Oscar Davis, often stopped by the radio station to shoot the breeze. During one such stopover, Neal invited Davis to come out to the Eagle's Nest, where Elvis was performing. As fate would have it, Davis was in Memphis doing scouting work for Jamboree Productions, a national booking agency run by Colonel Tom Parker.

For Presley, it was the beginning of an odyssey that would have no end.

Chapter 5

The Shaping of a Hero

A teacher affects eternity; he can never tell where his influence stops.

— Henry B. Adams, U.S. historian

Despite the economic hardships suffered throughout their childhoods, Presley and Nixon were fortunate; they each had parents and teachers who encouraged their dreams.

Nixon credited his father with having had the most profound effect on his life. Chief Newman, his college football coach at Whittier, ran a close second. Gladys was the heart of Elvis's world during his formative years, making certain he got an education and nurturing his musical development at every opportunity. Presley's boyhood idol, Mississippi Slim, inspired him to keep practicing his guitar. Mrs. Grimes was responsible for his appearance at the fair.

Without the influence of these early mentors, it is unlikely that Presley or Nixon would have gained the strength of character needed to reach their particular goals. For Nixon, the lesson was to look inward for courage and survival, to rely on himself to get the job done. Although he continued to watch and learn from those around him after the fund scandal, he never forgot who controlled his political survival; the Checkers Speech had proven self-reliance was the key to success.

Presley, too, had gained confidence in his own abilities, but that confidence was limited to only one aspect of his chosen career. Nixon had climbed the ladder at a slower pace, learned the business of politics step by step. Elvis, like many young, aspiring artists, knew nothing about contracts and percentages, he just wanted to be a singer. Given the circumstances, he had no choice but to put his faith in someone else. He was extremely lucky that his someone turned out to be the highly reliable and artistically driven Sam Phillips.

Music and politics may appear to have little in common on the outside, but beneath it all, the gears spin in the same direction. Nixon's conclusion that people were his friends only as long as there was something in it for them applies equally to the entertainment industry; yesterday's teen idol is lucky if he winds up doing commercials for a used car dealer.

The situation was no different during Presley's rise to fame. He was a naive, poor kid who saw the dream of his lifetime dangling within reach. Phillips could have handed him a contract written in a foreign language, and he probably would have signed it. Instead, trust and honesty were the order of the day. Sam never made a promise he could not keep.

While this scrupulous relationship hindered Elvis in making decisions later on, it left him free to concentrate on developing his talent when it mattered the most. Regardless of what else happened, he learned he must always remain true to himself. "I don't think there's anybody who can decide what I can do best," he said later, when asked if he would continue to choose his own material. "I think it would be a big mistake if I had somebody else telling me what to record and how to record it."[1]

Phillips did, of course, offer guidance while Elvis was learning. "Sam had an uncanny knack for pulling stuff out of you," Scotty recalled. "Once you got a direction, he'd work you so hard you'd work your butt off, he'd make you so mad you'd want to kill him, but he wouldn't let go until he got that little something extra sometimes you didn't even know you had."[2]

In Presley's case, Sam's role extended far beyond the studio walls of Sun Records. Certainly, Gladys's encouragement remained vital to Elvis's development as an artist, but because he felt responsible for taking care of her, especially once he became a man with a full-time job, her position as a role model began to diminish. Vernon, meanwhile, had grown increasingly comfortable sharing his adult responsibilities with his son. When Elvis mentioned he might abandon his electrician plans in order to concentrate on his music full time, the elder Presley responded that he had never known a guitar player who was worth a damn.

Standing at the crossroads of his life, 19-year-old Presley had never been more on his own — until Sam Phillips pulled him under his wing.

"He had confidence in me," Phillips related when discussing Presley's first appearance at Overton Park on July 30, 1954. "When I got there he was standing on the steps at the back of the shell looking kind of pitiful — well, maybe pitiful is the wrong word, I knew it was the way he was going to look: unsure." Elvis hugged Sam and confessed that he was terrified of going on stage. What if the people didn't like him? "Well," Sam explained, "you know, it's like when somebody's mother is real sick and you tell them everything is going to be all right, and yet you know there's the possibility that his mother might die. I said, 'Look, Elvis, we'll find out whether they like you or not.' And then I said, 'They're gonna love you.'"[3]

Sam was all business when he needed to be, but he made sure that Elvis

5. The Shaping of a Hero

continued to enjoy what he was doing. Marion Keisker recalled seeing a lot of laughing and goofing off during those early sessions; confirmation of this exists on many of Presley's out-take recordings. In later years, such antics were viewed by his producers as a waste of recording tape and studio time. None of them ever realized what Sam had figured out during that first session with Scotty and Bill: in order for Elvis to be successful, he had to have fun.

It is difficult to speculate how long Sam expected his association with Elvis to last, but given his business savvy, he must have known that Presley was destined for bigger and better things than Sun Records could ever provide. So, too, did Bob Neal. Elvis and the boys were drawing enthusiastic crowds on the Southern circuit, but Neal realized it would take national exposure to bring in the big money. Introducing Elvis to Oscar Davis was a logical move in that direction. At the time, of course, Neal had no way of knowing just how big a move it would turn out to be.

After watching Presley's performance at the Eagle's Nest on Friday, Davis invited the boy to drop by Ellis Auditorium for Eddy Arnold's show on Sunday evening. Eddy was always looking for new talent, Davis added; perhaps he could arrange a backstage meeting after the show.

By the time the big night arrived, Presley must have been walking on air. Not only was he able to attend the concert for free, he got to shake hands with the star of the show. Elvis also met Eddy's backup group, the Jordanaires, one of the day's top vocal groups, who would provide background and harmony for Presley's records in the not-too-distant future.

Watching the introductions from across the way, with a seeming disinterest in the whole affair, was Colonel Thomas Andrew Parker.

To this day, Parker's personal history remains somewhat cloudy. Was he actually Andreas Cornelius van Kuijk, born on June 26, 1909, in Breda, Holland, the descendant of a French mother and Dutch father? And did he, at age 18, enter the United States illegally in 1929, stowed aboard a ship?

In *Elvis and Gladys*, Dundy cites possible confirmation stemming from a 1983 lawsuit filed against Parker by Presley's estate, in which Parker claimed he could not be sued under federal laws because he was "a man without a Country." The unique line of defense was never put to the test, as a settlement was reached prior to the trial date. More recent research, conducted by Dutch journalist Dirk Vellenga and published in 1988 in his book *Elvis and the Colonel*, uncovered a birth certificate and other official papers from Holland supposedly connected to Parker.

Records confirm that a Thomas Parker served in the army from 1930 to 1932. Several accounts have suggested that van Kuijk obtained legal papers from the government during his time of service, thus becoming Tom Parker, while others contend he did so illegally, stealing them from the body of a dead man.

In 1960, the Colonel told *Time* magazine that he had been orphaned at an early age and spent his teenage years working for his uncle's Great Parker Pony Circus. Parker listed his official birthplace as Huntington, West Virginia, a town that borders three other states. The simple truth, or a resourceful way around it? Tracing a family tree with the common name of Parker spread over four states would most surely result in numerous possibilities.

In 1987, a group of Belgian and Dutch fans traveling on an extensive tour of the U.S. to coincide with the tenth anniversary of Presley's death met with Colonel Parker in Las Vegas. "We conversed with him in our language," recalled one fan. "He still remembered enough to understand it *and* respond."[4]

While the precise facts, whatever they are, were buried with the infamous Colonel in January 1997, an Associated Press article covering his death reported that the immigration theory had been confirmed by Parker's wife, Loanne, and his longtime friend, Bruce Banke.

Regardless of his ancestry, events following Parker's army days are, for the most part, quite well documented. Upon his discharge, he joined up with a traveling circus, where he learned the ins and outs of managing various entertainment acts. From there, he dabbled in just about everything — from managing country singer Gene Austin to serving as a dogcatcher in Tampa, Florida.

Parker finally found his true calling in 1944, when he was hired by the Grand Ole Opry to manage its Traveling Tent Show. Convinced that the show's top act, Eddy Arnold, was destined for greatness, Parker soon took over as the singer's personal manager. Although Arnold was already quite well established, the hit of the Opry and under contract to RCA, it was under Parker's stern guidance that he rose to national fame.

The Colonel, as the manager had taken to calling himself, was actually no colonel at all. The "commission" was merely a gesture of friendship from the governor of Louisiana, Jimmy Davis, who presented his old carny friend with the honorary title in 1948. But Parker liked the sound of the impressive title and thus became Colonel Tom Parker from that point forward. In 1953, he received similar credentials from the governor of Tennessee, Frank Clement, for having assisted Clement in his successful election campaign.

Parker's lucrative association with Arnold lasted until 1953, when Eddy, by then America's most popular country singer, decided he had had enough of the Colonel's controlling interference in his life, both on and off the stage. Parker retreated to Nashville, where he gathered together a small staff headed by Tom Diskin and Jim O'Brien, both of whom would remain with him for the rest of his working days. By 1954, Parker was managing Hank Snow, a Canadian star whose popularity had finally taken hold in the States, thanks to his regular appearances on the Opry and a contract with RCA. Together, Parker and Snow formed Jamboree Productions, a national touring company.

Having represented such proven artists as Austin, Arnold, and Snow, the Colonel could afford to take a wait-and-see attitude toward the unconventional

5. The Shaping of a Hero

kid from Memphis whom Oscar Davis seemed so excited about. A disappointed Bob Neal remained persistent in his contact with Davis and Parker, but it was February 1955 before the Colonel agreed to book Elvis on a tour with Hank Snow.

Once the decision was made, the Colonel's lukewarm attitude evaporated into the steamy crowd. Regardless of his personal opinion regarding Elvis's talent, there was no question that audiences loved the kid with the gyrating hips and the sensuous, yet innocent smile. When it reached the point where even Hank grew uneasy following Presley's act, Parker knew he had discovered the hottest star since Eddy Arnold. There was only one problem: Elvis already had a manager, local DJ Bob Neal. After mulling over the possibilities, Parker took Neal aside and suggested, in a casual, offhand manner, that perhaps the two of them should become partners in young Presley's career.

Neal saw the opportunity as a great career move, both for himself and Elvis, but Sam Phillips was skeptical. Not surprising, considering that Parker had been so brazen as to suggest — to Sam's face — that Presley would never get anywhere if he stuck with Sun's small-time label. Sam voiced his concerns to Elvis and Neal but did not attempt to stand in the way. Like it or not, he realized that national exposure, both for Elvis and Sun Records, would come more quickly through Parker's connections.

The Colonel's reputation lived up to the hype, though not all of his contacts were ready to embrace Presley with open arms. On the strength of the February tour with Hank Snow, Bob Neal arranged an audition with the Arthur Godfrey talent show in New York, the very program that had launched the career of Elvis's longtime idols, the Blackwood Brothers Quartet. As had been the case with Richard Nixon some 20 years earlier, however, the Big Apple sent Presley on his way with a "thanks but no thanks." In the words of Godfrey's assistants, Elvis had a long way to go before he was ready for prime time.

A full schedule kept Presley from dwelling on the rejection. In addition to regular monthly appearances on the *Hayride*, Elvis, Scotty, and Bill continued to play one-nighters from Cincinnati to Dallas. Many of these early bookings can be attributed to another of Parker's connections, popular Cleveland DJ Bill Randall, who was impressed enough with Elvis to advertise his upcoming appearances during his radio show, thus giving Presley his first real exposure above the Mason-Dixon line. Randall even went so far as to suggest to Freddy Bienstock, a heavyweight at RCA's publishing house, Hill and Range, that he consider putting Elvis under contract. Bienstock, no doubt overwhelmed with similar suggestions from amateur talent scouts, initially passed on Randall's suggestion.

The month of May brought another Jamboree tour, coinciding with the release of Elvis's fourth single, "Baby, Let's Play House." By the time the tour was over, the Colonel had arranged enough dates that Elvis would be kept busy performing through September.

If Parker harbored any doubts about the heights his young protégé could reach, they were alleviated by the success of the May tour. He could see where Elvis was headed, and he had no intention of sharing the limelight with an amateur. Unbeknown to his "partner," the Colonel began calling Presley's home to discuss business matters without Bob Neal listening in.

Elvis, of course, was thrilled by the individual attention Parker was devoting to his career. He tried to explain to his parents and Dixie what an important connection he had made in the Colonel, how the man could take him places a local guy like Neal could never even dream about.

Vernon agreed with Elvis. Gladys and Dixie had their doubts.

Gladys just could not understand why her boy continued to push himself so hard, given that he had already made more money than she had ever dreamed of. Privately, she confided to an old Tupelo neighbor that all she really wanted was for Elvis to come home and stay with them in Memphis, to be a family again.

Dixie, on the other hand, understood all too well. She knew Elvis loved what he was doing and that he would never stop, regardless of how much money he made. She also knew there was more truth than rumor to the girls on the concert tours, the one night stands following the shows. Consequently, she put her dream of living happily ever after with him on the back burner and began to date other boys.

While this may seem a minor detail in the scope of things — their relationship was, after all, a teenage romance — it was no small thing to Elvis at the time. Friends said he never really got over the rejection. Understandable, considering there was far more at stake for the budding star than a bruised ego. Dixie had loved him *before* he was famous. She remained his link to the simple, ordinary life. When put in perspective, Presley didn't lose a girlfriend as much as he lost a part of himself. Never again would he know for certain whether a woman loved him for the person he was — or for the image he represented.

Nixon was married years before he entered the political arena. Pat understood his dream, shared his joy in the victories, his agony in the defeats. In his writings, he credited her with being the rock in his life, and rightly so: she stood by him through the most difficult times of his life.

After his breakup with Dixie, Elvis had to struggle through the ups and downs on his own. He had friends, of course, but none he could really confide in, as they had only become his friends after the fact. "They used horrible language," Dixie recalled. "They all smoked, everybody had a drink — it was a group of people I felt totally uncomfortable with."[5] While a part of Elvis must have shared her feelings, his new, worldlier side welcomed all the attention. Finally, he was star of the show *after* the performance had ended.

Meanwhile, he continued to drift further away from Gladys's vision of a normal family life. Colonel Parker's emergence on the scene only served to

5. The Shaping of a Hero

escalate the distance. "We all used to wonder about the Colonel," Gladys's older sister, Lillian Smith, recalled. "He'd come busting into the house and never had a smile for anyone, never made a joke or passed the time of day. Never so much as nodded at any of us who was there. He was all business, always in a hurry — dashing, dashing all over the place, making money, dashing like he was going to grab it right out of the air."[6]

As life on the home front began to fall apart, offers to buy Elvis's contract from Sun were pouring in. Sam said he might be interested if the price were right, but he rejected all of them for one reason or another. He was worried that things might get too big too fast, especially with Colonel Parker waiting in the wings.

Sam's concern proved a legitimate one. In early August, Parker had a contract drawn up specifying himself as "special advisor to Elvis Presley (artist) and Bob Neal (manager)." Because Elvis was not yet of legal age, the Colonel needed the senior Presleys' signatures on the document. Initially, Gladys refused, but by mid-month, Elvis and Vernon had convinced her it would be in everyone's best interests if the Colonel took over.

Like Gladys, Bob Neal seemed to accept the inevitable. While technically he remained Presley's manager until his contract expired the following March, it was Parker who made 90 percent of the decisions regarding Elvis's career from mid-August 1955 onward.

From a business perspective, they were not bad decisions. Elvis was added to the Hank Snow Jamboree on a permanent basis, receiving national exposure alongside such popular stars of the day as Slim Whitman, the Carter Sisters, and Faron Young. By the end of October, Parker had negotiated a deal with RCA, which agreed to buy Presley's contract from Sun for $35,000 — an unprecedented figure at the time.

Like any good businessperson, Sam's first loyalty remained with his company. If he expected Sun to compete on a national level, he needed cash to promote his other artists. Offers of $35,000 did not come along every day. While he truly believed Elvis's popularity would continue to climb, he was unwilling to gamble away his company's future waiting for it to happen. On November 21, 1955, with what must have been great artistic regret, Sam signed away full interest in Elvis's recordings, including the five singles already released on Sun's label.

The Colonel wasted no time in taking over as Presley's full-time mentor. "Heartbreak Hotel," Elvis's first song for RCA, was recorded about six weeks later and eventually topped the charts nationwide, due largely in part to Presley's television appearances with the Dorsey Brothers, Steve Allen, and Milton Berle — all courtesy of deals closed by his manager, hot on the heels of his new recording contract.

As national success grew at a fast and furious pace, criticism of Presley's style continued to mount. Northern journalists, unfamiliar with the deep

South's expressive, Praise-the-Lord gospel sing-ins during church on Sunday mornings, denounced Elvis's stage behavior as indecent. Parents and social committees, on a constant yellow alert for the "enemies" hell-bent on demoralizing their youth, were quick to join in. Following the broadcast of Elvis's second appearance on the *Milton Berle Show*, the *Daily News* concluded, "[Popular music] has reached its lowest depths in the 'grunt and groin' antics of one Elvis Presley.... Elvis, who rotates his pelvis, was appalling musically. Also, he gave an exhibition that was suggestive and vulgar, tinged with the kind of animalism that should be confined to dives and bordellos."[7]

Colonel Parker was overjoyed by all the controversy, which amounted to unlimited free publicity, but Elvis did not see it that way. His character and integrity were being challenged, just as Nixon's had been by the fund scandal. He knew how badly the personal attacks were hurting his mother, that they were taking a toll on her physical and mental well-being.

Still, he was convinced the good outweighed the bad. His mother would never have to empty another bedpan as long as she lived. He could finally buy the expensive clothes and fancy cars he had always dreamed of — not only for himself, but for his friends and family. Best of all, he was able to provide his parents with a brand-new home of their very own.

What the budding star did not yet realize was that no matter how much money he made, he would never become one of the elusive haves.

In March 1956, the Presleys moved to 1034 Audubon Drive, a one-story, ranch-style home, located in one of Memphis's more fashionable neighborhoods. Gladys insisted they bring along their old furniture, though most of it wound up in the den when Elvis convinced her they should have new furnishings to go along with their new house. According to neighbors, the Presleys chosen decor consisted of "all the furniture in a store you wouldn't buy."[8]

In reality, it was not Elvis's taste in loud clothes or gaudy wallpaper that were at issue. From day one, the established residents of upscale Memphis wanted nothing to do with the hillbilly Presleys, and they were not shy about saying so. They complained to the police about the noise, cars coming and going at all hours, teenagers hanging around.

Most families probably would have sold the place and moved on. Presley erected a brick and iron fence around the property and remained there until April of the following year. Unlike Nixon, who continued to search for acceptance among the social elite, by the time 1957 rolled in, Presley had resigned himself to the fact that he would never fit in. Thanks to Colonel Parker, it no longer mattered. He was an established phenomenon: Elvis Presley, teenage idol of millions, the most sought-after artist of the day. He could darn well do as he pleased.

Although Nixon had not yet attained such prestige, his election to the second-highest office in the country had afforded him a position of considerable leverage within the Republican party. The new VP had no intention of carrying out the traditional "be seen but not heard" role associated with the second-in-command. He was one step away from reaching his ultimate goal, one step from securing the long-awaited respect of the rival haves. Not even his new mentor, President Eisenhower, could stand in his way.

Ike may have been an outsider as far as Washington was concerned, but the former general knew how to play the political game. Regardless of his personal feelings, he hugged the middle ground on all major issues, never taking a stand too far to the right or the left. His ultimate goal was to remain a popular president, to preserve the war hero image that had allowed him to capture the White House. He was able to implement this strategy quite effectively, thanks to his aspiring protégé. When the situation called for talking tough on any given issue, Dick Nixon, Communist-busting pal of the blue-collar voter, was his voice.

It was a philosophy that fit neatly into Nixon's plans. Representing the administration on controversial issues was a risky affair, making the job all the more attractive. As was the case with Colonel Parker, Nixon did not worry about the negative effects of the exposure; what mattered was the result — that his name remain in the headlines throughout his tenure as vice president.

By the time Eisenhower had taken office in January 1953, the fanfare surrounding the Hiss case was long over, but America's fear that Communism would continue to spread throughout the nation lived on. Fueling the flames was Joe McCarthy, an ambitious Republican senator from Wisconsin. Taking a cue from Nixon's early days, McCarthy was determined to find a Communist around every corner. Initially, his investigations were conducted with some caution, but he soon grew tired of obtaining proof before slinging accusations.

Eisenhower realized he had to distance himself from McCarthy's extremism, but he was concerned that denouncing the senator's efforts would make him appear weak on Communism. Assigning the duty to Nixon left him on comfortable ground; if the public reacted unfavorably, it would be to the vice president's position, not his.

A nationally televised address — to be delivered by the trusted VP — was scheduled for March 13, 1954. Nixon worked on the material for five days before presenting it to the president for his approval. In *RN* (page 145), he said that while Eisenhower was satisfied he did not need advice on writing a political speech, he should try to "work a smile or two into the program." Nixon agreed.

The speech was delivered in typical Nixon style, flavored with language aimed at rallying the common people. He referred to the Communists and their supporters as traitors and related that many voters he had spoken with considered them nothing but a bunch of rats who ought to be shot. After agreeing that they were indeed "rats," Nixon went on to explain that it was important, when going out to "shoot rats" that the shooter not strike out aimlessly at anything that moved, but rather, take careful aim. "We have to be fair," he calmly explained, "for two very good reasons: one, because it is right; and two, because it is the most effective way of doing the job."⁹

Nixon's speech satisfied most party activists, who had been pushing the administration to distance itself from McCarthy before the upcoming election. As it turned out, their action had not come a moment too soon. Congressional hearings on the senator's conduct began a month later and carried on throughout the summer. In December, he was formally reprimanded for his behavior, becoming only the third senator ever to be censured by his colleagues.

Not coincidentally, the move came too late to spare Republicans a disastrous off-year election: Democrats increased control of both houses by substantial margins. It was a discouraging time for Nixon, who had campaigned long and hard on behalf of his party. From mid-September to election eve, he had covered more than 26,000 miles, sleeping an average of five hours per night.

Eisenhower, meanwhile, had monitored the campaign from his chair in the Oval Office. Unwilling to risk a loss of popularity by supporting candidates whom some voters might not approve of, he had opted to remain in Washington and "act presidential."

Nixon took the party's loss so personally that he considered quitting politics altogether unless "exceptional circumstances intervened."¹⁰ Nearly 11 months later, on September 24, 1955, President Eisenhower suffered a heart attack.

As Presley toured the country, capturing the hearts of swooning teenage girls, Nixon contemplated the possibility of finally realizing *his* dream. Public speculation that he would soon inherit the presidency was impossible to avoid, but Nixon, still meticulously planning ahead, made every effort not to appear overly anxious. He continued to conduct all business from his own office. When attending cabinet meetings, he refused to sit in Eisenhower's chair. Whatever documents he signed were "on behalf of the president."

Nixon doubters were not impressed. Several cabinet members openly accused him of seeking publicity at Eisenhower's expense. Like the religious leaders hell-bent on exposing Presley as a threat to the morality of America's youth, the Republican elite were determined that Nixon be kept in his place. Utilizing his bond with the common people to secure their votes had been quite acceptable, but the possibility of a Nixon presidency was out of the question.

The impending power struggle was postponed temporarily when, 48 days after being stricken, Eisenhower returned to the White House as thousands lined the streets, cheering him on. The question of his health remained a concern, however, causing a flurry within the party as to whom would be nominated the following year, should the popular general decide not to seek reelection.

Nixon's experience and leadership — qualities he viewed as essential to

5. The Shaping of a Hero

obtaining his goal—proved of little value to his peers. What concerned them was his popularity rating among voters, which paled miserably when compared to Ike's. Communism was no longer the hot topic it had been in the midst of McCarthy paranoia. People were turning their attention to other issues: rising unemployment and an unstable economy. The president's supporters were concerned that Nixon's usefulness to the party had evaporated, many going so far as to suggest his presence on the ticket would prove a liability.

Their fears were not unfounded. Recent polls had Nixon trailing well behind Democrat Adlai Stevenson in a head-to-head contest for the presidency. Ironically, even Presley, who in later years refused to publicly endorse any candidate, came out in favor of the Democratic challenger. "I'm strictly for Stevenson. I don't dig the intellectual bit, but I'm telling you, man, he knows the most."[11]

No doubt Nixon had anticipated that key Republicans might withhold their support, as many of them had their own sights aimed toward a presidential bid. When Eisenhower himself refrained from offering an endorsement, however, the loyal VP must have wondered what he would have to do to prove himself worthy. For three long years, he had done whatever had been asked of him on behalf of the party, accepted the dirty jobs in order to preserve Ike's hero status. While his reasons for doing so aided his own self-interests, that could hardly be considered a unique motivation. What politician, at some point in his career, does not envision himself occupying the White House?

Unfortunately for Nixon, he did not fit the image of a president. Physically, he was not an attractive man, and he came across even less so on camera. On the social scale, he led a middle-class life. Throughout his career, he had tried to exploit those characteristics to his advantage, to prove to blue-collar America that he was still one of them. The strategy had been successful prior to the fund scandal and might have continued to work had Nixon been able to secure his colleagues' support. Ultimately, though, they refused to accept him for who he was.

While there is no question that Presley's and Nixon's upbringings were responsible for their successes, it is just as obvious that their backgrounds served to hinder their climbs. Each had been taught to value family, loyalty, and honor. When seeking guidance, they chose mentors who appeared to share their ideals.

Because the Colonel was able to project a fatherly image when needed, Elvis envisioned him as a more successful version of Sam Phillips. While the mistake in judgment would greatly enrich the singer's life financially, on an artistic level, it cost him dearly.

Nixon chose to align himself with Eisenhower for similar reasons: the general was a common man who, like Nixon's own father, had achieved success through old-fashioned hard work. Due to the poor treatment he received from his mentor during the fund scandal, however, Nixon proved better equipped than Presley to handle the disappoints that would later result from the relationship, as the following incident clearly illustrates.

On December 26, 1955, Eisenhower summoned the vice president to his office and suggested that perhaps he might want to consider taking a cabinet post rather than remain on the ticket. He added that accepting a position such as secretary of defense would provide administrative experience, a skill he found essential for a president. In his memoirs, Nixon admitted that he was surprised by Ike's suggestion, although the general seemed to have made it in a "friendly and sincere" manner.

Nixon's comment is hard to fathom, given the circumstances. Judging from Eisenhower's behavior, he cared about Nixon's personal welfare even less than Colonel Parker did Presley's. Yet Nixon, longing for acceptance and approval from his oracle, wanted to believe that he did. Speculating about why Ike did not ask him to remain on the ticket, Nixon said he believed Eisenhower's staff and friends had convinced him that Nixon's presence on the ticket would hurt the president's chance of reelection.

Elvis defended the Colonel in a similar manner throughout his career. Unlike Presley, however, Nixon was able to separate emotion from business. Although he realized that the president's supporters, and probably Ike himself, would have liked nothing better than if he *offered* to resign from the ticket for the "good of the party," Nixon had no intention of making such a sacrifice. If Eisenhower wanted him off the ticket, he was going to have to say so in no uncertain terms.

Of course, Eisenhower realized that forcing Nixon out would divide the party, fueling the Democrats' campaign in the process. Thus, clinging to the strategy that had made him such a popular president, he sidestepped the issue when confronted directly. On February 29, 1956, after formally declaring his bid for reelection, he was asked if Nixon would again be his running mate. Ike responded that it would be improper for him to designate Nixon, or anyone else, as his running mate, given that his party had yet to choose its presidential nominee.

Shortly after the press conference, an article in *Newsweek* appeared detailing the conversation Nixon had had with the president about taking a cabinet post. Nixon later stated that he was never able to trace the source of the leak. On March 7, the press questioned Eisenhower about the story. He replied that he had simply told Nixon to "chart his own course."

The president's remarks caused Nixon to reevaluate his position, but any thoughts he had of quitting evaporated a week later when 23,000 New Hampshire voters wrote his name in on their primary ballots. On April 26, he finally decided to follow the president's suggestion that he "chart his own course" by informing Eisenhower he would be honored to continue under him as vice president. Ike, impressed by the write-in campaign, responded that he was happy to hear it and arranged for Nixon to make the announcement to the press.

Nixon had won a round, but his expectations of a smooth ride to the convention stalled five weeks later when Eisenhower was admitted to the hospital again. The president was operated on for ileitis, an inflammation of the small intestine. Doubts surfaced as to whether he would even be able to run again, let alone finish out a second term. The dump Nixon movement quickly resumed, led by the president's advisor on disarmament, Harold Stassen.

Luckily for Nixon, time was on his side. Key Republicans feared an eleventh-hour split in the party would have a disastrous effect on their upcoming convention. Stassen was silenced, clearing the way for the vice president's renomination in San Francisco on August 22.

Ironically, Nixon was not present to bask in the triumph. Earlier in the day, he had been notified that his father had suffered a ruptured abdominal artery and was not expected to live. The elder Nixon was feeling better by the time Richard arrived at his bedside — well enough, at least, to deliver a final pep talk. "You get back there, Dick," he snapped, referring to the convention in San Francisco, "and don't let that Stassen pull any more last-minute funny business on you."[12]

Nixon watched the convention from his parents' living room later that afternoon. He was renominated by a vote of 1,323 to 1.

Francis Nixon lived to hear his son's acceptance speech, but his condition took a turn for the worse a few days later. In *RN*, Nixon described the event as if he were an omniscient narrator: "He knew that the end was near, so he gave my mother instructions for his funeral and asked to be allowed to die at home rather than in the hospital. He died at 8:25 P.M. on September 4, 1956" (176).

End of subject. No details are given about the funeral, the weather that day, the clothes he wore. Nothing personal that might give the reader insight as to how the death of his father — arguably, the most important person in his life — had affected him. To Nixon, emotions had become just another enemy to be conquered. Over the next four years, he would make great strides in holding them at bay.

As the fall campaign kicked in, it was obvious a more aggressive Nixon had emerged from the San Francisco convention. In a bold move, he chose to disregard Eisenhower's wishes regarding their game plan. Ike wanted to refrain from attacking the Democrats in favor of touting the administration's accomplishments. Nixon tried out the "give 'em heaven" strategy for two days before concluding it would not be successful. The press was disappointed with the lack of campaign rhetoric and tough talk they had become accustomed to, claimed Nixon, and so, after a particularly disastrous appearance in Oregon, the disheartened VP decided to take matters into his own hands. Returning to the Nixon of old, he rose at dawn and began work on a new speech. Later that morning, the adrenaline still flowing, he celebrated his sense of renewal at the piano, engaging in a spirited version of Brahms's *Rhapsody*.

Stevenson, preying on Nixon's lack of popularity within his own party, made Eisenhower's health the prime issue of his campaign. His strategy appeared to elevate his position in the polls, but he went too far for most voters' tastes during a televised speech on election eve.

Gazing flatly into the camera, Stevenson reminded viewers of Eisenhower's poor health and suggested, "distasteful" as it was, that there was a strong possibility that the popular general would die in office, should the people choose to reelect him. What voters should ask themselves upon entering the polls in the morning, he continued, was whether they thought the country could afford to take the chance, considering their decision would very probably result in a Nixon presidency a few months down the road.

The Eisenhower-Nixon ticket won 57 percent of the popular vote, carrying 41 of 48 states. The question of Ike's health faded from the headlines until November 25 of the following year, when he suffered a stroke.

Proving that he had learned more from his mentor than even he had realized, Nixon played both ends of the spectrum when a weakened Eisenhower returned to the White House. Speaking as a friend, he suggested to the president that he cut back on his work load while recovering — there was, after all, no reason why his cabinet members could not make more decisions on their own. Switching to concerned politician, Nixon dutifully added that, on the off-chance the president's health worsened unexpectedly, the administration must be prepared to continue, business as usual, so as not to lay America's government open to question among other world powers.

Eisenhower agreed. A plan was drafted, specifying that the president's fitness for duty would be determined between the president and the vice president. If both parties concurred that the president could no longer perform his duties, the vice president would take over as acting president with full authority until the president was judged able to resume his obligations. If the president was incapable of making or expressing a decision, the vice president would act on his own authority after seeking "appropriate consultation." A decade would pass before a formal document regarding the delegation of presidential power was added to the Constitution in the form of the Twenty-fifth Amendment.

As it turned out, the agreement between Eisenhower and Nixon proved unnecessary. Nixon reported that Ike was back to normal within a few months' time, attending to the daily business of the presidency.

Nixon resumed his duties as VP, intent on reaching his objective, which by now had become twofold. The issue of Communism might not have been as important to voters as it once was, but to Nixon, it had become the main obstacle toward achieving his ultimate goal: world peace.

"Nixon knew that to be a great leader, he had to set a great goal, and he did so," concluded biographer Stephen Ambrose. "It was world peace. The phrase was one he used too often; it was a concept he sometimes abused, and yet it was the cause to which he dedicated his life. Not always effectively, not always wisely, not always selflessly, but always."[13]

Cynics scoff at this deduction, but a study of Nixon's later writings prove that, at least in his own mind, he truly believed he was destined to lead the world in a unified movement toward establishing permanent global peace. Misguided or not, this assumption remained the driving force behind his actions from the time he was elected vice president until Watergate drove him from office.

CHAPTER 6

The Survival of the Fittest

In a battle all you need to make you fight is a little hot blood and the knowledge that it's more dangerous to lose than to win.

— George Bernard Shaw

The period of 1958 to 1960 marked a significant turning point in both Nixon's and Presley's careers. Eisenhower's acquiescence had played right into Nixon's hand, allowing the vice president to emerge from his tenure as an experienced leader at home and abroad. Meanwhile, Presley's rebel image had been cleverly transformed by the Colonel, courtesy of the U.S. Army.

In March 1958, as Nixon prepared for a trip to South America, 23-year-old Presley traded in his blue suede shoes for a pair of combat boots.

Elvis's induction into the service was a major press event, capturing headlines across the world. Acting on the Colonel's advice, Presley passed up the opportunity to serve his time entertaining the troops in favor of regular army duty. Strategically, it was a brilliant move by Parker. The Colonel knew from experience how fickle the music business could be. His boy was currently the most popular entertainer in the country, but who knew what the future held? Elvis mania was limited to teenagers. Stiff competition had already crept into the market with rockers such as Jerry Lee Lewis and Gene Vincent. The tamer, smiling faces of Ricky Nelson and Bobby Vee graced the covers of teen magazines as their songs climbed to the top of the charts. Even the squeaky-clean followers of Pat Boone saw their hero make successful covers of songs first made popular by black musicians.

Shipping Elvis off to the army meant visibly removing him from the teen idol contest, a risky move, but one that had potential to pay huge dividends down the road. If Parker convinced the teenagers' parents that Elvis was really a respectable, God-fearing boy at heart — such a good boy, in fact, that he was willing to put his red-hot career on hold for two long years to serve Uncle Sam — the hip-shaking kid with the curled-up lip would exit the army a reputable soldier, ready to conquer an entire new legion of admiring fans: adults.

6. The Survival of the Fittest

This future scenario may not have been exactly what Presley had in mind, but he had no intention of churning out rock-and-roll records for the rest of his life either. He knew as well as the Colonel that his style might be a passing fad. "Teenagers are my triumph," he admitted to reporters shortly after his second appearance on Ed Sullivan's show in October 1956. "I'd be nowhere without them."[1] Grabbing a page from Nixon's Book of Success, he hoped to use his current popularity as a steppingstone to future endeavors, namely an acting career in Hollywood. Bing Crosby and Frank Sinatra had made the jump from singer to film star, so why not Elvis?

By the time Uncle Sam came knocking, Presley had already laid the groundwork for his transformation. A screen test with producer Hal Wallis two years earlier had resulted in his first big screen effort, *Love Me Tender*, a western starring Richard Egan and Debra Paget. While Elvis's performance left a lot to be desired — as did the film itself — critics grudgingly admitted it was not all that bad for a first attempt. The story in film number two, *Loving You*, was tailor-made for its young headliner: a poor boy hits it big as a rock-and-roll star. Released in 1957, it contained an album of musical numbers, all of which fit neatly into the story line. Presley's acting was noticeably improved.

When his draft number came up on December 17, 1957, Elvis was enjoying mixed reviews on his third film, *Jailhouse Rock*. "While Presley may not be everyone's idea of a favorite star," read the review in the January 25, 1958, edition of *Picturegoer*, "at least now he looks like a performer with a screen future." He showed improvement again in his final pre-army movie, *King Creole*. "Elvis Presley does his strongest acting job so far," proclaimed *TV Radio Mirror*. "Two years ago, Presley on the screen was a laughing stock. But nobody's laughing now."[2]

While it is true that three of Presley's first four films contained enough songs to warrant two full-length soundtrack albums (*Loving You* and *King Creole*) and several extended plays, there was a decent plot to accompany them, and a lead character to challenge Elvis's ability as an actor. Hollywood noticed. Upon his return from the army, he was cast in *Flaming Star*, *Wild in the Country*, and *Kid Galahad*, all dramatic roles with limited musical numbers.

After viewing these encouraging performances, one is left with the mind-boggling question of how such a promising young talent wound up making a decade of B-grade bikini movies. Several factors combined to produce the tragic result, but the catalyst for each was Gladys's death.

Bothered by stomach problems throughout the summer of 1958, Mrs. Presley had finally been diagnosed as having what doctors thought to be a rare type of hepatitis, and she was admitted to the hospital on Saturday, August 9. Elvis, in the midst of basic training at Fort Hood in Texas, was granted emergency leave three days later, after remarking to friends that he would go AWOL to reach his mother's side if need be. He arrived at the hospital late in the evening of August 12 and spent several hours reassuring his parents that everything would be all right. Gladys's condition improved the following day, but she awoke in the early morning hours of the fourteenth, struggling for breath. Vernon summoned help, but Gladys died before the doctor arrived.

"She's all we lived for," a teary-eyed Elvis confessed to reporters as he sat on the steps of Graceland with his father later that day. Leaving the cemetery after her funeral, he stared out the window of the limousine and moaned to friends, "Oh God, everything I have is gone."[3]

A person's character is most clearly revealed in times of tragedy. Francis Nixon's last message to his son had been to keep fighting, and Richard dutifully complied. It is important to note, however, that honoring his father's memory was not the major factor in his quest for the presidency. Nixon believed his destiny — to achieve world peace — was dependent upon his becoming commander-in-chief. Gladys's happiness had always been the driving force behind Elvis's dream; he was determined to make life better for *her*. There is no question he loved the fame and adulation that accompanied his success, but it was a satisfaction he was unable to fully enjoy because of the strain it put on his mother.

Presley had done everything he could think of to alleviate that strain, short of giving up his career. In the spring of 1957, realizing that Gladys was uncomfortable living among neighbors who would never accept them, Elvis had sent his parents on a house-hunting trip that resulted in the purchase of an 18-acre estate in Whitehaven, a suburb eight miles south of Memphis. "Graceland," named in honor of Grace Moore, an aunt of the former owners, provided adequate privacy with its generous, parklike grounds. The 18-room colonial was large enough to accommodate all of the things Gladys had accumulated through the years and still left plenty of space to grow. Elvis paid what Vernon thought to be an inflated asking price of $102,500 and instructed his father to spend whatever else necessary to get the home customized to Gladys's taste.

Mrs. Presley was as proud as any mother would have been under the circumstances, but beneath her glowing cheeks lay a haunting, inner sadness. Beautiful as it was, Graceland marked the ultimate symbol that her son had arrived; there would be no more dreams of leading a "normal" family life. "She never did go nowhere after they moved out there," her sister Lillian recalled. "She used to go to the grocery store, but she quit going to the grocery store. She never was satisfied after she moved out there."[4]

In the wake of her son's more frequent, prolonged absences, Graceland must have seemed all the more overwhelming to Gladys. Maids did the cleaning, cooks prepared the meals. What, exactly, was she to do? Lacking a sense of purpose, it is understandable that, as some accounts contend, the occasional beer she had enjoyed during sultry afternoons on Audubon Drive had become more routine. "When we would come downstairs probably at two or three in the afternoon, his mother would always be there, sitting in the kitchen drinking a beer," related Hank Snow's son, Jimmie Rogers Snow, in an interview.[5]

6. The Survival of the Fittest

If Elvis thought his mother had a problem, he kept it to himself. Vernon, meanwhile, vowed to maintain the comfortable lifestyle his son had provided. If his wife wanted to have a cold one now and then, who was he to stand in her way? "She was getting real sick," Lillian said. "She was drinking a lot. At the end she was drinking all the time. Vodka. Where'd she get it from? Vernon — he gave it to her. Just to keep her quiet."[6]

Despite Elvis's well-meaning efforts, Gladys simply could not adapt to the new world he had provided. Whether the resulting lifestyle contributed to her death or not, Elvis must have entertained the possibility. For years he had struggled to understand why he had survived instead of Jesse Garon. Was it because of his God-given talent? If so, he had done right by his dead twin, used his gift to build a better life for his family. Or so he had thought. Was it possible his goal had been a selfish one after all? Had he been so determined to overcome the humiliation caused by his classmates' teasing that he had lost sight of his true intent? If his dream had caused his mother's death, how could he possibly continue to enjoy the luxuries it provided?

For Elvis, Gladys's passing could not have come at a worse time. His induction into the army had already caused concern regarding the future. Upon completion of basic training, he was scheduled to leave for Germany. Would his fans remain loyal in his absence or forget all about him? Despite the Colonel's assurances, there were no guarantees.

As long as Presley felt responsible for his mother's security, he could overcome the doubts. When she died, most of his motivation was laid to rest beside her. He was on his own now, a grown man, financially secure. The fame and glory he had so coveted as a child had matured as well, baring its ugly guise.

"It affects your home more than it does yourself because you know what to expect," John Lennon said, reflecting on the changes he had experienced during the Beatles' rise. "But your parents and your family don't know what's happening."[7] By the time Gladys figured it out, she was trapped in her son's fame with no visible means of escape.

The Colonel wasted no time stepping in as surrogate parent following Gladys's death. From the beginning of their relationship, Parker had realized the value of Presley's homespun upbringing, that once the boy signed on the dotted line, he would honor the deal whether he liked it or not. He had already secured Vernon's trust. With Gladys out of the picture, no one was left to stand in his way.

Somewhere amid this appealing scenario, Parker had neglected to consider one very important factor: Private Presley would be serving his tour of duty thousands of miles across the ocean. While the distance was not a significant problem insofar as the Colonel's plans for Elvis's career — RCA had several songs in the can, scheduled for intermediate release during his absence — it made for a sticky situation on the public relations end. For the next 18 months, Elvis's personal life would be completely out of Parker's control.

Clinging to each other amid the tragedy of Gladys's death, the Presleys vowed to remain a tightly knit family. Vernon and Grandma Minnie-Mae "Dodger" (Vernon's mother) accompanied Elvis to West Germany, along with Memphis buddies Red West and Lamar Fike.

Upon his arrival, Elvis reported for duty with the Third Army Division, stationed near Friedberg, a town of 18,000 situated about 20 miles from Frankfurt. Presley was a typical soldier during the day, refusing any special treatment because of his celebrity status. Evenings, he was Elvis again, retiring to the rented suites he shared off base with his family and friends in the posh Hotel Grunewald, located in nearby Bad Nauheim.

Predictably, the Presleys proved as unwelcome at the Grunewald as they had been in the upscale neighborhoods of Memphis. Red and Lamar got into bar fights. Vernon would offer to buy the house a round, but often failed to bring along enough cash to pay. Pillow fights and wrestling matches between Elvis and his pals drifted into the hallways, upsetting other guests. By late December, the hotel management had officially requested that the brash Americans vacate the premises.

The task of locating new accommodations proved difficult, thanks to the Presleys' well-established reputation. Elvis searched high and low before finally settling on a modest, four-bedroom rental at 14 Goethestrasse, which he found ridiculously overpriced at 3,000 Deutsche Marks per month (then amounting to the equivalent of about $800). Making matters worse, the owner, Frau Pieper, insisted on remaining in the house.

Red and Lamar were responsible for maintenance and repairs, while Minnie Mae busied herself cooking the daily meals and shopping. Like Gladys, Grandma Presley was known to enjoy a drink or two, a habit she shared with her new housemate, Frau Pieper. According to various German sources, the two were often seen together in local cafes, having coffee and cognac.[8]

Bored in the wake of Elvis's daily absence, Vernon began to spend considerable time in the company of another army couple, William and Dee Stanley. A noncommissioned officer, Stanley had plenty of interesting yarns to pass on, having served as General George Patton's personal bodyguard. Bill Stanley grew to enjoy the elder Presley's company so much that he gave his blessing when Vernon offered to entertain Mrs. Stanley at social functions in his absence. The friendship between Vernon and Dee quickly blossomed into an affair.

As his father courted Dee behind her husband's back, Elvis busied his evenings with various girlfriends, among them Priscilla Beaulieu, the stepdaughter of an air force captain he had met at a party. Presley's initial attraction to the dark-haired beauty was tempered by her age, which he learned after several dates was a mere fourteen and a half. Although he continued to see her periodically during the final six weeks of his stay in Germany, years would pass before the relationship turned serious.

6. The Survival of the Fittest

Elvis's father had no intention of waiting that long. After convincing Bill Stanley that he and Dee were meant to be together, Vernon helped her secure a divorce so that she could join him in Memphis after Elvis's discharge. The couple would officially tie the knot on July 2, 1960. The Stanleys' three sons, David, Rick, and Billy (ages four, six, and seven), who had been sent to a boarding school in the States while Dee's romance was in progress, moved into Graceland that summer and began calling Vernon "Daddy."

Whether the Colonel could have prevented the romance from developing is open to question, though certainly he would have voiced his disapproval, easily foreseeing the effect Vernon's actions would have on his plans for Elvis's new clean-cut image. Presley, meanwhile, went into a state of shock from which he never fully recovered. Two years had not yet passed since his beloved mother's death and already his father had replaced her with another woman, a woman he had stolen from another man, a woman with three young sons, all of whom considered Elvis their new big brother.

The age of innocence had ended, in ways the Colonel had never imagined.

"Elvis died the day he went into the army,"[9] John Lennon once said. A crude remark on the surface, yet very astute. The Elvis who emerged from his tour of duty in March 1960 was Colonel Parker's version of Elvis. The dreamy-eyed boy with the sultry grin, who Sam Phillips had challenged to remain true to himself, no longer existed. In his place stood a confused young man in a dark suit and a polished smile. Nowhere is this more apparent than on Presley's first post-army TV appearance, *Welcome Home Elvis*, taped in the Grand Ballroom of the Fontainebleau Hotel in Miami Beach on March 26.

"Many of Elvis' fans were surprised that he first appeared on a Frank Sinatra television special," noted George Klein, Presley's DJ friend at WHBQ in Memphis.[10] Indeed, in the tape of the program, Elvis appears as uncomfortable with the situation as his fans must have been. Performing his newest RCA single, the ballad "Fame and Fortune," he stands center stage in a dark suit and bow tie, periodically glancing up to the heavens, as if searching for divine guidance. Most striking is the lack of interaction with his audience, a give-and-take present since the inception of his act. No teasing grins or winks as he glances into the crowd, no leg or hip gyrations, suggestive or otherwise. The one-time rebel stands straight and tall, snapping his fingers, shrugging an occasional shoulder, tapping his foot to the beat.

Sinatra must have been pleased to see the rebellious, free-spirited Elvis of the fifties replaced by a younger version of himself; he had detested Presley's early stage act and rock-and-roll music in general. "Rock and roll smells phony and false," he had been quoted in a magazine article several years earlier. "It is the most brutal, ugly, desperate, vicious form of expression it has been my misfortune to hear."[11]

The Colonel had promised a new Elvis, and as far as Sinatra was concerned, he had delivered. "I'm glad to see the army hasn't changed you," he said after Presley performed "Stuck on You," the upbeat flip side to "Fame and Fortune." With a victorious grin, Old Blue Eyes slung his arm across the young man's shoulders and introduced the next number, an odd duet of Presley's "Love Me Tender" and "Witchcraft," one of Sinatra's bigger late-fifties hits.

Parker saw his supreme hope realized in critics' reactions to the television special. "A Conservative Elvis!" read magazine headlines following the show's air date on May 18. "It's the end of an era," announced movie stylist Sy Devore. "The new Elvis now takes his place alongside such conservative and stylish dressers as Frank Sinatra, William Holden, Peter Lawford and even JFK himself. He could pass for a Wall Street banker."[12]

Although Elvis had some trouble adjusting to his new look, he appeared satisfied with the direction the Colonel was taking him. Clearly, the James Dean image he had once coveted had been buried along with Gladys. "I don't want to push my luck," he said in 1962, when asked about his future plans. "I don't like to take chances."[13]

Parker concurred, opting to follow the safe route from this point forward. Shortly after his discharge in March 1960, Elvis reported to Hollywood to make his fifth movie, suitably titled *G.I. Blues*. Not surprisingly, the plot revolved around a singer in the army — serving his hitch in Germany, no less.

In keeping with Presley's new image, the soundtrack album was customized for the toned-down audience of Frankie Avalon and Bobby Vinton. A pleasant mix of ballads and upbeat pop, the songs do not exhibit a trace of the originality present in Presley's early work at Sun. In sharp contrast, *Elvis Is Back*, recorded at RCA's Studio B in Nashville during March and April, represents a classy mix of rock, blues, and soulful ballads, all of which challenged the young master to attempt new heights. Also cut at these sessions were the blockbuster singles "Are You Lonesome Tonight?" and "It's Now or Never," which sold a combined 3 million copies over a period of just a few months.

Elvis Is Back peaked at number two on Billboard's album chart. *G.I. Blues* shot to number one and remained on the charts for 111 weeks. The movie did nothing to enhance Presley's reputation as an actor, but it mattered little to the Colonel, as fans jammed the theaters in record numbers, returning again and again to enjoy the celebrated musical score. Elvis's performances would improve steadily with his next two efforts, but neither the western *Flaming Star* nor *Wild in the Country*, a drama in which Elvis portrayed a juvenile delinquent, came close to matching the box office receipts for *G.I. Blues*.

Not to worry. Supported by facts and figures that must have made even the IRS crack a smile, an elated Colonel assured his boy the wheels would continue to turn smoothly as long as he stuck to what he did best: singing *and* acting. Presley's entourage, consisting of high school buddies and new pals he had met in the army, smiled and agreed.

By now Scotty and Bill, the only associates close to Elvis who actually worked for a living, had been effectively cut off. The two had been unhappy with their contract since the Colonel had taken over and rightfully so. Each had earned a mere $200 per week, out of which they covered their own traveling expenses. As an added slap in the face, they were retained as Elvis's musicians exclusively, which left them unable to pick up extra income playing in other bands or doing endorsements.

The boys had submitted their resignations in August 1957 but were lured back into the fold a few weeks later, after several less-than-lucrative solo appearances. Both sides claimed there were no hard feelings, but things were never the same. Bill's last recording session with Presley was in February 1958. Scotty continued to play on most of Elvis's sessions until 1968 but was employed by the studio, not Presley. Neither was allowed near Elvis again on a social basis.

Jerry Leiber, of the songwriting duo Leiber and Stoller, experienced similar treatment. Bored with the songs he had been commissioned to write for *King Creole*, Leiber had come across what he felt would be the perfect movie for Elvis in which he would play a "handsome, innocent victim." When he attempted to pitch the idea to Parker, one of the Colonel's assistants told him, "If you ever try to interfere with the business or artistic workings of the process known as Elvis Presley, if you ever start thinking in this direction again you will never work for us again."[14]

Rather than encourage Elvis's creativity, the Colonel did everything in his power to stamp it out. He had already chosen his star's persona. Nothing would stand in his way — nothing, that is, that he had foreseen.

Across the ocean, four young men who called themselves the Beatles were causing quite a stir in their native England. Raw and hungry as Presley had once been, they rose from the rundown pubs of Liverpool to challenge his throne. It is ironic, yet fitting, that Elvis served as their inspiration.

"He just looked perfect," Paul McCartney said, recalling a promo ad for *Heartbreak Hotel*. "When I was sixteen, Elvis was what was happening," John added. "I thought, that's it. This is the guru we've been waiting for. The messiah has arrived."[15]

Like Presley, the Beatles struggled through hard times before success arrived. Several members of the group, first known as the Quarry Men, came and went during the early years. The most famous of the "almost weres," Pete Best, played drums for the group's unsuccessful audition at Decca Records on January 1, 1962. Best was replaced by Ringo Starr in August, shortly before the band signed its first recording contract at EMI. Subsequent sessions provided a polished version of "Love Me Do," the group's debut single. Coupled with the flip side, "Please Please Me," the disc reached number 17 on the British charts.

By year's end, the Beatles' popularity had surpassed expectations in England, but EMI did not have enough confidence in the records to back their release in the United States. As a result, Brian Epstein, the boys' manager, cut several deals with small American labels. EMI's business savvy proved on the mark; the songs met a swift, silent death on American airwaves.

Elvis, meanwhile, remained at the top in the States as well as abroad. Early in 1961, he had played three benefit concerts, two at Ellis Auditorium in Memphis and one in Hawaii. Performing classics such as "That's All Right Mama" and "Heartbreak Hotel," he showed signs of returning to his old form, but Parker quickly smothered the fire. The March 25 show in Hawaii proved Presley's last live performance until he would rock Las Vegas some eight years later.

How much did the Beatles affect Elvis' popularity? Prior to the group's emergence, Presley had racked up 27 top tens in a span of nine years, 14 of which hit number one. During the Beatles era (1963–70), only six Elvis singles reached number ten or better. "Suspicious Minds" was the lone number one.

While the Beatles must be credited with an important role, they were not the only factor in Elvis's declining record sales. Just as Presley set the tone for his American rivals, so the Beatles paved the way for an onslaught of British groups vying for the top of the U.S. charts, among them such giants as the Rolling Stones, the Hollies, and the Dave Clark Five.

As the mid-sixties approached, rock and roll was growing with the times. Songwriters — the bread and butter of the industry — began recording their own material. Folk music edged its way into the contemporary market, led by Bob Dylan and Joan Baez. Lyrics of discontent jammed the airwaves, questioning the war in Vietnam, the government, society in general.

A victim of his own success, Presley was stuck on the side of the road, watching the parade march by. His dream of becoming a serious actor was all but over, thanks to the commercial success of the beach-blanket movies that had begun with *Blue Hawaii* in 1961. The film was a smash at the box office, far surpassing any of his earlier work, even the fantastically popular *G.I. Blues*. On the musical end, the accompanying soundtrack remained at number one on Billboard's album charts for 20 weeks, selling in excess of 5 million copies.

Semi-dramatic roles in his next two films, *Follow that Dream* and *Kid Galahad*, left a glint of hope for creativity, but ticket sales for the next Presley vehicle, *Girls! Girls! Girls!*, essentially a remake of *Blue Hawaii*, sealed his fate. The fans were not concerned with Presley's acting, they wanted to see him sing — and if he wore swimming trunks in the process, all the better.

Elvis made no secret of the fact that he detested his plastic, movie star image. Unfortunately, the only one he could turn to for guidance was the very man responsible for the situation. Whatever credibility Vernon had managed to acquire over the years had ended with his marriage to Dee, leaving Colonel Parker the sole role model in Presley's life.

Nixon's parents had stood behind him through the rough times, urging him to fight for what he believed in. More important, he had a strong supporting partner in Pat, who proved his equal on every front.

Presley's decision to pursue his romance with young Priscilla Beaulieu after his discharge from the service put him at the opposite end of the spectrum. After two years of exchanging phone calls and letters, Priscilla finally became Elvis's live-in girlfriend in October 1962. Considered mature for her age of 17, she was, nonetheless, still a child — able to recognize that Elvis was unhappy with the current status of his career, perhaps, but ill-equipped to offer advice as to how he might remedy the problem. "He blamed his fading popularity on his humdrum movies," she recalled in her 1985 autobiography, *Elvis and Me*. "He loathed their stock plots and short shooting schedules. He could have demanded better, more substantial scripts but he didn't."[16]

While Priscilla's theory — that the fault lay in Presley's inability to stand up to the Colonel — may have been a plausible assumption, it failed to take into account the personal influence Parker had on Elvis. Nor does it address the responsibility Presley felt for those around him, an entourage that had grown to a dozen or so buddies, their wives or girlfriends, and distant family members, most of them poor and undereducated, who had appeared on his doorstep looking for work.

Once Elvis realized where his film career was headed, there was nothing he could do about it, short of refusing to honor his contract — hardly something the well-mannered boy from Tupelo would consider, especially with the above-mentioned obligations weighing on his conscience. So he continued to make the movies and record the dismal soundtracks, putting forth less effort with each new release.

Artistically speaking, no one blamed him. The scripts were all the same, the songs progressively worse. "If you think some of the songs he *did* record for those pictures were bad," exclaimed Presley's drummer at the time, D. J. Fontana, "then you ought to have heard some of the ones he *wouldn't* record."[17]

The lack of good material was linked to the growing number of popular artists. Colonel Parker's deal with Hill and Range, the publishing company that supplied most of Elvis's songs, allocated a share of the writer's profits to the singer. While this had once been an acceptable practice, times had changed. As competition for their products grew, quality songwriters were able to pick and choose among hundreds of eager prospects. As would be expected, not many opted to sign away a percentage of what was rightfully theirs.

By the time the Beatles played Ed Sullivan's show on February 9, 1964, the die was cast. Elvis was turning out three movies a year with an average shoot time of six weeks per film. Meanwhile, he was producing virtually no new studio recordings. The soundtracks, usually cut at the movie studio's expense, sold so well that RCA did not concern themselves with the content. In addition, the movies provided an outlet to showcase the star's current music without incurring the cost of a nationwide tour.

It was the best of both worlds, for everyone but Elvis. It was no wonder the Beatles were able to overtake him when competing against the likes of such dubious offerings as *Kissin' Cousins* and *Do the Clam*. Obviously, the group had an advantage in that they were able to pen their own material — and were encouraged to do so by their producer, George Martin. Elvis's contract left him little say in what he recorded, thanks to the Colonel's agreement with Hill and Range. Unless an artist managed to hand-deliver his song to Elvis, she had no chance of getting it heard by Presley, let alone recorded.

Even the Beatles had trouble breaking through the Colonel's barricade. "We tried to meet Elvis during our first tour of the States in 1964," John Lennon recalled, "but couldn't make it because of his commitments and ours."[18] The boys did manage to arrange a meeting the following year, when Elvis was in Hollywood. According to Lennon, they spent the evening together jamming and talking. "We were joined by some of his staff, as well as Colonel Parker."[19] Speculation as to whether the historic jam session was recorded continues to this day though, as of this writing, no evidence to support the theory has surfaced.

In retrospect, the songwriting duo of Lennon and McCartney was arguably one of the best ever, but whether the Beatles were more talented entertainers than Presley remains doubtful. The group quit touring altogether in 1967, citing frustration with the inability to be heard over their screaming fans. Presley, on the other hand, thrived on his audience's frantic shows of affection. Even in later years, when his act suffered from a lack of fresh material, he continued to sell out show after show.

Ultimately, the deciding factor that gave the Beatles their edge was not musical superiority but business savvy. Whereas Elvis maintained undying loyalty and confidence in the Colonel, the Beatles were willing to go with the flow, to allow their own instincts to guide the way, much as Nixon had done throughout his successful political climb.

Realizing he had found his stronghold in foreign policy, Nixon did not hesitate to exploit the opportunities. In eight years as vice president, he represented the United States in 58 countries, the Virgin Islands, Puerto Rico, Wake Island, and Guam, covering a total of 159,232 miles.[20] Every time, his message remained the same: the United States would not be intimidated.

When taunted by rock-throwing rebels outside San Marcos University in Peru during the spring of 1958, Nixon defied the violent crowd by standing in his convertible, waving his fist at his taunters, and calling them "cowards." Several days later, his motorcade was trapped by an angry mob in Caracas and held at bay for 12 minutes. This time, the energized VP was not so cocky. Recalling the incident in *RN*, he admitted having been terrified that the crowd would turn over the car and set it on fire, killing everyone inside. A large press truck traveling ahead managed to break free from the crowd, and Nixon's party escaped behind it, shaken but unharmed. Upon his return home, Nixon was lauded as a hero for having stood up to the bullies. His popularity among voters soared, pulling him even with the Democrats' top challenger, Jack Kennedy, in a trial run for the 1960 presidential race.

Nixon continued the trend the following year, when he was chosen to represent the United States at the July opening of the American National Exhibition in Moscow. While exploring the kitchen of a working model home on display at the exhibit, Nixon took issue with Nikita Khrushchev, the Communist party leader, who was boasting to nearby reporters that the Soviet Union would soon overtake American technology. As the topic drifted from the merits of washing machines to the strength of rockets, Khrushchev quickly lost his temper. "We, too, are giants. You want to threaten — we will answer threats with threats."[21] Somewhere in the conversation, Nixon poked his finger into Khrushchev's chest to emphasize a point. As luck would have it, a nearby photographer captured the moment on film. The photo appeared on the front pages of newspapers throughout the world.

In view of the voters' increasing support, even Nixon's doubters should have realized he was their most viable candidate for the 1960 election. But such was not the case. Power struggles continued to divide Republicans, many of whom expected to glide to victory on the coattails of fellow elitist Nelson Rockefeller.

Republicans had cause to worry. The Democrats, fresh from a unified convention in June, had chosen to pool their efforts in support of their most likely victor in November, the handsome and very wealthy young senator from Massachusetts, John Fitzgerald Kennedy.

A graduate of Harvard, JFK truly did have it all: a family with political clout and unlimited financial means, charisma, and a physical attractiveness Nixon could only dream of. Like Nixon, Kennedy was a navy veteran, though his tour of duty had proven far more active. While in command of PT-109, Kennedy's boat was sunk by a Japanese destroyer. Rescuing several crew members from the frigid water, he aggravated an old back injury and later contracted malaria. "It was absolutely involuntary," he joked, when asked how it felt to be a hero. "They sank my boat."[22] Kennedy received his discharge early in 1945. The following year, he ran a successful campaign for a Democratic seat in the House of Representatives.

As with Nixon, Kennedy dreamed of bigger and better things. In 1952, he conducted a successful Senate campaign against Republican incumbent Henry Cabot Lodge. His losing bid for the vice presidential nomination four years later, however, gave Nixon a clear edge when comparing their early careers.

Presley lost ground during the Beatles era because Colonel Parker refused to acknowledge the competition and update his marketing strategy accordingly. What cost Nixon the edge over the ultimate "have" was not the actual factors of Kennedy's financial advantage and appealing charisma but rather his refusal to admit their importance.

In 1956, Nixon had clearly been the most qualified candidate to serve as Ike's running mate during the president's bid for reelection, yet he managed to secure the nomination only after a bitter fight within his own party. As noted earlier, it was not his experience or loyalty that had been at issue but rather his lack of popularity in the polls. His final term as second-in-command had him confronting Communist demonstrators in Caracas and Khrushchev in Moscow. As the election year approached, figures showed him running even with Kennedy in a head-to-head race; still, it was not until the Republican convention in July that he finally secured his party's nomination.

With the presidency a breath away, common sense suggests his strategy in the upcoming election would reflect the painful lessons he had learned over the years. Instead, he clung to the very tactics that had made his climb such a difficult one. "I believed the key issue of the campaign would be experience," he wrote in *RN* (216), "and in my acceptance speech I brought home that message." Just as Presley was a prisoner to his emotions, Nixon was trapped by left-brain logic.

Party elitists knew all too well that JFK's personality would be a key issue and thus had fought for Nelson Rockefeller, governor of New York, to head the ticket. Rockefeller rivaled Kennedy's charisma and could compete with his endless supply of campaign funds. Nixon tried to appease the haves by asking the governor to be his running mate, but Rockefeller declined.

In the end, Nixon chose Henry Cabot Lodge of Massachusetts, the United Nations ambassador. It was no coincidence that Lodge originated from Kennedy's home state. The Republicans were desperate to achieve balance on their ticket, as Kennedy had done by choosing the Senate majority leader, Lyndon Johnson, an experienced southern politician.

Ultimately, the candidates' choice of running mates proved far less significant than the series of nationally televised debates that preceded the election. Nixon realized the exposure would benefit Kennedy far more than it would him, but there was no way he could refuse to meet his challenger without having the decision become a major campaign issue. Thus he agreed to a four-program schedule to commence in late September.

In the meantime, he took to the campaign trail, pledging to personally visit all 50 states before the election. A fateful stop in Greensboro, North Carolina, put a damper on his plans and proved an omen of things to come. While attempting to get into his car, Nixon bumped his knee. The resulting bruise appeared to be nothing out of the ordinary, but infection set in 12 days later, requiring hospitalization. As he lay in bed recovering, Gallop polls showed Kennedy closing the gap.

Nixon had not come so far only to lose by default: two days after his discharge, he embarked on a whirlwind tour covering 15,000 miles and 25 states. The hectic pace took its toll. In his memoirs, he described his condition as he prepared to face off against Kennedy on the evening of September 26 as being

6. The Survival of the Fittest

"mentally alert," but he conceded that he looked underweight and physically exhausted. In contrast, he thought Kennedy appeared "tanned, rested, and fit" (*RN*, 219).

As if the downturn in the economy and Nixon's subpar health were not enough to ensure a Kennedy victory, the challenger landed a fatal blow, courtesy of President Eisenhower. A month earlier, when asked what major ideas Nixon had contributed as vice president, Ike had flippantly responded, "If you give me a week, I might think of one."[23] Naturally, the incident was raised during the debate. Nixon defended the president's comment in later writings, claiming that what Ike had really meant was for the reporter to ask him again at next week's press conference. Regardless, the damage had been done. While a survey conducted among radio listeners gave the upper hand to Nixon, post-debate polls of the much larger television audience declared Kennedy the clear winner.

Nixon made a strong comeback in the next match-up, but the novelty had worn off as far as viewers were concerned: 20 million fewer watched the second debate. Much to the dismay of the Nixon camp, the figures held for the remaining two programs. By then, JFK had edged ahead in the polls, 51 to 49 percent.

With the election too close to call, support from Ike as the hour of reckoning approached probably would have put Nixon over the top. In *RN*, he stated it was his plan all along to limit the president's appearances on his behalf until the final two weeks of the campaign, when they would have the most impact. If so, the strategy backfired dramatically. Using his health as an excuse, Eisenhower remained a non-presence in the final days.

After spending what he called "the most tantalizing and frustrating" election night he ever experienced, Nixon watched his dream evaporate in the early morning hours. Kennedy was declared the winner by a margin of 113,000 popular votes, the closest election since Harrison–Cleveland in 1888.

Even in the darkest shadow of defeat, Richard Nixon continued to plan ahead. Despite talk of vote tampering in Chicago and Texas, he vetoed fellow Republicans' advice to demand a recount. Too much was at risk. Should the final tally substantiate Kennedy's victory, Nixon would be branded a "sore loser," permanently damaging his political future.

The battle had been lost, but the war was far from over. In January 1961, as Presley settled into his post-army suit and tie, Nixon left Washington confident that he would return a winner. Until that time, however, he had to make a living. Pat wanted to return to California, as did daughters Julie and Tricia, so Nixon accepted a position with the Los Angeles law firm of Adams, Duque, and Hazeltine. Having tasted the excitement of high-level politics, it is no wonder he found the work as boring as the job at Wingert & Bewley years earlier.

While understandable, his need to supplement the monotony with local politics proved far less advantageous the second time around. Acting against the advice of nearly every trusted political aide, as well as his partner and top supporter, Pat, Nixon made the ill-fated decision to run for governor of California in 1962.

In no election did Nixon's political views prove less relevant. Californians were convinced that his bid for governor was nothing more than a steppingstone to a presidential campaign in 1964 and thus rejected him in favor of the Democratic incumbent, Pat Brown, by a margin of nearly 300,000 votes.

Still simmering from his loss to Kennedy two years earlier, Nixon's emotions finally got the better of him. He blamed the media for having given Kennedy preferential treatment throughout the presidential campaign. He blamed fate for the timing of the Cuban Missile Crisis. (On October 22, the president had ordered a naval blockade of Cuba, placing the world on the brink of nuclear war; headlines about the crisis dominated the news for the final weeks leading up to the election. In Nixon's mind, the publicity gave his Democratic challenger a decisive advantage.) Most of all, he blamed himself for having allowed his love of politics to overcome better judgment.

Unlike the nail-biting match with Kennedy two years earlier, the gubernatorial contest was over by midnight. As his defeat to Brown became evident, the press gathered outside Nixon's hotel, clamoring for a concession. He rewarded them with one of the most memorable speeches of his career. After admitting defeat and thanking those involved in his campaign for their support, Nixon got down to what he called the "main theme" of his statement.

> For sixteen years, ever since the Hiss case, you've had a lot of fun — a lot of fun — that you've had an opportunity to attack me, and I think I've given as good as I've taken.
>
> I leave you gentlemen now and you will now write it. You will interpret it. That's your right. But as I leave you I want you to know — just think how much you're going to be missing.
>
> You won't have Nixon to kick around anymore, because, gentlemen, this is my last press conference.
>
> And I hope that what I have said today will at least make television, radio, the press recognize that they have a right and a responsibility. If they're against a candidate, give him the shaft. But also recognize if they give him the shaft, put one lonely reporter on the campaign who will report what the candidate says now and then. Thank you, gentlemen, and good day.[24]

Whatever damage his premature farewell speech inflicted on his career, Nixon felt that his decision to "tell it like it was" had been worth it. While he was obviously referring to a sense of personal satisfaction, the gamble paid off in the literal sense as well: his comments generated as much publicity, perhaps even more, than winning the governor's election would have.

Colonel Parker might have done well to pull the old free publicity trick out of his hat, considering how well it had worked in the early years of Presley's career. Instead, he remained content to let his bank account do the talking, as Beatlemania swept his boy off the charts.

As the sixties progressed, Lennon and McCartney continued to break musical ground with each new release. Like Dylan and Joni Mitchell, the Beatles' songs reflected the changes going on in the world around them, from the innocence of "I Wanna Hold Your Hand" to the eerie loneliness of "Eleanor Rigby."

Colonel Parker, meanwhile, was too busy nailing down the marketing deal for his boy's latest movie souvenirs to care that kids were not rushing out to buy the latest copy of "Frankie and Johnny." The film deals were in the can, the money in the bank. Only when sales crumbled to record lows in October 1967 with the release of *Clambake*, which reached a pitiful number 42 on Billboard's album chart, did executives at RCA sit up and take notice. By then, of course, the damage had been done. Elvis was viewed as a joke by serious music lovers and a has-been to all but his most loyal fans.

On the outside, he appeared to take his celluloid image in stride. Was his marriage on May 1, 1967, his way of accepting what he had become or simply another image enhancement forced on him by the Colonel? Several members of his entourage insist that Parker, troubled by falling revenues, put pressure on Elvis to end his live-in arrangement with Priscilla because he felt it was bad for his "clean-cut" look. Priscilla herself alluded to the possibility. "I know that Colonel Parker asked him to take a long look at our relationship and decide where he wanted it to go," she wrote in *Elvis and Me* (223). "Curiously enough, after his talk with Colonel, it didn't take him long to decide the time was ripe."

According to Presley's stepbrother Billy Stanley, Elvis had been feuding with the Colonel over their contract for several months prior to the wedding. Stanley is convinced that the marriage was only one of several conditions included in the eventual settlement. "Colonel was to desist from making further movie deals — Elvis would decide what pictures he would act in; Colonel was to pursue Elvis's wish to reestablish himself as a performer, through the media and on tour; Colonel was to provide Elvis with the best songwriters and musicians so that Elvis would record and perform only quality music, not movie songs. In return Elvis would fulfill the existing movie contract; would agree either to marry or drop Priscilla; and would pay the Colonel fifty percent of all proceeds after Elvis's expenses."[25]

Subsequent events tend to support Stanley's claim. Prior to Elvis's final movies, *That's the Way It Is* and *On Tour*, both documentaries, he would make only one more film that warranted a full-length soundtrack. *Speedway* peaked at 82 on Billboard's album chart in May 1968.

For Elvis, the dark clouds would burst open to reveal the shiniest of silver linings. Just as the success of *Blue Hawaii* and *G.I. Blues* had retarded his career, the failure of *Speedway* served to revive it. Whether or not the Colonel had agreed to the stipulations mentioned by Stanley, he had to admit the well had finally gone dry; multiyear deals of a million dollars per picture were no longer an option. The huckster needed a new angle, and it conveniently materialized in the form of Lisa Marie Presley on February 1, 1968, nine months to the day after Elvis and Priscilla had wed.

"Elvis Is a Daddy!" read headlines in movie magazines throughout the world. The accompanying photos of an elated Mr. and Mrs. Elvis Presley leaving the hospital with their brand-new daughter in their arms said it all.

Anxious to cash in on this turn of good fortune, Parker approached NBC about a possible television special. The idea was to promote the "family" image by putting Elvis in a suit and tie and having him sing Christmas songs. (*Elvis' Christmas Album*, number one in 1957, was so popular it had been re-released several times throughout the years. His spiritual albums, *His Hand in Mine* and *How Great Thou Art* had also sold well, the latter earning him a Grammy in 1967.) Naturally, this brilliant marketing strategy was not mentioned to Presley until after the contracts were signed.

Nixon, who had battled his own *Speedway* of sorts with his loss to Governor Brown, had used the experience to formulate a new comeback strategy: leave them guessing. As editors and politicians scrambled to debate the effect his "final" press conference would have on the Republican party, Nixon moved his family back to the East Coast, where he accepted a position with the prestigious Wall Street firm of Mudge, Stern, Baldwin, and Todd (which soon became Nixon, Mudge, Rose, Guthrie, and Alexander).

The job proved the perfect intermediate step, allowing the former VP to remain close enough to the political hot seat to keep abreast of all major events happening in Washington while making important new East Coast connections. In addition, his work with the firm afforded numerous opportunities to travel abroad. Not only was Nixon able to maintain current knowledge of foreign affairs—a necessary step in his preparation for a second presidential bid—he was able to do so at company expense.

Nixon had learned a valuable lesson from his loss to Governor Brown: never enter a race without confidence in your ability to win. As the 1964 election approached, Republicans were once again battling Republicans. Right-wingers wanted a Barry Goldwater nomination, a move many insiders feared would chase off all but the most conservative party members. Rockefeller's liberal views threatened to split the party down the middle.

In *RN*, Nixon said moderate Republicans encouraged him to seek the nomination, but he declined, certain that Kennedy would be reelected regardless of whom he faced. If that had been his sole reason for staying out of the race, then the California loss proved more costly than he had ever imagined.

Kennedy's assassination on November 22, 1963, put the upcoming election in an entirely new light. The Democrats were suddenly without their popular incumbent; Johnson was not blessed with JFK's youthful good looks, charm, or charisma. Given Nixon's recent trouncing in his home state, however, there was little he could do but stand by and watch his former running mate, Henry Cabot Lodge, challenge Goldwater for the Republican nomination.

According to Nixon, Johnson's ability to comfort America in the wake of the national tragedy and his superb conduct in the months that followed made him as unstoppable as JFK would have been. While his landslide victory over Goldwater lends credence to that theory, it is interesting to speculate how a more middle-of-the-road Republican candidate might have performed.

Johnson's continuation of the economic and foreign policies of the Kennedy administration resulted in both more social programs and an escalation in the number of U.S. troops in Vietnam, causing confusion among liberal supporters. Although the South would seem a stronghold for a born and bred Texan, Johnson's views regarding racial equality had evolved over the years, causing him to fall out of favor with former allies. In 1957, his support had been instrumental in the passage of the first national civil rights legislation since the Civil War. As president, he managed to push an even stronger bill through Congress in 1964, attacking discrimination in all institutions and public places across America.

Goldwater told the Confederate flag wavers what they wanted to hear, but he hugged the conservative end of the platform too tightly for many voters' tastes. His biggest personality problem was his ego. He did not share Nixon's view that unifying the party was essential to a Republican victory.

Following Nixon's call for togetherness at the San Francisco convention, Goldwater took the podium and firmly stated that while he certainly welcomed every member of the party to hop aboard his bandwagon, "those who don't care for our cause, we don't expect to enter the ranks in any case." His closing remarks provided the basis for his campaign. "Extremism in the defense of liberty is no vice! Moderation in the pursuit of justice is no virtue!" Nixon described the crowd's reaction as split down the middle following Goldwater's speech. Half jumped to their feet, shouting and cheering, while the others sat with their mouths open, stunned into silence.[26]

Americans did their talking at the polls, soundly rejecting Goldwater's parochial philosophy in November. A Democratic tidal wave nationwide sweetened President Johnson's victory; Republicans lost 37 House seats, two in the Senate, and more than 500 in state legislatures. The devastating turnabout left Nixon more determined than ever to eliminate bickering among his fellow Republicans. If he were to have a chance of becoming president in 1968, he knew strengthening the party base during the off-year election was a must.

The task proved far easier than Nixon could have imagined. Due largely in part to Johnson's handling of Vietnam and, to a lesser extent, his vision for a Great Society — a collection of social programs with a price tag far too high for most citizens' budgets — voters decided they were ready for a change. When all was said and done, Republicans gained more seats in 1966 than they had lost two years earlier.

Ironically, one of the most stunning victories occurred on Nixon's former home turf. California's new governor, retired actor Ronald Reagan, had edged his way onto the national scene in 1964, making several well-received speeches on Goldwater's behalf. Although his views were as conservative as Goldwater's, he presented them in such a way as not to offend anyone. This ability, in conjunction with his film star charisma and irresistible sense of humor, made him Nixon's most formidable opponent since JFK.

As Republicans basked in their victory, Nixon used the "leave 'em wanting more" gambit also subscribed to by Colonel Parker. Downplaying talk of his impending bid for the presidency, Nixon insisted that he had not yet decided if he would be a candidate. The strategy proved effective. His name remained in the headlines amid speculation as to if or when he would announce his candidacy. Meanwhile, he continued to travel abroad at his firm's expense, increasing his knowledge of foreign affairs.

Just as Presley's declining soundtrack sales provided the basis for his resurrection, the Republicans' stinging defeat with Goldwater at the helm had provided the perfect forum for a Nixon comeback. As the election neared, conservatives had no choice but to accept what the former VP had been telling them all along: extremism was the kiss of death. Reagan had the winning personality the party was searching for, but his views paralleled Goldwater's so closely that many feared a repeat of 1964 should he become their nominee.

Everything appeared to be falling into place for Nixon, but, like Presley, he was destined to reach the pinnacle of success without his beloved mother beaming proudly from the sidelines. Hannah had been confined to a nursing home in Whittier since suffering a stroke in 1962. Despite her deteriorating state, Nixon had continued to visit her often. In his memoirs, he insisted that although she never acknowledged his presence, he felt certain that she knew who he was.

Given Nixon's controlled emotional state, it comes as no surprise that he failed to shed tears when his brother Don called to inform him of their mother's death on September 30, 1967. What is significant, however, is that he admitted to breaking down at her funeral, literally weeping in the arms of evangelist and friend Billy Graham, as dozens of people looked on.

Also worth noting is the space in his memoirs devoted to the incident. Unlike the brief description of his father's passing, Nixon wrote two full pages about Hannah's funeral and his feelings afterward. As had been the case with Presley following Gladys's death, the sweet taste of success left a bitter taste in his mouth. "My principal thought was a feeling of regret that I had not done as much for her as I might have if I had not been so busy with my own career and concerns," he concluded in *RN* (288).

Both Gladys and Hannah were instrumental in their sons' quests for the American Dream, but it was their mothers' respective reactions to the achievement of those dreams that helped determine how each would deal with his success in later years. Whereas Gladys had kept her true feelings to herself, secretly hoping Elvis would quit, Hannah echoed Francis's last words, encouraging her son to keep fighting. "Don't you give up," she told him after his foiled bid for governor. "Don't let anyone tell you you are through."[27]

Nixon's chance to capture his dream had never looked better as 1968 began. The inner workings of the Democratic party reflected the confused society it represented. President Johnson had fallen out of favor with voters and party members alike, a victim of Vietnam. Meanwhile, the memory of JFK was alive and well in the form of his younger brother Bobby, who had been elected to the Senate in 1964. Challenging Kennedy for the left-wing vote was Eugene McCarthy, the outspoken, antiestablishment senator from Minnesota. On the opposite end of the spectrum, Alabama governor George Wallace, running as an independent, appealed to die-hard bigots by promoting a racially divided society.

Rockefeller's name remained in contention on the Republican side, but his support was strongest on the more liberal East Coast. Governor Reagan's popularity had ballooned among conservatives, especially in the South, making him a viable threat. Neither candidate appealed to moderate voters, however, leaving Nixon the leading choice of Republicans in most national Gallop polls.

Nixon received a belated birthday present on March 21 when Rockefeller, citing a need for party unity, proclaimed that he would not be a candidate for the presidency. An additional surprise arrived ten days later. Exhausted from dealing with a war he was convinced could not be won, President Johnson announced he would not be seeking reelection.

The nation's shock over Johnson's announcement had barely dissipated when civil rights giant Martin Luther King, Jr., was assassinated on April 4. Nixon met with King's family three days later to express his condolences. On the ninth, he returned to Atlanta to attend the funeral and, as an added gesture, canceled all political appearances for the next two weeks.

The sudden turn of events left Nixon with little to celebrate. By the end of April, Rockefeller had done an about-face, proclaiming it was his duty to offer his services to a nation in desperate need of direction. Sensing that Rockefeller's decision left Nixon vulnerable, Reagan, still professing he was not a formal candidate, "allowed" his name to be placed on key primary ballots.

Johnson's withdrawal pitted the vice president, Hubert Humphrey, against Kennedy and McCarthy in a three-way race for the Democratic nomination. Echoing the Republican contest eight years earlier, the party was sharply divided. Humphrey supported the war in Vietnam; Kennedy and McCarthy strongly opposed it. McCarthy stood little chance of securing the nomination due to his harsh criticism of the administration. While Kennedy held similar views, he displayed more tact in presenting them. Like the former president, Bobby was a handsome, charismatic speaker whose antiwar message and call for racial equality appealed to a diverse group of voters, especially the younger generation.

Following a primary win in California, Kennedy's campaign appeared to be picking up steam, but the jubilation came to a screeching halt when he was shot after delivering a victory speech in Los Angeles. His death on June 6 sent the nation whirling into disarray. Violence between police and protesters became a nightly event on the six o'clock news, causing many Americans to embrace the Republicans' call for stricter enforcement of law and order.

The inner turmoil plaguing the Democrats gave Nixon's campaign a decided edge. When it became clear that his moderate views were leading the way with Republican voters in primary balloting, Eisenhower finally lent his support, publicly endorsing Nixon on July 18. Two weeks later, Nixon took the stage in San Francisco to deliver his acceptance speech.

Presley, meanwhile, had won an unexpected victory of his own. Thanks to the courage of a young producer named Steve Binder, Elvis did not appear in a tuxedo and croon "Silent Night" to a room of cameramen for his upcoming Christmas special. In a move slated to recapture the excitement of what had once been Elvis Presley, Binder (who had been given full control of the program's content by NBC, thanks to encouragement from the network's business affiliate, RCA) reunited the star with Scotty Moore and DJ Fontana (Bill Black had passed away in 1965) for several mini-concerts performed in front of a live studio audience. Elvis re-created his rebel image by dressing in a black leather jacket and matching pants.

Edited film of the 30-minute concerts comprised about half of the hour-long special that aired on December 3, 1968. Taped studio sequences were added into the program though, unfortunately, due to final editing at the insistence of the ever-present Colonel, the plot line suffered dramatically. The original idea had been to tell the story of a guitar man encountering temptations and evil along the road to success. The "evil" was represented by a racy bordello scene, which wound up on the cutting room floor.

The strength of Presley's performances kept viewers enthralled nonetheless. Donning a classy white suit for his finale, Elvis put his heart and soul into "If I Can Dream," a message song specifically written for the program. The lyrics reflected on the recent assassinations of Robert Kennedy and Martin Luther King, exactly the type of material the Colonel had previously avoided.

RCA was so anxious to promote the record that they released it well before the show's broadcast, no doubt hindering sales. Regardless, "If I Can Dream" proved Elvis's biggest hit in more than three years, climbing to number 12 in

6. The Survival of the Fittest

the United States and to 11 on the British chart. The accompanying soundtrack album reached number eight and two, respectively.

"I'll never sing another song I don't believe in," Presley told Binder, after watching a tape of his performance. "I'm never going to make another movie that I don't believe in."[28]

A newly energized Presley emerged from the special determined to regain control of his career. In the two months following the screening of the NBC special, he recorded his most innovative material since the Sam Phillips era. In January, six sessions at American Sound studios in Memphis produced a whopping 19 new songs, spanning the genres of country, pop, and rhythm and blues. He returned in February to cut 14 additional tunes. *From Elvis in Memphis,* the first album to showcase Presley's revamped sound, was released in June 1969. Sales rivaled that of the recent television special soundtrack. The accompanying single, "In the Ghetto," climbed all the way to number three on Billboard's chart. On the Beatles' home turf, the album hit number one. "In the Ghetto" reached number two.

Presley's summer engagement at the International Hotel, during which he performed 57 shows from July 31 to August 28, capped his return to the throne. "Oozing the sullen sexuality that threw America into a state of shock in the 50's, he groaned and swiveled through a medley of 'Jailhouse Rock,' 'Don't Be Cruel,' 'Heartbreak Hotel,' 'All Shook Up,' and 'Hound Dog.' It was hard to believe he was 34 and no longer 19," exclaimed *Newsweek.* "Elvis is back," *Rock Music* reported. "He had been away."[29]

As Elvis basked in the glory of critics' praise for the first time in nearly a decade, the Beatles were penning the material for their final album, *Let It Be.* Citing irreconcilable differences, the foursome disbanded in 1970 to pursue individual careers. None would equal, or even come close to, the success of their combined efforts.

Presley managed to survive his competition by returning to his roots, remaining true to himself. Even more amazing than his comeback itself was the fact that he was able to do so not *because* of his manager's efforts but *in spite* of them. Had Elvis been in control of his emotions like Nixon, rather than dependent on them, he would have told the Colonel to pack up his tent and move on. As it was, he allowed the carny man to remain ringside, cracking his whip.

CHAPTER 7

The New America: Hippies, Drugs, and Vietnam

> *History teaches us that the great revolutions aren't started by people who are utterly down and out, without hope and vision. They take place when people begin to live a little better — and when they see how much yet remains to be achieved.*
>
> — Hubert H. Humphrey

Nixon's personal triumph at the Republican convention was soured by the changes sweeping the country as the sixties neared an end. The counterculture — a generation intent on defying the adult establishment, yet clamoring for its respect — was growing at a feverish pace. Scraggly young people flocked to communes, experimenting with drugs and sex. Students organized rallies and teach-ins attacking the administration's policy in Vietnam, while tens of thousands marched in the capital, demanding an end to the war. Revolutionary groups sprang up in support of Ho Chi Minh, advocating terrorism to achieve their goals. From Nixon's home town of Whittier to Presley's Graceland in Memphis, America was at war with itself.

Nixon's decision to nominate Spiro Agnew as his running mate assured that the Republican ticket would offer little chance of bridging the gap. A moderate conservative, Agnew's career had paralleled Nixon's in many ways: he was a World War II veteran who had gone on to practice law in his home town before running for office. As governor of Maryland, he provided a geographic balance to Nixon's ticket, much as Johnson had for JFK. It was not the governor's eastern location nor his inner city experience, however, that had put him at the top of Nixon's list. What most impressed him, he said in *RN*, was Agnew's "inner strength." And while it was true that the governor had virtually no experience in foreign policy, Nixon was satisfied that Agnew's views on the subject were very similar to his own. As with most who would serve in the upcoming administration, Spiro Agnew was not likely to rock the Nixon boat.

Conversely, the Democrats' campaign reflected the chaotic society it hoped to govern. By the time the party gathered in Chicago for its August convention, most of Bobby Kennedy's supporters had migrated to McCarthy's camp, sparking a bitter right-left showdown. Conservatives edged out a victory for Humphrey, but it was far from satisfying. As the vice president prepared his acceptance speech on the eve of his nomination, tear gas fumes engulfed his hotel suite, bringing tears to his eyes. Scrambling to the window, Humphrey watched in horror as police dressed in riot gear swung clubs at thousands of chanting protesters gathered outside the hotel. Quick-thinking volunteers turned McCarthy's headquarters, located two floors below the vice president's, into a makeshift hospital where they bandaged the wounded with cut-up bed sheets.

The tumultuous beginning to Humphrey's campaign did little to enhance Nixon's cross-country travels during his quest for the presidency. In *RN*, he recalled the events as the "saddest" of his 1968 campaign. Whether he appeared alone or with his family at his side, angry demonstrators followed his every move, waving antiestablishment signs and interrupting his speeches with obscenities. The chaos was, as Nixon put it, "symbolic" of what was currently wrong with the country.

The Wallace campaign dumped oil on the fire, stirring up hatred between blacks and whites. Although his support was strongest in the South, polls revealed that nearly 20 percent of the nation embraced the Alabama governor's views. In addition to promoting racial discrimination, Wallace advocated a reversal of Johnson's Great Society. His call for fewer government programs and stricter enforcement of law and order in the streets made him an attractive alternative for conservative Republicans disenchanted with Nixon's refusal to endorse segregation.

Polls following the Democratic convention gave Nixon a 12-point lead over Humphrey, but despite their differences, Democrats eventually narrowed the gap, aided by the staunch support of organized labor, a party stronghold for decades. Humphrey's running mate, Senator Edmund Muskie of Maine, proved a solid addition to the ticket. The media favored him so highly over Agnew that even Humphrey began telling voters, "If you have any doubts about the top of the ticket, please settle it on the basis of Number Two."[1] Chants of "Dump the Hump" faded as he closed in on Nixon's lead. Two weeks prior to the election, McCarthy called for party unity by publicly endorsing Humphrey. Rumors of an impending peace agreement in Vietnam throughout the following week, spurred by a temporary bombing halt, pulled the vice president virtually even in the polls.

By election eve, it was obvious the country was in for a nail biter, reminiscent of 1960. Once again, Nixon spent most of the night secluded in his hotel room, monitoring results via network TV. When the final count was tallied on the morning of November 6, Nixon had won by just over one half of a percentage point, half a million popular votes. The final electoral count had given him 301 to Humphrey's 191. Wallace had siphoned off 45.

Alluding to his ill-fated contest with JFK, Nixon told a crowd of cheering supporters that one thing was certain: it was a lot more fun to win a close election than to lose it. He celebrated by retiring to his library, where he listened to the musical score *Victory at Sea*. The music, he explained years later, "captured the moment" much more than any words, written or spoken, could ever express.

As Presley and Nixon had each learned at an early age, music reflects the mood of its listeners — from the triumphant sound of victory in Nixon's long-fought battle to the outrage of the defiant generation he sought to lead. The counterculture dominated the airwaves as the new Republican administration moved into office. While the Beatles' call for peaceful change in "Revolution" might have helped bridge the generation gap, the no-guilt morality of "Why Don't We Do It in the Road," from the group's top-selling *White Album*, left little hope for a tranquil unity of the masses. The free-love theme of the youth culture, epitomized in Dylan's smash hit "Lay Lady Lay," came full circle on August 15, 1969, when half a million war resisters, hippies, and flower children gathered on a farm near Woodstock, New York, for a three-day festival. Chanting peace slogans, making love while the news cameras rolled, couples grooved to the sounds of Jimi Hendrix and the Grateful Dead as they tripped out on marijuana, heroin, and LSD.

Like its musical counterpart, Hollywood is a reflection of the community at large. As Nixon's presidency began, the rebel image personified by James Dean, the suave cult hero of Presley's generation, was modernized by director Dennis Hopper. Drawing from his experiences in *Rebel Without a Cause* and *Giant*, in which he had costarred with Dean, Hopper skillfully explored the mood of the current generation in his classic film *Easy Rider*. Jack Nicholson's portrayal of a disillusioned, alcoholic lawyer who joins a couple of hippies on a motorcycle trip in search of the meaning of life, won him an Academy Award nomination. Conservatives, crossing their fingers for the lighthearted musicals *Hello Dolly* and *Goodbye Mister Chips*, watched in disbelief as the academy voted *Midnight Cowboy*, the story of a young stud who heads for New York to become a male prostitute, best film of the year. Needless to say, Nixon's relationship with the motion picture industry remained as strained as it had been in the days of the Hollywood Ten.

Meanwhile, the senseless violence glorified in the 1967 film *Bonnie and Clyde* had hit home with the real-life murders of actress Sharon Tate and four friends at her Bel Air estate on August 10. The killing spree continued later that day in Los Angeles, taking the lives of supermarket chain president Leno LaBianca and his wife, Rosemary. Cult leader Charles Manson, who many conservatives claimed had been inspired by the chaotic Lennon-McCartney tune, "Helter Skelter," released on the group's *White Album* some nine months prior to the killings, was later linked to all seven deaths and sentenced to life in prison. Perhaps the most telling sign of the new America came from the publishing world when the *Saturday Evening Post*, a fixture on newsstands for 148 years, closed its doors as *Penthouse* readied its debut.

Amid the upheaval, Nixon concentrated on fulfilling his campaign promise to end the war. Significant troop withdrawals during the summer of 1969 (25,000 in June, with an estimated 60,000 by year's end) signified his commitment to achieving peace in Southeast Asia. Characteristic of his fighting nature, however, he refused to be bullied into accepting terms that would not assure at least a face-saving settlement for the United States.

The administration's "peace with honor" strategy suffered a major setback six months later when Nixon, reacting to intelligence reports that the North Vietnamese were invading the border countries, ordered the expansion of the war into Cambodia and Laos. The counterculture responded with massive demonstrations at universities across the nation, but the message was garbled by the violence accompanying it. Pat Moynihan, one of the president's most liberal advisors, concluded that the biggest problem facing the country was not the war in Vietnam, but rather the "eroding authority of the principal institutions of government and society."[2] Nixon readily agreed.

As the fighting in Vietnam raged on, America's tension continued to mount on the home shores. On May 4, 1970, the administration's plea for law and order turned bloody at Kent State University in Ohio when several members of the National Guard, taunted by rock-throwing students, opened fire on the crowd. Four students were killed, and several others wounded. Nixon said the days that followed were among the darkest of his presidency. "I wrote personal letters to each of the parents," he wrote in *RN*, "even though I knew that words could not help" (457).

The attack triggered a new wave of fires and bombings. Students and faculty members responded with strikes, causing many colleges to close their doors. A national day of protest in Washington, D.C., was scheduled for May 9. In a well-meaning attempt to communicate with those who opposed him, Nixon paid a surprise late-night visit to a group of students gathered at the Lincoln Memorial on the evening prior to the scheduled demonstration. Ultimately, it was a move that emphasized just how wide the generation gap had grown. Rather than address the protesters' reason for being there, Nixon tried to soften the students' mood by talking about sports, travel, and other nugatory events. When confronted point-blank, he attempted to relate to their concerns by comparing their disillusionment with Vietnam to the struggles he had encountered growing up as a poor boy in Whittier.

Nixon was blasted in the press for his failed attempt at understanding, the march went on as scheduled, and violence continued to erupt. On May 15, another clash with the National Guard, at Jackson State in Mississippi, resulted in the deaths of two more students. The president's "silent majority," those citizens who supported the administration and its effort to achieve "peace with honor," responded with a rally of its own on May 20 when 100,000 marched through the streets of New York. A *Newsweek* poll conducted amid the outbreak of violence backed the administration's claim that the government was reacting to the turmoil, not causing it: 58 percent believed the demonstrators were responsible for the deaths at Ohio State, while only 11 percent blamed the National Guard.

The counterculture insisted the fault lay solely in Nixon's lap and conveyed its message at every possible opportunity. Akin to his face-off with the demonstrators in Caracas 12 years earlier, Nixon refused to be intimidated. Spurred on by polls that predicted a substantial victory for Democrats in the upcoming November elections, he abandoned Ike's stay-at-home-and-look-presidential strategy and took to the road, openly campaigning for his fellow Republicans. Following a speech in San Jose, a crowd of 2,000 protesters confronted him as he walked to his limousine. Irritated by the foul language and obscene gestures, Nixon responded by standing on the hood and giving the vocal crowd his trademark V-for-victory sign. He was rewarded with a barrage of flying rocks, eggs, and tomatoes. Secret service agents rushed him into the car and began emergency evacuation procedures. Several agents were hit by broken glass as rocks smashed the windows.

Never in the history of modern America had a president been physically attacked by a mob while he traveled within his own country. As far as Nixon was concerned, the incident had separated the nation into "them" and "us." He said that while it was not important what the demonstrators thought of him on a personal level, if they refused to respect the office of the presidency, "people should be made to recognize that fact and take sides on it."[3] And take sides they did, putting the country on the brink of civil war.

Having been the focus of the youth revolution some 15 years earlier, Elvis was better equipped to deal with the changes afflicting society than was Nixon, although the focus of the revolt was oddly reversed. In the fifties, *adults* had been the ones reacting with rebellion. DJs smashed rock-and-roll records over the air, politicians and preachers deemed Presley's wiggling provocative and indecent, promoting juvenile delinquency. Elvis had been considered as anti-establishment by the conservative sector then as was the counterculture of the late sixties — an unjustified comparison, taking into account that it had been Presley's music and his way of performing his music that had earned him the label, not his personal or political views regarding his country.

Ironically, it was Presley's patriotic ideals that now led him to side with the very establishment that had so despised him. Although his experience gave him a better understanding of the hippie culture than Nixon had, he did not embrace the movement, let alone join it. Still Gladys's respectful, God-fearing boy at heart, Elvis could not relate to the hippies' total disrespect for everything he had come to hold dear. Nor did he appreciate fellow celebrities who used their fame to influence their generation. "He was particularly upset with Jane Fonda when she was carrying on about Vietnam," Billy Stanley recalled. "The Smothers Brothers got his goat as well. While we laughed, Elvis fumed and exploded at their political satires. But if a national leader said the same thing, Elvis had no quarrel with him."[4]

It is here, of course, where Presley's homespun upbringing comes most strongly into play. He had been raised to respect his elders, and he did so without question. He had served his hitch in the army without complaint and come out a better person for it, at least in his mind. Why, then, would he expect any less of the youths who followed? Elvis viewed the flag as a symbol of the American Dream — *his* dream — a poor southern boy rising above his hardships to become a world-famous entertainer. He could not understand why the current generation had abandoned similar hope for a better life.

That is not to say that Presley was out of touch with the changes going on around him. He was deeply saddened by Martin Luther King's assassination. Upon learning that several of his associates had made snide comments on the subject, he called everyone together and made it clear such attitudes would not be tolerated in his presence. "Today we lost a great man. A man who has done a lot for his own people. It's bad for Memphis. But more than that this whole country has suffered a tragic loss. I don't want to hear anything different than that said around here."[5]

Publicly, Elvis let his music do the talking. His emotional performance of "If I Can Dream" on his television special had said more about his hope for the future than a hundred speeches might have, while "In the Ghetto" reflected his understanding of the hopelessness and sorrow present in the world. Clearly, the problem he had with the counterculture was not the basic argument that changes were needed, but rather how those changes should be brought about.

Elvis had no interest in becoming a politician; he was merely a concerned citizen who wanted to do whatever he could to help his country. His return to live performing had provided the perfect opportunity. In addition to having given his career a well-needed boost, working the nightclub and tour scene allowed him to observe the inner workings of the generation he sought to understand.

For the past several years, Presley had been doing some soul searching of his own. Always fascinated with religion, he had expanded his horizons to include studies in Buddhism, Islam, and other non–Christian faiths. His interest had been stimulated by many night-long conversations with Larry Geller, a philosophical hairdresser he had befriended in 1964.

A native New Yorker, Geller had moved with his parents to Los Angeles in 1947. His interest in spiritual studies began at age 12, ignited by the violent murder of his grandmother, who had been robbed and strangled by a stranger while taking an afternoon stroll in Santa Monica. What began as a means to deal with his grief evolved into a lifelong search for the meaning of life.

Intrigued that Elvis shared so many of his interests, Geller had eagerly accepted a full-time slot in Presley's entourage. Predictably, the relationship hit rough waters from the beginning, as Larry's "interests" were not among those shared by the majority of Elvis's long-time buddies. Presley eventually gave in to majority rule, led by the Colonel and Priscilla, who claimed Geller was causing Elvis to retreat into himself. While Presley's well-being might have been a concern to some, the idea that Geller might acquire a more prominent position with Presley ranked as the most likely common denominator in the united "dump Geller" movement.

Regardless of his friends' well-meaning efforts, Elvis continued his theological search in Larry's absence. Among the most pressing questions remained the age-old puzzle of why he had survived and not Jesse Garon and what, if anything, was expected of him in regards to the influence he had, via his music, on millions of people throughout the world. "Once Elvis saw Jesse's death as an act of God, or destiny," Geller explained, "it logically followed that Elvis' living wasn't an accident of fate, either."[6] Stepbrother David reached a similar, if less philosophical, conclusion. "He always knew that his popularity was a gift from God," Stanley related in *Life with Elvis* (115), "but he was never sure what to do with it, or why he'd been the one chosen for it."

Many a related quest for understanding had led the counterculture to experiment with marijuana and LSD — though a one-time experience with the latter had been enough to convince Presley they were on the wrong track. "Realizing it was too dangerous a drug to fool around with," Priscilla admitted, "we never tried LSD again."[7]

Nevertheless, drugs and one-night stands were a way of life for most musicians as the decade neared an end. Presley's group was no exception, nor was Elvis himself, although in his mind, the legally prescribed pills he took had nothing in common with the mind-altering hallucinogens being passed around among his entourage. The argument may have been legitimate at this point as, according to Priscilla, his chemical intake at the time was limited to Dexedrine to control his weight and the ever-present sleeping pills he used to combat his chronic insomnia.

David Stanley concurred. "In fairness to Elvis, he really didn't know about the drugs, at least in those early days. Some of the guys in the group used drugs, but they tried to do it behind the boss's back. He didn't like it, and everybody knew it. In fact, Elvis's after-concert parties were usually pretty tame. We'd sit around drinking champagne, making small talk, and trying to find girl friends for the evening. Later on, we'd break out the booze and the grass, and things would really get going. But that would be without Elvis."[8]

According to Stanley, it was about this time that Elvis's long-time hobby of collecting guns and police badges graduated to a more serious, hands-on interest in the business of law enforcement. Both David and his brother Billy spoke of Elvis's disgust with the drugs plaguing the schools. At one point, Elvis even pressured his stepbrothers to get personally involved by becoming informants at their high school, reasoning that their long hair and hip attitude would give them an in with dealers.

Despite Presley's heightened awareness of society's woes as the seventies rolled in, he was enjoying life as never before. He had managed to rescue his career and redeem himself in the eyes of critics and fans alike. "Suspicious Minds," his latest single, released to coincide with his Vegas opening, had given him his first number one record in seven years. Meanwhile, the August engagement had been so successful that he had signed a contract to return in February.

On the home front, he was a devoted husband and doting father, making family the center of his life. Even when he and Priscilla were apart, she felt confident he remained faithful. "During his first couple of engagements he still seemed humbled by lingering doubts of whether the public was fully accepting him," she wrote in *Elvis and Me* (276). "At this point he had no interest in outside affairs or flirtations, his concentration on daily rehearsals and performances every evening excluding everything else."

As a family man, Elvis became increasingly concerned for the safety of those he loved, especially in view of the numerous death threats he had received since his return to live performances. When the fevered state of the country began to affect his own security, Presley decided it was time to take action. He began carrying a gun on a regular basis and went out of his way to make friends in police departments and law enforcement agencies across the country.

One of Elvis's closest associates at this time was John O'Grady, a former narcotics agent turned private investigator. The two had met when the entertainer hired O'Grady to investigate a paternity suit filed against him. The case was eventually dismissed when blood tests proved Presley was not the father, but Elvis and O'Grady remained friends. It was through O'Grady that Presley became involved in the International Narcotics Enforcement Officers Association, an antidrug brigade that has since been disbanded.[9]

Elvis's participation in this association shows a clear desire on the singer's part to become active in the administration's war against drugs, but it was only one of many steps. In November 1970, Presley initiated a meeting with Vice President Agnew in Palm Springs, in which the two discussed the nation's current problems. Expressing his concern, Elvis told the vice president he wanted to use his position as a popular entertainer to do something positive for his country.

A brief account of this meeting is related in the notorious "bodyguard book" published shortly before Presley's death, *Elvis: What Happened?* According to the authors, Elvis spent about 30 minutes visiting with Agnew at the

VP's rented house in Palm Springs. In what would soon be viewed as an ironic twist, the vice president refused to accept Elvis's gift of a gold-inlaid .357 Magnum revolver, informing Presley that, as an elected official, it was inappropriate for him to accept gifts. When Agnew was forced from office shortly afterward, Sonny West recalled having told Elvis that Agnew would probably accept the gift now, to which Presley replied, "No, screw him. He got caught as a crook."[10]

Around the time of his meeting with Agnew, Presley also visited Los Angeles police chief Edward Davis. Stressing the importance of keeping his visit out of the public eye, Elvis presented Davis's department with a check for $7,000 and threw in a Colt .45 as a personal gift for the chief. According to later accounts, the money donated by Presley was used to buy toys for needy children, uniforms for the LAPD's marching band, and special flak jackets for explosives-sniffing dogs.

As with his membership in the International Narcotics Enforcement Officers Association, these meetings show a clear desire on Presley's part to become actively involved. Being an entertainer, not a politician, however, he was limited in what he could do to bring about the changes he felt were needed to heal society's ills — at least from a public standpoint.

Given the impact music had on the counterculture and Presley's age-long "what purpose is my God-given talent supposed to serve" quest, his next step seemed a logical progression. Elvis was ready to be of service. Who better to ask what he could do for his country than the president himself?

CHAPTER 8

The King Meets the President

I have touched the highest point of all my greatness, and from that full meridian of my glory, I haste now to my setting.

—William Shakespeare

As with any event involving Elvis, speculation abounds as to why he initiated a meeting with President Nixon. The most common theory, revolving around the entertainer's hobby of collecting police badges, first surfaced in *Elvis: What Happened?* During his discussion of the Presley-Nixon meeting, coauthor Sonny West recalled a conversation that took place during the fall of 1970 with Elvis, John O'Grady, and "a very well-known show business celebrity." Reportedly, the unnamed personality was an undercover agent for the federal narcotics bureau and had the badge to prove it.

Later sources identified the mystery man as Paul Frees, an actor best known for his voice in television ads and Disney cartoons. Like Presley, he was a police fan who had followed the activities of the drug enforcement team for years. The documents in his possession identified him as an agent "in general service" with the Bureau of Narcotics and Dangerous Drugs and were signed by the bureau's chief, John Ingersoll. In Sonny's words: "As soon as Elvis saw that badge, he was both surprised and very impressed. His mind started working right away. He wanted one."[1]

Rock music biographer Jerry Hopkins claimed the singer's idea of collecting police badges came from O'Grady. In his 1980 offering, *Elvis: The Final Years*, Hopkins quotes the PI as saying he knew Elvis was on pills and thought if he started carrying police badges around, "maybe he'd stop taking that shit" (4). The author thus concluded it was O'Grady who arranged an appointment for Presley at the Bureau of Narcotics and Dangerous Drugs. No mention is made of O'Grady in any White House or FBI memos contained in the National

Archives' official Presley File, making this assertion highly suspect. Moreover, Hopkins's claim that the PI started Elvis collecting police badges is clearly erroneous: a number of Presley's badges are on display at Graceland, some dating back as early as 1964.

While it is certainly possible that Elvis wanted a narcotics badge for his collection, to suggest that obtaining one was the sole reason for his trip to Washington displays gross misunderstanding of the entertainer's homespun ideals, exemplifying the mental gap that existed between Presley and the majority of his entourage. Likewise, Priscilla's analysis, that Elvis wanted the badge because he thought it would give him the legal right to carry prescribed drugs and weapons wherever he went, sheds light on her growing discontent with their marriage. By this point, she had tired of the hoopla surrounding her husband's resurgent career and was pursuing interests of her own. His frequent, prolonged absences left her feeling resentful and suspicious. Given the current state of their relationship, her lack of understanding regarding Elvis's intentions does not seem unreasonable, and it does tend to explain his reluctance to discuss his proposed trip to Washington with her beforehand.

In retrospect, it seems amazing that people who lived at Presley's side on a daily basis could have been so unaware of the significance of events taking place before their very eyes. Billy Stanley clearly recalled Elvis's disgust for the Smothers Brothers and his unyielding support of the Nixon administration. He and his associates were well aware of their boss's involvement in the narcotics association and his subsequent visits with the vice president and the Los Angeles chief of police. Rather than put two and two together, they asserted that Presley's trip to Washington was a spur-of-the-moment decision, fueled by a childish desire.

The fact that Elvis told no one about his plan suggests he was aware of the way his friends and family would view it. Additionally, he was concerned about leaks. How could Elvis Presley, world-renowned superstar, be of any help if his intentions were splattered all over the newspapers? The media would have viewed the event as a clever publicity stunt by Colonel Parker and dismissed it as a joke.

In Presley's mind, nothing could have been further from the truth. He was a man on a mission, a mission he had plotted out in every detail, as his actions throughout the episode clearly illustrate. Slipping from the protective walls of Graceland without his usual array of bodyguards on December 19, 1970, Presley drove himself to the airport in Memphis. Traveling first class under the alias Jon Burrows, he took a flight to the capital and checked into a room at the Washington Hotel. Step one complete, he phoned Jerry Schilling, a close member of his entourage and instructed him to assure friends and family that he was fine. Whether or not he mentioned his current location to Jerry is unknown, but his request that Schilling meet him in Los Angeles later that evening suggests that he did not.

8. The King Meets the President

Elvis arrived in Los Angeles for his rendezvous with Schilling about 1:30 A.M. on December 20. At 10 P.M. that evening the two returned to Washington aboard another commercial flight, with Presley now traveling as John Carpenter. Also aboard the aircraft was Senator George Murphy, a conservative Republican from California. Whether this was a coincidence or part of the plan is unknown, but in any event, Elvis struck up a conversation, informing Murphy of his wish to be of service in the administration's antidrug campaign. The senator promised he would contact John Ingersoll on Presley's behalf and also agreed to pass on the entertainer's request to meet with the FBI director, J. Edgar Hoover.

Following his talk with the senator, still in flight, Presley composed a personal letter to the president, informing Nixon of his concerns for the country and expressing his wish to be of help in any way that he could. Upon touching down in the capital, Elvis and Jerry drove to the White House, where Elvis hand-delivered his letter to a security guard. He and Schilling then returned to Presley's room at the Washington Hotel. Sonny West arrived shortly thereafter, most likely for security purposes, as Jerry had to return to Los Angeles later that evening due to personal obligations.

Back at the White House, the president's advisors read Presley's letter. Bud Krogh, one of Nixon's aides assigned to drug control policy, was asked to meet with Presley in order to determine if the singer's intentions were sincere. Krogh phoned Elvis at the hotel and requested that Presley stop by his office about 10 A.M. By 10:15, Elvis was gone, and Krogh was busy drafting recommendations to the president on how best to employ Presley's assistance. Among his suggestions:

- Work with White House staff.
- Cooperate with and encourage the creation of a one-hour television special in which Presley narrates as stars such as himself sing popular songs and interpret them for parents in order to show drug and other antiestablishment themes in rock music.
- Encourage fellow artists to develop a new rock musical theme, "Get High on Life."
- Record an album with the theme "Get High on Life" at the federal narcotics rehabilitation and research facility at Lexington, Kentucky.
- Be a consultant to the Advertising Council on how to communicate antidrug messages to youth.

While Krogh brainstormed, Nixon aide Dwight L. Chapin sent a memo to the president's chief of staff, H. R. Haldeman, noting, "It would be wrong to push Presley off on the Vice President since it will take very little of the President's time and it can be extremely beneficial for the President to build some rapport with Presley." Haldeman approved the meeting for later that day.

Shortly after speaking with Krogh, Presley arrived at the Bureau of Narcotics and Dangerous Drugs for an appointment with John Finlator, who was serving as temporary director. Finlator had asked Elvis to stop by his office to determine what could be worked out regarding the entertainer's requests. At the meeting that followed, Presley expressed his concerns and reiterated his offer to help in any way he could, including financially. Finlator informed Elvis the bureau was unable to accept gifts or financial assistance and denied Presley's request for a federal narcotics badge, telling Elvis the best he could do was to offer him an "honorary" one. Presley then asked Finlator, "You won't mind if I ask the President for the badge?" to which the director responded that would be the only way for Elvis to obtain one.[2]

Judging by his request to meet with Hoover, it is obvious Presley had more in mind than offering his assistance in a musical capacity. The idea of becoming an informant had already surfaced when he had tried, unsuccessfully, to convince his stepbrothers to spy on pushers at their high school. Paul Frees's agent-at-large credentials had probably convinced him that his celebrity status could be a plus rather than a minus, if used correctly. But a real agent needed a *real* badge. An honorary one, while a nice addition to his collection, would not suffice.

When Presley returned to his hotel, he was informed, via a phone call from Krogh, that Nixon would meet with him around noon. Upon arriving at the White House, Elvis had to leave his gift for the president — a Colt .45 from World War II, complete with seven silver bullets and housed in a decorative wooden case — with Bill Duncan, the head of the Secret Service Protective Detail. (This gun is presently on display at the Richard Nixon Library and Birthplace in Yorba Linda, California.) He was then escorted to the Oval Office.

Reports indicate the meeting took place in a relaxed atmosphere. Elvis showed the president a few family photos and some of his police badges. He explained to Nixon that he had been an avid collector for years and had been appointed sheriff or deputy in several cities across the nation. Nixon agreed that Elvis could reach young people with an antidrug message but said it was important for the entertainer to maintain a credible image. Presley responded, "I have to reach people in my own way, by singing." The conversation drifted to a discussion of the drug culture, the anti–American spirit sweeping the nation, and the destructive influence of Communism.

Krogh, who remained present throughout the meeting, related in a follow-up memo: "Presley indicated to the President in a very emotional manner that he was 'on [his] side.' Presley kept repeating that he wanted to be helpful, that he wanted to restore some respect for the flag which was being lost. He mentioned that he was just a poor boy from Tennessee who had gotten a lot from his country, which in some way he wanted to repay."

Elvis also expressed the opinion that the Beatles' influence on young people in America contributed to the anti–American spirit, which brought a surprised reaction to Nixon's face and a nod of agreement.³

The president went on to say it was his opinion that "those who use drugs are also those in the vanguard of anti–American protest. Violence, drug usage, dissent, protest, all seem to merge in generally the same group of young people."

When all was said and done, Nixon must have been convinced of Presley's sincerity, as he granted the entertainer's request for the "official" badge. As the meeting wound down, Elvis again expressed his support of the president and then, according to Krogh's report, "in a surprising, spontaneous gesture, put his left arm around the President and hugged him."

The shock that must have spread across Nixon's face at that instant defies description. Here was a man who, as a boy, had felt the need to ask his mother's permission before hugging his own brother. Presley, on the other hand, was so used to showing his emotions that the move came spontaneously. While amusing when taken in context of the story, the stark contrast proved a significant factor in shaping each man's destiny a few short years down the road.

All of his life, Elvis had thrived on emotions. He was so encouraged by his rapport with the president that he felt comfortable hugging the man. Who among Nixon's advisors would have had such a thought, let alone carried it out? To Presley, the move came naturally, a logical extension of his concord with the president. If he was aware of Nixon's discomfort, he did not let on. Rather, he continued with the spontaneity, asking his new friend a favor. Would the president mind meeting two of his employees, who were waiting outside?

Whether Nixon was beginning to enjoy Presley's impulsiveness or was simply too shocked to refuse is hard to say, but he granted the request. Years later, Schilling spoke of the event with host George Klein in the television special *Elvis Memories*.

> Elvis introduced us to the President, and he took over. It was like we were at Graceland, not at the White House. So, [Elvis] said, "Mr. President, they would like some of those key-chains too." You know, the President had just given Elvis a Presidential Seal key chain. So the President went over and got that, and he came back, and [Elvis] said, "You know, they got wives too." He had the President running around the White House.... There's where I knew that nobody could really say no to Elvis.¹¹

As they left the Oval Office, Krogh invited Elvis and his friends to dine in the White House mess. Presley happily accepted. Before sitting down to the meal, Krogh phoned Finlator to inform him the president had authorized Presley's narcotics badge. If the Director was upset by being overruled, he kept it to himself. Krogh later stated that Finlator personally handed the badge to Elvis and promised to send him an official "consultant's commission" to go with it.

Presley had the badge with him the following week, on December 30, when he returned to Washington yet again, this time in the company of former Memphis sheriff William Morris and six bodyguards, for the purpose of touring the FBI headquarters and a possible meeting with Hoover. Elvis's party was informed that the director was out of town, but that Assistant Director Casper would set up a special tour of the bureau on the following day. In early January, Elvis received a note from Hoover. The director apologized for his absence during Presley's recent visit and assured the entertainer he would keep Elvis's offer of assistance in mind.

While it appeared Presley's efforts were given serious consideration at the time, backstage events proved otherwise. In the original memo issued from Chapin to Haldeman, discussing the possibility of Elvis meeting the president, Chapin suggested, "If the President wants to meet with some bright young people outside of the Government, Presley might be a perfect one to start with," to which Haldeman responded with the caustic, written reply, "You must be kidding," in the margin of the memo.

Similar cynicism reverberated within the FBI. In a December 22 memo, a Presley-Hoover meeting was discussed. Included was a summary of Elvis's conversation with Senator Murphy from the day before. After informing the bureau of the entertainer's offer of assistance, Murphy had expressed his personal opinion that Presley was "a very sincere young man, ... deeply concerned over the narcotics problem in this country and ... interested in becoming active in the drive against the use of narcotics, particularly by young people." The memo concluded with a paragraph stating that Elvis was presently involved in a paternity suit and had been the subject of considerable criticism from the public and press back in the fifties.

Denying Presley's request to meet Hoover, a December 30 memo concluded: "Presley's sincerity and good intentions notwithstanding he is certainly not the type of individual whom the Director would wish to meet. It is noted at the present time he is wearing his hair down to his shoulders and indulges in the wearing of all sorts of exotic dress." A recent photo of Elvis, clipped from the *Washington Post*, was attached. (Presley's hair had been shoulder length when the photo was taken several months earlier. Serving as best man at Sonny West's wedding, he had worn a dark velvet suit for the occasion.)

From a conservative point of view, the FBI's reluctance to enlist Presley's help was understandable, given the current state of the country. Regardless of what he said or did, the bureau continued to view him as antiestablishment because of the rebel image created in the fifties. While this atmosphere of mistrust might also explain why no mention was ever made of involving Elvis in the "suggested Presley activities," a closer examination makes it appear more likely that Presley himself gave the plan a thumbs down.

Although he had made tremendous strides in closing the gap between his movie soundtracks and the turn popular rock and roll had taken, Elvis was still not considered very much "with it" as far as the teenage population was concerned. Had he agreed to the television special outlined by Krogh, he would have further alienated himself from the youth culture rather than closing the gap, as in all likelihood, the other "stars" enlisted by the administration would have been along the lines of Andy Williams and Pat Boone, not Led Zeppelin or the Steve Miller Band. Similar problems would have plagued the "Get High on Life" projects.

Colonel Parker's influence must also be considered. While Presley had made great strides in recovering artistic control of his career over the past several years, Parker remained in charge of contractual decisions. Two years earlier when Elvis, along with 80,000 other individuals listed in *Who's Who in America*, had been asked by then president-elect Nixon to recommend exceptional individuals for executive positions in the federal government, Parker released the following statement: "Elvis doesn't comment on political matters." No doubt he had evaluated how his boy's affiliation with one political party would affect his status with the other and in turn what effect that status would have on ticket and record sales. The "Get High on Life" projects posed a similar threat. In addition, Elvis would have done them as a public service, generating little revenue for Presley or his manager.

The last of Krogh's suggestions, that Elvis be made a consultant to the Advertising Council on how to communicate antidrug messages to youth, would have been, by far, the most workable — and the most beneficial to all parties concerned. Certainly Presley, mingling with other entertainers as well as having fans of diverse ages, would have had useful input, workable suggestions to pass on to the council. In addition, fellow members might have offered Elvis the push he needed to make the connection between the street drugs he so despised and the various pills he deemed safe and respectable, simply because they were prescribed by a doctor.

Regardless of the numerous incentives, securing Presley's approval on the council would have been difficult, given the tone of the memos circulated between the FBI and Nixon's staff. The administration had already made up its mind that Elvis would be no benefit in its war on drugs. His possible sincerity aside, how could a man who dressed as outrageously as some of the people he was trying to reach be of any help in bridging the generation gap?

While there is no direct evidence that Nixon agreed with his aides' evaluation, it is probable that he did. He had personally selected every member of his staff, most of whom held similar philosophies, especially regarding the counterculture. The FBI was another matter, where, behind closed doors, criticism of the director was harsh and prevalent. Outwardly, however, Hoover remained one of the most respected men in the country. At the helm of the FBI since 1924, just three years after its inception, he had instituted many of the techniques that had made the bureau famous for apprehending legendary criminals such as John Dillinger and Al Capone. By the time Nixon took office, Hoover had become such a powerful figure that even his own supervisors, the attorney general and the president, feared repercussions should they question his actions. If he expressed the opinion that Elvis would be more of a hindrance than a help, it is unlikely Nixon would have dared to challenge that assessment. Bottom line: the administration felt it had a responsibility to uphold a certain image, and Presley did not fit the bill. Had he arrived in the Oval Office wearing a brown wool suit, perhaps things might have gone differently. But then he would not have been Elvis. His ability to stand out from the crowd as an individual, while still lending his support to the conservative effort, is what would have proven useful to the administration, not a blind willingness to conform.

Presley realized this, as the following incident clearly illustrates. When recounting their visit with Nixon at the dinner table one evening, Sonny West said, "E, tell them about Washington's portrait." Elvis laughed and replied, "Well, I walked up to this portrait of George Washington and I looked at his powdered hair and the frills on his shirt and cuffs and I said to Nixon, 'This dude dressed kind of funny.' And the President looked at my velvet suit and cape and said, 'Uh, Elvis, I could say the same thing about you.' And I said, 'Mr. President. You've got your show to run and I've got mine.'"[4]

Clearly, neither Nixon's nor Hoover's aides were impressed with the way Presley ran his show. Had Elvis been aware of the events being planned behind the closed doors of the administration he so admired, chances are he would have had similar misgivings.

As attacks from the Black Panthers and the Weathermen continued to escalate, Nixon turned to the inner reliance that had faithfully served him thus far. His instincts told him to fight fire with fire, and that is exactly what he decided to do. Because the terrorists had such efficient underground communication, it was impossible for the police to anticipate when or where they would strike next. Banks, universities, and courthouses had all become common targets. Nixon reasoned that the only way to get advance notice of their activities was to spy on their leaders. For help on how to implement the process, he turned to the one man in Washington whom Lyndon Johnson had advised him could always be trusted. It was thanks to J. Edgar Hoover, the exiting president had reportedly told Nixon, that he had been able to carry out his duties as president. Johnson assured his successor that he, too, would come to rely on the director again and again whenever matters of security were in question.

Regardless of what Nixon thought of Johnson's assessment, he had little choice but to seek the director's approval, as the retaliatory measures he

8. The King Meets the President

planned to put into effect would obviously involve bureau personnel. Among the ideas discussed were a resumption of covert mail opening, expanded electronic surveillance, and an increase in campus informants, all of which had been common practice during the anti–Communist frenzy of the fifties. Most had been phased out by 1967, thanks to increased pressure from Congress, a move Hoover deemed responsible for the current wave of chaos plaguing the country.

Although Nixon gave serious thought to implementing what came to be known as the Huston Plan (named for Tom Huston, a White House attorney who drafted the proposal), in the end, he became convinced it would be too risky given the present state of the nation. Looking back on the situation in *RN* years later, he second-guessed those doubts, wondering whether the Huston Plan might have brought about a swift end to the country's bloodshed.

The aborted plan was not the only action considered. One of Nixon's first moves as president had been to remove the tape recorders that had been installed throughout the White House during the previous administrations. Some two years into his presidency, he began to wonder whether Johnson's so-called paranoia had been justified. In 1969 alone, the CIA had reported 45 separate newspaper articles containing what it considered serious breaches of security.[5] Increased leaks from within the National Security Council, the organization responsible for policy discussions regarding Vietnam, had already resulted in Hoover's authorization of FBI wiretaps on 17 individuals — four reporters and 13 White House, State, and Defense Department aides. None of the suspected individuals were ever caught in the act, spreading concern that the leaks might be originating among the president's most trusted advisors.

As 1971 began, Nixon was not about to sit on his hands, watch his dream of achieving world peace destroyed by trouble at home. As he saw it, the radicals of the counterculture were working hand in hand with the North Vietnamese in the hope of achieving his early retirement and thus his failure to make the world safe from the threat of Communist domination. Determined to find out whom he could trust, Nixon ordered that voice-activated tape recorders be installed in the Oval Office, the cabinet room, and his office in the Old Executive Building located behind the White House. Additional machines were put in the Lincoln Sitting Room (where guests relaxed while awaiting their appointments with the president) and attached to Nixon's office phone at the presidential retreat, Camp David.

"Sometimes the letter of one law will conflict with the spirit of another and that is when the President must choose," he wrote, reexamining the ethics of the Huston Plan. "He cannot throw up his hands in dismay, because inaction may be as devastating as wrong action. The question is: What is the law, and how is it to be applied with respect to the President in fulfilling the duties of his office?"[6]

While Nixon would be accused of many things over the next several years, inaction was certainly not one of them.

CHAPTER 9

No Man Is an Island

A man, Sir, should keep his friendship in constant repair. If a man does not make new acquaintance as he advances through life, he will soon find himself left alone.

— Samuel Johnson, English author

Nixon's and Presley's shy, private natures — a hindrance in making friends since childhood — continued despite their successes. While both had managed to develop an outgoing persona to further their careers, it was a game-day face. Nixon smiled as he waved to the masses from a limousine, secretly counting the minutes until he was away from the crowd, alone with his thoughts. On stage in front of 20,000 people, Presley appeared the epitome of confidence, balancing the audience in the palm of his hand; prior to his arrival on stage, he literally shook with fear at the prospect of fulfilling his destiny. Beneath the halo of glory, each man continued to question his own self-worth, making the process of establishing close relationships an ongoing struggle. The problem was no longer a lack of willing friends, but rather developing skills in choosing them.

"The image is one thing, the man is another," Presley commented during a press conference prior to his sold-out appearances at Madison Square Garden in June 1972.[1] His sequined jumpsuits and elaborate jewelry were an expression of the image he wanted to project — be different and show it — but beneath it all, he remained a poor country boy, preferring the company of pals of similar backgrounds with whom he could connect.

Whereas Presley found solace in his roots, Nixon preferred to bury the memory of his less-fortunate days. He chose his friends not based on his ability to relate to them, but rather on their usefulness in helping him achieve his goals. While this strategy may have been necessary in order to climb the political ladder, it limited his ability to trust those around him as time wore on. Had he abandoned the practice once he became president, he might have avoided the mistakes that eventually led to Watergate, but by then self-reliance had served him far too effectively to consider discarding it.

As with Presley, most of Nixon's friends doubled as business associates. Discussing his appointment of cabinet members in *RN*, he said he wanted people who would fight for what they believed in, but when all was said and done, would agree to support his decision once he had made it. Among those chosen for positions of power were Bill Rogers (secretary of state), a personal friend who had served as attorney general under Eisenhower; Bob Haldeman (chief of staff), Nixon's campaign manager since 1962; and John Mitchell (attorney general), a lawyer Nixon had worked with at the Wall Street firm in New York.

One of the few exceptions to the buddy system was Henry Kissinger. Born in Furth, Germany, Kissinger became a U.S. citizen in 1943, studied politics at Harvard, and went on to teach at the university from 1954 to 1969. The theories discussed in his first book, *Nuclear Weapons and Foreign Policy*, published in 1957, led him to serve as a consultant on foreign policy to the Kennedy and Johnson administrations and, later, as an advisor to Rockefeller. Impressed with Kissinger's knowledge of and influence on world affairs, Nixon appointed him to head the National Security Council.

Despite a supportive cabinet, Nixon's term began on shaky ground. He was the first president in 120 years to have been elected with opposition in both houses of Congress. Having won the popular vote by such a narrow margin, he felt compelled to prove himself not only to his colleagues but to the American public as well. His age-old battle with the media continued to escalate as he pursued his peace with honor strategy in Vietnam. Meanwhile, his growing inability to relate to the counterculture threatened to split the nation in two.

Surrounded by what he viewed as a sea of enemies, skepticism became a way of life. Leaks from his hand-picked NSC in the summer of 1969 had convinced him that no one was above suspicion. Although Hoover's wiretaps had proven inconclusive, the door to "anything goes" had clearly been pried open. Nixon's ill-fated decision to reinstall tape machines in February 1971 was a direct result of his increased paranoia, much of which had been caused by "friends" telling him that other "friends" could not be trusted.

By condoning borderline methods to determine personal loyalty, Nixon raised the inevitable question of his own merit. Two years into his presidency, he found it impossible to know who his true friends were because so few outside of his immediate family were exempt from suspicion. Long-time acquaintances Bob Abplanalp and Charles G. "Bebe" Rebozo were exceptions to the rule, although even they did not pass the ultimate litmus test. "You can't enjoy the luxury of intimate personal friendships," Nixon related in an interview years later. "You can't confide absolutely in anyone."[2]

As Nixon had, Abplanalp had worked his way up the ladder the hard way.

The son of a Brooklyn auto mechanic, he had contributed to the meager family income during his teenage years, washing dishes at a local restaurant after school and on weekends. His interest in engineering produced the aerosol valve, a nifty little invention that left him a multimillionaire. Abplanalp's business became one of Nixon's first clients at the Wall Street law firm during Nixon's "wilderness" years. Finding they had much in common, including a love of boating, swimming, and professional sports, the two struck up a lasting friendship.

Nixon and Rebozo had been friends since Nixon's Senate days, when the two had shared many a Sunday boating off the Florida coast. The youngest of nine children born to Cuban parents, who had emigrated from Havana to Florida at the turn of the century, Rebozo, too, was well acquainted with the hardships of life. The Spanish-speaking family struggled to get by on the senior Rebozo's income as a cigar maker. Determined to better his life, Charles took an evening business course after high school, which provided the basis for his training in various local enterprises. His knack for selling boats and real estate proved more lucrative than he could have imagined. By the time he met Nixon in 1951, Rebozo had acquired a yacht to go along with his expensive beachfront home in Key Biscayne.

Like Nixon, Rebozo was perceived by others to be the strong, silent type — friendly, but from a distance. Just the sort of guy Nixon would feel comfortable with. "Rebozo was just part of the landscape," commented Senator George Smathers, who had been responsible for introducing the two, "but always attentive and helpful if required.... It's a profound relationship. Two men who separately trust nobody yet when together they trust each other absolutely."[3]

The key, of course, was that both Abplanalp and Rebozo were self-made men with lives of their own *outside* of the political arena. They could be trusted completely because neither wanted nor expected anything in return for his friendship, a situation that could not be duplicated once Nixon was elected president.

Adding to the problem of White House isolation was Nixon's natural tendency toward introversion. Throughout his political career, he had had to set aside his shyness in order to relate to his public, be they constituents or foreign leaders. But when the day was over, he had been able to relax with friends and family behind closed doors. As president, the office was also his home. Regardless of time or place, every incident had the potential to become a bold-faced headline. "This is just a pressure-box atmosphere," daughter Julie said during a White House interview. "Phones are always ringing. People are always around. It's not really a home."[4] Surrounding himself with familiar faces helped to alleviate the strain, but Nixon still found the transition to center stage a difficult one. "Any moments of real privacy suddenly seem especially precious," he confided in his memoirs. "I discovered how isolated from the reality of American life a President can feel in the White House."⁵

Effectively shut off from outsiders, Nixon relied more and more on his own decision-making ability. Having chosen aides whom he expected to support those decisions left him with few — if any — opposing points of view to consider.

As his power increased, so too did his trademark determination to identify and conquer his enemies. While he had pursed his causes with similar vigor in the early days of his career (the Hiss case and the Hollywood Ten), he had taken care to remain within the strict boundaries of the law. Midway into the third year of his presidency, those boundaries had become blurred, subject to Nixon's interpretation.

Confrontation regarding such judgment was inevitable. In June 1971, the debate went public when the *New York Times* published the first report on what would become known as the "Pentagon Papers." The documents, consisting of a 7,000-page study done by Robert McNamara, President Johnson's secretary of defense, provided an in-depth look at U.S. policy in Southeast Asia from WWII through 1968. Included were many top secret and classified papers originating from the Defense and State departments, the CIA, the White House, and the Joint Chiefs of Staff. The *Times* promised publication of the actual documents in the near future, setting off a storm of criticism and panic within the affected departments.

Anticipating that disclosure of past transgressions in the Kennedy and Johnson administrations would interfere with current prospects for a negotiated settlement with North Vietnam, Nixon moved for an immediate injunction to prevent publication of the documents. The administration's argument to the Supreme Court — that national security was at risk — was defeated in favor of the First Amendment, six votes to three.

The president was outraged that the Court valued freedom of the press over the security of the nation and vowed to expose the person responsible. He suspected Daniel Ellsberg, a former Pentagon aide already under suspicion of leaking classified information. Mitchell claimed sources at the Justice Department believed Ellsberg, a member of the research team hired to gather information for McNamara's study, had provided the Soviets with a copy of the report, along with other classified information, prior to publication of the Pentagon Papers on June 13. Kissinger went so far as to call Ellsberg the most dangerous man in America and insisted he must be stopped, whatever the cost.

On June 28, Ellsberg was indicted by a Los Angeles grand jury for theft of government property and unauthorized possession of documents relating to national defense. Undaunted, he took to the airwaves, using his position in the hot seat to attack the administration's policy in Vietnam.

Kissinger's opinion, combined with Mitchell's accusations, led Nixon to believe that Ellsberg was part of a larger conspiracy, thus he asked the FBI to conduct a more thorough investigation. According to Nixon, Hoover's longtime friendship with Ellsberg's father-in-law left him unwilling to pursue the case, forcing the president to take matters into his own hands. In mid-July, an investigating committee was assembled, consisting of White House lawyers Bud Krogh and David Young; Howard Hunt, formerly with the CIA; and G. Gordon Liddy, a former FBI man. Because they were in charge of plugging leaks, the group jokingly dubbed themselves the "Plumbers."

In an attempt to gain information that might discredit Ellsberg, the group authorized a Labor Day break-in at the office of his psychiatrist, Dr. Lewis Fielding. Nothing useful was gathered, and Ellsberg was eventually cleared of any wrongdoing. In his memoirs, Nixon said he did not recall having been told of the break-in at the time, but had he been, he would not have thought it "unprecedented, unwarranted or unthinkable," given the fact that national security was involved.

As the most respected leader in the world, Richard Nixon was no longer in awe of anyone. Extensive travels abroad had made meeting with foreign leaders as commonplace as a casual dinner with friends. His self-confidence had risen to such a level that he was unable to view what were clearly illegal acts as morally wrong. Because he had carefully selected his staff, there was no one within the tight circle willing to voice an opposing opinion — least of all those who had broken the law themselves. Gradually, Nixon became convinced that whatever actions he took as president could be sanctioned by the very fact that he *was* the president.

Behind the sturdy walls of Graceland, Presley was cultivating a similar attitude. A prisoner of his own notoriety, he had long been sheltered from the real-life world. Like Nixon, he relied on others to determine what day-to-day matters were pressing enough to demand his personal attention. During the early days of his career this may have been an adequate solution, but times had changed. Old pals thought less about friendship and more about their spot on the payroll. Anyone requesting to meet with Presley on a business matter was first scrutinized by the Colonel as to how the situation would affect Parker's share of the impending profits. Likewise, social acquaintances needed clearance from the live-in gatekeepers, who were anything but anxious to share their golden goose.

Elvis openly embraced this "funnel-through" lifestyle, but was it because he deemed it necessary or because it provided a convenient cover to live as he pleased behind closed doors? Most probably, it was a combination of both. Obviously, his fame necessitated taking safety precautions. The poor boy from Tupelo had risen to such prestige that he was known by his first name throughout the world, including China and the Soviet Union, where his recordings were officially banned. His Las Vegas engagements, now a mainstay on the schedule, sold out well in advance, drawing reservations from as far away as

Germany and Japan. Cross-country tours had been added to the mix, selling out as fast as tickets could be printed.

Given the circumstances, the argument is not whether Presley needed protection, but rather how much was enough. Upon leaving Graceland, he had not one or two guards at his side, but half a dozen, sometimes many more. While it is true that members of Presley's entourage were also his buddies on a social level, the fact remains that their "job" was to protect their boss.

Numerous threats had been made on his life, some of which were reported to the FBI and remain on file today. In addition, he lived in constant fear that his daughter — his only child — would fall victim to kidnappers. "Elvis became almost paranoid about Lisa's privacy and physical safety," Presley's karate instructor and friend Ed Parker confided. "Once when we were staying at his Palm Springs residence, he requested that I sleep on the couch in her room. He wanted to see to it that she would have personal security at a time when there was no live-in nurse to stay with her."[6] Certainly Elvis' growing dependency on prescription drugs — partly attributable to the overall mounting pressure — further intensified the paranoia.

To suggest that any of his friend-employees exaggerated the situation for personal gain would be irresponsible, considering the evidence. But that is not to say they were above taking advantage of it. The more wary Elvis became of strangers, the more unlikely it was that he would break free from his stagnant circle of friends, as it was they whom he relied on for his personal safety.

The trend to limit Presley's association with outsiders in order to secure their own positions had begun years earlier, first with Scotty and Bill and, later, with Larry Geller. In Geller's case, his physical presence was not the only worry: Priscilla and company did not stop until they thought they had flushed from Elvis's mind the very ideals the profound friseur stood for. Elaborating on the subject in *Elvis and Me*, Priscilla wrote:

> After Larry left, Elvis locked away many of his books. I told him I was glad, that they were literally destroying us. We were engaged to be married. "Would it make you feel better if I just got rid of them all?" Elvis asked. I nodded. That night, at three in the morning Elvis and I piled a huge stack of his books and magazines into a large box and dumped them into an abandoned water well behind Graceland. We poured gasoline over the pile, lit a match, and kissed the past goodbye. (234)

In fact, the past retained its hold on the entertainer until his death. Despite his quest for the meaning of life, Presley either could not or would not let go of the very things preventing him from finding the answers he so desperately sought. His long-time buddies might have understood where he had come from, but they had no idea what being Elvis Presley, idol of millions, was all about. Having chosen Graceland as his main residence, Elvis rarely mingled with other celebrities on a social basis. This was commendable in that it probably kept him from delving into the fast lane of hard-core drugs and alienation from his own roots, but what of the positive aspects? Had Presley become acquainted with others in similar situations, he might very well have found the outside world was not as lonely as he perceived it to be.

"That was the good thing about being four together," former Beatle George Harrison recalled in an interview. "Not like Elvis, you know. I always felt sorry later for Elvis because he was on his own. He had his guys with him but there was only one Elvis. Nobody else knew what he felt like. But for us, we all shared the experience."[7]

With Gladys gone and Vernon preoccupied with his new family, Elvis felt emotionally abandoned. Everyone around him was dependent on him for financial support: his entourage and their families, his cousins, aunts, and uncles, even Priscilla. While a spouse is often one's best source of understanding, the age difference between the two was in itself an added pressure. Prior to her relationship with Elvis, Priscilla had lived a very sheltered life. The well-to-do stepdaughter of a career army man, she had never gone hungry or experienced the humiliation of living on the wrong side of the tracks. Since she had no idea what her famous husband had gone through prior to his success, how could she have been expected to relate?

Barely 17 when she moved in with Elvis, Priscilla viewed the world through his perception. Surely her willingness to do so played an important role in their budding relationship. A born and bred southerner, Presley held to the belief that the man was the head of the family, in charge of all decisions, and — right or wrong — a woman's job was to support her man. Due to Priscilla's tender age, Elvis was able to mold her into the type of woman he wanted her to be. While an appalling idea by today's standards, it was not uncommon for the era, especially in the South. Many girls married young — and with their parents' blessing, no less. Singer Jerry Lee Lewis, another of Sam Phillips's discoveries, had married his 13-year-old cousin, causing outrage in the foreign press. Stateside, the move did little to adversely affect his career.

Living as a fairy princess in a magic castle, Priscilla had been more than happy to comply with Elvis's every whim. Slowly, as she matured, she gained more and more control — over herself, Elvis, and, eventually, their situation as a whole. Now a 25-year-old woman, she had her own ideas regarding her responsibilities as a wife and mother. Pleasing Elvis with every move she made was no longer a top priority.

Presley, meanwhile, struggled with his own sense of values. The insecurity of surviving Jesse Garon had never really gone away. As a little boy, he had felt the constant need to please his mother; now the head of a much-extended family, he was torn between wanting to keep everyone happy and doing what was best for himself. Further complicating the matter was the knowledge that many of his long-time pals had become more concerned with finances than friendship. "Of all those people and everybody in the band, he knew exactly who he could count on," Presley's bass player, Jerry Scheff, concluded. "Who he couldn't count on, who was given to be Elvis Presley's friend and who was out for whatever they could get. He knew all of that stuff, he had that all wired in."[8]

Assuming Scheff's assessment is correct, a major housecleaning seemed in order. Undoubtedly, Presley would have benefited from such action, yet his reluctance is understandable. Perhaps many of his friends *were* using their relationship for personal gain, but who was to say that any new associates would not exhibit the same tendencies? How could they not? His status as a superstar was what attracted people to him in the first place. Everyone wanted something; better to give it to those who had once been his friend just for the sake of friendship than to risk being used by a total outsider.

Vernon wholeheartedly agreed. With a wife and three boys to support, he had long ago adopted a "fewer the better" policy in regards to his son's entourage. Not only was he leery of new additions to the pack, he encouraged a reduction in the number of existing members. It is common knowledge that Elvis delighted in giving away expensive cars to friends and strangers alike; less well known is the family friction such acts of generosity created. In charge of Elvis's checkbook, Vernon insisted the Presley bankroll could not afford such extravagance. The fewer on staff, the fewer checks he would be required to write.

Like Nixon, Presley had some friends who proved exceptions to the what's-in-it-for-me rule. Among the most influential of the independent spirits was Kempo karate expert Ed Parker.

A sociology graduate of Brigham Young University, Ed's love of karate urged him to concentrate on the sport as a career. Having grown up on the rough side of town, he felt that conventional karate, when used as a means of self-defense, left something to be desired. "As a former street-fighter in Honolulu, I knew that many of the traditional movements from the orient were not effective in an American back alley brawl. Oriental methods did offer more variables, but adjustments and additions were definitely needed."[9] Upon his arrival in Los Angeles in 1956, he was shunned by traditionalists, who dismissed his methods as far too radical to be of commercial value. Taking his cue from another rebel who was currently riding a wave of unprecedented success with his "radical" style of music, Parker chose to follow his heart. He opened his own school in Pasadena and remained self-supporting for the duration of his lifetime.

An avid fan of the martial arts since his army days, Elvis had already achieved a brown belt by the time he crossed paths with Parker at a karate tournament in 1960. When the two spoke at length after the event, Ed was surprised — both with the entertainer's personal humility and with his obvious passion for the sport. "Our discussion delved deeper into theory," he recalled. "I was impressed at the depth of his intelligence. The more we talked, the more it became apparent that Elvis was a much deeper person than his public image portrayed."[10]

The kindred rebels crossed paths occasionally throughout Presley's Hollywood career, but it was not until Elvis's triumphant return to Las Vegas in 1969 that the friendship truly blossomed. Utilizing karate as a form of expression, Presley incorporated many of the rhythmic poking and jabbing movements into his stage act. Encouraged by the audience's favorable response, he turned to Parker for more personal instruction, eventually earning an eighth-degree black belt in 1974.

Never accepting payment for his services, Parker accompanied Elvis on tour occasionally, working as a bodyguard in later years. (He can be seen on the 1977 CBS television broadcast *Elvis in Concert*, helping the entertainer off stage after the performance.) While it is important to note Parker's absence from the payroll, the telling factor was his lack of dependency — on Presley's money or his name. Like Nixon's friends Abplanalp and Rebozo, Ed had established his own life prior to his relationship with Elvis. In addition to his successful karate school, he participated in numerous tournaments across the nation and worked as a bit actor in films and television.

Ironically, it was Parker's very independence that kept him from providing the emotional support so lacking in Elvis's life. The same was true of Presley's long-time friend and classmate George Klein.

As with the excommunicated Geller, Klein had traveled with Presley's entourage on occasion during the movie era. Unlike Larry, however, he was never perceived as a threat by the rest of the entourage and for good reason: when George and Elvis got together, they discussed music or the local entertainment scene, not the mysteries of life. George was one of a chosen few who was also embraced by the Colonel. Not surprising, considering that Klein's position at WHBQ offered endless promotion of Presley's recordings, free of charge.

Geller, on the other hand, had never been perceived by Elvis's cronies as anything *but* a threat. If their boss followed Larry's quest for spiritual knowledge and they refused to follow, they would be left behind to fend for themselves. Why complicate their lives with studies they had no interest in learning when all they had to do was remove the troublemaker from the scene, problem solved?

Geller did not think in such small-minded terms. Despite the back stabbing he had encountered prior to leaving the group, he continued to hold his friend in high regard, patiently awaiting the chance to renew their relationship when circumstances permitted. The long-awaited opportunity materialized in August 1972, when singer Johnny Rivers, a client of Larry's, made arrangements to attend Presley's performance in Las Vegas and invited Geller to join him. Unfortunately, Larry found the reunion bittersweet. "I had only to see Elvis onstage for five minutes for it to be clear to me how deeply in trouble he was. Everyone else in the audience was so overwhelmed by him that they couldn't possibly have guessed the truth.... Clearly, Elvis had lost his center, and the drugs numbed his emotional pain."[11]

Presley invited Larry backstage after the show, where the two exchanged hugs and promised to get together soon. It wasn't until late that same year, however, that a lengthier meeting occurred. By then no longer worried about the effect his decision would have on Priscilla or the Colonel, Elvis expressed regret over having allowed others' judgment to overrule his own feelings and asked that Larry rejoin the entourage full time. Geller was unable to accept the invitation due to prior business commitments, but he remained a constant force in Elvis's life — albeit at arm's length.

Had these independent friends been accessible on a daily basis, Presley most surely would have grown beyond the "good old boy" circle. As it was, he continued to serve as the lone role model for an extended family, unable to break free of the daunting responsibilities that had weighed on him since childhood.

Nixon's problem was not the lack of an on-site mentor but rather his refusal to consider the possibility that he might benefit from one. He had captured the highest office of power in the world without the aid of a wealthy family or the support of his peers. Why would he need help now? His close ties to Rebozo and Abplanalp — both self-made men like himself — only served to reinforce his opinion.

Previous teachers had come and gone, never to be replaced. While it is obvious from the text of Nixon's memoirs that he thought very highly of Eisenhower as a person, it is just as apparent he did not respect the former general's political leadership abilities. Rather than explain how observing Ike's methods had prepared him for the presidency, he pointed out the weak spots and noted how best to improve upon them.

Surrounded by "yes men" and with the most important counselors of his life — his parents — both dead, Nixon was dependent on his family for emotional guidance. At first glance this seems a positive situation, as, unlike Presley, he had a loving wife and two admiring daughters. Pat had remained at his side through good and bad times alike; Nixon described her as "the strongest member of my family, personal or official."[12] Daughters Tricia and Julie, now adults with lives of their own, remained close to their parents and fully supportive of their father's political decisions.

Ultimately, Nixon's problem was not a lack of support but rather his inability to embrace it. Regardless of how hard he tried, he remained a man who loved from a distance. A prime example of this is related in his memoirs, when, on the eve of Tricia's wedding (March 15, 1971), he admits having slipped a note under her door *after* she had gone to bed, expressing his thoughts on her upcoming marriage to Eddie Cox. The note, fully related in *RN*, is as warm and affectionate as most fathers could hope to achieve, but the key here is Nixon's inability to speak the words to Tricia's face. A similar episode is related by biographer Jonathan Aitken in *Nixon: A Life*, when he tells of Julie's marriage to David Eisenhower several years earlier.

Expressing emotion, even in the presence of those he cared for deeply, remained an unmet challenge throughout Nixon's life. While Hannah and Francis's contribution cannot be denied, there is also the factor of Nixon having watched not one, but two of his brothers die. Seven-year-old Arthur's passing was unexpected and swift, leaving painful but fond memories of a happy child. In Harold's case, it was a matter of the young man's body literally wasting away over a span of ten years, an experience no one would be able to forget.

Nixon's goal of achieving the presidency had, at least in part, been derived from the need to prove himself worthy of surviving his brothers. When the time finally arrived for his victory celebration, it came without his parents cheering from the sidelines. Watching those close to him pass away left an undeniable void, one he appeared unwilling to fill as the years progressed. His emotional shield may have been a result of his increasing self-confidence but, more likely, it was a defense mechanism built up over the years. By keeping his distance, he was able to minimize the loss if or when it occurred.

While Presley may have found such a strategy useful, it was nearly impossible for him to carry it out. Joy was experienced by sharing it with others, be it a hug for a fan or an expensive gift for a stranger. Literally a prisoner of his emotions, he could no more stop feeling than cut off an arm or leg. Naturally, such dependence had positive and negative repercussions. When he loved, he loved deeply. And when he lost that love, it touched the very depths of his soul.

As 1971 began, Elvis was more in demand than ever, playing to one adoring, sellout crowd after another. Meanwhile, his young wife was stuck at home with their three-year-old daughter, alone. Priscilla did her best to cope, filling the empty hours with dancing lessons and art classes. Spurred on by a wave of creativity, she redecorated Graceland, then enticed Elvis into purchasing a house in Beverly Hills to serve as their "home away from home."

Elvis responded favorably to her domestic efforts, but when they did not bring the desired result—more time alone together—she began to look elsewhere for company. In early 1972, she found it in the form of karate instructor Mike Stone. Ironically, she had taken up the sport with Elvis's blessing, in the hope that it would draw them closer together.

In *Elvis and Me*, Priscilla credited both her teacher and the sport with opening her eyes to the real world, forcing her to see that the guarded life she lived with Elvis was abnormal and detrimental to her own well-being. She left Graceland with Lisa Marie later that year, intent on establishing a life away from her famous husband. While her affair with Stone would prove temporary, her separation from Elvis did not.

9. No Man Is an Island

To Presley, the failure of his marriage was nearly as devastating as Gladys's death. His ego was damaged beyond repair: his wife had left him for another man, and everyone within his tightly knit group knew it. As previously noted, Mike Stone was only one of many factors that forced Priscilla from Elvis's life. Considering Presley's status as a universal sex symbol, however, it is unlikely he was able to put this situation in any type of perspective other than having not been "man enough" to hold his woman. Not surprisingly, his first reaction was anger. Some members of his entourage say he went so far as to threaten Stone's life. After a cool-down period, it was back to business as usual — or so he tried to make it appear.

"Elvis wasn't the same person," Billy Stanley said. "If he'd been moody before, the bad moods didn't last long, and then he was soon exuberant, daring, fun-loving, and in control again. If he was angry — well, that quickly passed as well. But now he was sad. The people who loved him didn't know how to react, so we all tried to pretend everything was the same."[13] But it was not, nor would it ever be. "Something behind those piercing blue eyes died," Ed Parker said of his friend after the divorce. "It was gone, never to return."[14]

Struggling to heal his wounded pride, Presley moved on to other women, dating such desirable starlets as Candice Bergen and Cybill Shepherd. But despite his rising popularity as an eligible bachelor, he found himself as uncomfortable with the Hollywood crowd as he had ever been. When Priscilla's affair with Stone ended and still she did not return, he was forced to face the ugly truth: his rival for her attention had been none other than his age-old nemesis, success. He had failed to address the problems his mother had had with regard to his fame until it was too late. Now he had done the same with his wife and child.

Longing to bare his soul to someone who understood, he found solace with Memphis local Linda Thompson. A former Miss Tennessee, Linda became acquainted with Presley through mutual friend George Klein, who was aware that she shared Elvis's passion for gospel music and higher religious understanding. Unlike young Priscilla, naiveté was not a problem for Linda. An English major at Memphis State University, her experience as third runner-up in the Miss America contest left her well versed on the pressures of life in the fast lane.

In retrospect, it is unlikely Presley could have found himself a better match. Whereas Priscilla struggled with selfhood, Linda brimmed with maturity and confidence. In addition to sharing many of Elvis's interests, her southern background made her sympathetic to his old-fashioned ideals regarding a woman's role in society. Perhaps most important, she passed the ulterior motive test. As a former beauty queen, the doors to the modeling and show business industries were already open; she didn't *need* Presley or his name, which was probably the reason she was able to penetrate his emotional armor so quickly. She moved into Graceland in August 1972 and remained his steady companion for the next four years.

"Linda was good for Elvis during a very bad period of his life," said Marty Lacker, an on-again, off-again member of Presley's entourage. "She was probably the last girl about whom Elvis was, in any way, serious."[15] Billy Stanley described her as a woman "who went with the flow and was part of Elvis's life both at home and on the road, who sang gospel music with him, laughed with him, cried with him, cared for him no matter what he did."[16] Larry Geller and Ed Parker both offered similar assessments in their respective books.

While Linda may have gone "with the flow" in regard to accepting Elvis's sexual encounters on the road, there were limits to her loyalty. Like Ed and Larry, her main concern was Presley's well-being. Rather than close her eyes and look the other way, she tried to help him with his problems. The trouble was that Presley — much like Nixon — was not able to admit he needed help.

CHAPTER 10

The Cancer Within

Show me a hero and I will write you a tragedy.

— F. Scott Fitzgerald

Judged from a critical standpoint, 1972 proved a banner year. Presley broke attendance records across the nation, while Nixon enjoyed some of the highest ratings for a president. To the masses, their images epitomized the true American ideal, but inside, each man continued trying to defy mortality, nurturing the seeds of a futile search for perfection.

Presley's commitment to his fans made it impossible for him to attain peace and happiness off the stage. Terrified of losing their devotion, he was unable to establish a meaningful one-on-one relationship with anyone, let alone put it first in his life. Nixon, meanwhile, had become so preoccupied with reaching his goal that he failed to exploit what Elvis so desperately needed: the loyalty and support of a loving family.

Regardless of how it would appear in the months to follow, Nixon's quest to achieve world peace remained the driving force behind his presidency. Following the Plumbers' less-than-lucrative break-in at Ellsberg's psychiatrist's office in the fall of 1971, the group had been ordered to disband. Nixon had concluded it was time to focus on more important matters. At the top of the list were issues most dear to his heart: a personal trip to China, a renewal of SALT talks with the Soviet Union, and an end to the Vietnam War.

Nixon realized that most Americans still viewed the U.S.S.R. (Union of Soviet Socialist Republics) as the supreme menace to democracy, but the Soviets were not his only concern. Russia's archrival, the P.R.C. (People's Republic of China), represented a growing nuclear threat. Aware that offering an outstretched hand to the Soviets while slamming the door in the face of the Chinese would spell disaster, Nixon worked behind the scenes with Kissinger to open communication on both ends. China was the first to respond with a formal offer in July 1971, requesting that Nixon come to Peking in February of the following year. The announcement prompted a quick reply from the Soviet leader, Leonid Brezhnev, offering to receive the president in May.

Few historians would argue that Nixon's weeklong visit to the P.R.C. was the crowning jewel of his political career. For him, it was a long-coveted personal triumph as well: the man who had built his career battling Communism now stood at its doorstep with a hand outstretched toward peace. Nixon described his initial face-to-face meeting with Premier Chou En-lai as the beginning of a new era. "The Star Spangled Banner," he recalled, had never sounded so sweet.

At his side, sharing in his moment of glory, stood his ever-faithful partner, Pat. Throughout the days to follow, as her husband sat at the bargaining table negotiating his dream, Mrs. Nixon socialized with Chou's wife and friends, quietly bridging the cultural gap that had separated the countries for more than 20 years. Although few specifics were agreed upon by week's end, neither side denied the impact the event would have on furthering relations. During his farewell dinner in Peking, Nixon appropriately dubbed it "the week that changed the world" (*RN*, 580).

The value of Pat's presence during that historic week was not lost on Nixon; several passages in his memoirs are devoted to describing her insights on the Chinese culture and how they bettered his own understanding. Nevertheless, when the couple returned to the U.S., it was the president who basked in the glow of the headlines.

Pat's ability to live in the shadow of her husband's career was a key factor in their successful relationship. Although Priscilla exhibited similar behavior during her early years with Elvis, the two situations do not equally compare. Priscilla entered Presley's life as an adolescent, anxious to please. From the moment Pat met Richard, she was an adult, fully conscious of her own decisions. Mrs. Nixon chose to share her husband's dream, Priscilla longed to chase her own. While neither can be faulted for her goals, the fact remains that their choices greatly affected the outcome of their partners' futures. Whether Elvis would have come to value Priscilla's input in the same way Richard did Pat's remains one of the biggest questions surrounding the entertainer's downfall. By the time Elvis's fairy princess had matured enough to communicate on an adult level, she was not the person he had fallen in love with seven years earlier. Rebelling against his ideal of the dutiful southern wife, she longed to become independent of his lifestyle rather than supportive.

As Presley struggled to accept the ultimate casualty of his career — the end of his marriage — Nixon embarked on his groundbreaking trip to the U.S.S.R., unaware that his commitment to peace was about to alter the course of his life and those of his loved ones, forever.

Rumors that the Soviets might cancel the May summit had arisen earlier

10. The Cancer Within

in the month, when Nixon, disgusted with the breakdown of talks with North Vietnam, had ordered the mining of Haiphong harbor and a massive bombing of key military targets in Hanoi, despite objections by key members of his cabinet. The president's hunch that the Soviets would be more worried about what had transpired with the Chinese during his visit than with their status with the North Vietnamese proved correct, and the summit went on as scheduled.

Ironically, Nixon's welcome meeting with Secretary General Brezhnev on May 22 at the Kremlin took place in the same office where he had met Khrushchev 13 years earlier. Nixon found the new Soviet leader to be as hardline as his predecessor in many respects but detected a warmer side to his personality. During their initial meeting, the two leaders exchanged joking remarks about the pitfalls of bureaucracy, which evoked a hearty laugh from Brezhnev. "It seemed to be a good beginning," Nixon recalled in *RN* (610).

And so it was. Four days into the talks, the ABM (anti-ballistic missile) treaty was signed, greatly limiting the defensive arms race on both sides. An interim agreement on strategic missiles was also reached, freezing the numbers of ICBMs (intercontinental ballistic missiles) to those that already existed or were presently under construction. In addition to the more widely publicized military agreements, both countries vowed to share information on science and technology. Research on medicine and public health was targeted, especially in the areas of cancer and heart disease. Nixon's commitment to space exploration was also addressed. Summit discussions produced an agreement on a joint orbital mission in space, which ultimately resulted in the landmark Apollo-Soyuz space docking in 1975.

Despite tremendous progress with the world's Communist superpowers, Nixon's short-term priority — peace with honor in Vietnam — continued to elude him. His frustration was not lost on the Democrats, who had decided the best way to regain the White House was to tout the present administration's failures in Vietnam. Their leading candidate, Senator George McGovern of South Dakota, favored an unconditional and immediate withdrawal of all U.S. troops from Southeast Asia. Early polls showed the senator trailing Nixon badly, but his nomination at the Democratic convention in July sent a surge of hope through Hanoi, further complicating the stalled negotiations.

As the Democrats rallied for peace at any cost, John Mitchell, who had resigned his post as attorney general to take the helm of the Committee to Reelect the President as a personal favor to Nixon, struggled to maintain a sense of order among fellow Republicans. Rumors of discontent plagued the local chapters, whose leaders complained that Washington bureaucrats were ignoring them. Adding to Mitchell's woes, his wife, Martha, was undergoing serious mental problems.

When word of the trouble infesting the CRP reached Nixon, he was reluctant to call his friend on the carpet for fear Mitchell would view the move as a personal reflection on his job performance. As a result, much of the leadership fell to the number two man, Jeb Magruder.

H. R. Haldeman later claimed that Watergate was a direct result of the ill-fated decision to leave Magruder in charge, for which he blamed himself. While the choice may very well have resided with Haldeman, Nixon cannot be exempt from blame, as it was he who insisted on hiring people to make such decisions for him. In *RN*, he admitted that he never actually confronted Mitchell about the burglary because he did not want to know if his pal had been involved. While it is likely their friendship played a role in Nixon's decision, a more complicated motive lurked in the president's subconscious: considering the possibility of Mitchell's guilt meant questioning his own judgment in having chosen the man as his friend in the first place. Believing in Mitchell's innocence allowed Nixon to maintain his image of self-perfection, an image he perceived as vital to retaining his presidency.

In Presley's case, it was his pals who were reluctant to confront him for fear of confirming the truth. By the summer of 1972, Elvis had become seriously addicted to prescription drugs. At home or on the road, his personal physician, George Nichopoulos (known as Dr. Nick) remained close at hand. Every member of Presley's tightly knit group knew what the doctor carried in his little black bag, yet few dared to question his intentions, let alone make an issue of it. Many were nursing similar addictions. Others feared for their jobs. Karate soulmate Ed Parker simply refused to admit his friend was capable of such poor judgment. Whatever the reasons, the lack of action by Presley's entourage, as despicable as it may have been, was, at best, a contributing factor to his dilemma. As new love Linda Thompson would soon find out, no one could force Elvis to do *anything* he did not want to do.

The same held true for Nixon. Although the massive U.S. assault he had launched on North Vietnam in May had not forced Hanoi back to the bargaining table as hoped, the president had no intention of allowing McGovern's chant for "peace at any cost" to dictate a change in policy. He had promised America peace with honor, and that is exactly what he intended to deliver.

Nixon's cohorts were every bit as determined to stay the course. Polls showed their candidate with a comfortable lead, but their respective spots on the power roster depended on the president's reelection. Discrediting McGovern was the surest way to ensure victory in November. Every vote for Nixon brought them one step closer to retaining — or improving — their current positions.

Nixon was too wrapped up in his presidential duties to worry about the tedious details of his reelection campaign. Following a busy week of receiving foreign dignitaries in mid–June, he took a much-needed break at Grand Cay, a small island in the Bahamas owned by his friend Abplanalp. The president spent two days relaxing on the island before flying to his Florida retreat in Key Biscayne. It was there, on Sunday morning, June 18, that he learned the first details of a sordid plot that would bring about the end of his presidency.

10. The Cancer Within

He began the day like many others, with a fresh cup of coffee and the morning paper. Skimming the front page of the *Miami Herald*, he noted an article reporting an attempted break-in at the Democratic National Headquarters in Washington, D.C. Five men, four of them Cuban, had been arrested. Recalling his initial reaction, Nixon said he found it "preposterous" and dismissed it as a joke.

The humor of the situation was lost the following evening when he spoke to Haldeman on the return trip to Washington aboard Air Force One. Haldeman had learned that James McCord, a former CIA security officer presently employed by both the CRP and the Republican National Committee, had been arrested at the Watergate office-apartment complex with the Cubans. Adding to the bad news, more than $1,000 in hundred dollar bills had been found on the burglars, traceable to the CRP.

The court's ruling on the Pentagon Papers may have dealt Nixon's pride a blow, but clearly, it had done little to erase his belief that the president was above the law. Reasoning that bugging the other guy had been common practice in politics for years, Nixon's first reaction to Haldeman's news was not to overreact. What bothered him was not the illegality of the break-in itself but rather the overall "stupidity" of the operation. Because the burglars had botched the job so badly, he entertained the possibility that the break-in had been a set-up, staged to demolish his reelection. Yet, as he admitted in *RN*, the trail of breadcrumbs "undeniably" led to the doorstep of the CRP.

Indeed, the trail to his own back door became clearer with each passing day. Address books found on the burglars contained the name of former Plumber Howard Hunt. On June 20, the *Washington Post* reported that Hunt had been employed at the White House as late as March 29, working as a consultant to Chuck Colson, special counsel to the president.

In his post–Watergate book, *The Ends of Power* (1978), Bob Haldeman described Colson as "the President's personal 'hit man,' his impresario of 'hard ball' politics."[1] He was a man who insisted that Richard Nixon was his only boss. Nicknamed "Wildman" around the White House, Colson had been suspected of concocting numerous schemes. Reportedly, his ideas ranged from spying on Senator Ted Kennedy in the hopes of catching him in an illicit affair to plotting a fire bombing at a liberal foundation in order to retrieve documents for the president.

While attempting to confirm or deny any possible involvement on Colson's part, Haldeman learned that committee money had indeed sponsored the burglary. Magruder insisted, however, that it had been the work of men "operating on their own" who "just got carried away."[2] One such zealot was former Plumber Gordon Liddy, then employed as a legal advisor to the CRP. Liddy had come recommended for the job by John Dean, the White House legal counsel. Haldeman had personally approved the request.

Over the next few days, John Ehrlichman, the president's chief advisor on domestic affairs, investigated the matter and concluded that Liddy bore full responsibility for planning the burglary. In a meeting with Nixon and Haldeman, Ehrlichman said a confession from Liddy would probably satisfy the Democrats and the media by giving them the White House "higher up" they were clamoring for. Nixon agreed. Haldeman added that they could "take care" of Liddy by paying his legal expenses and providing for his family in his absence, should Liddy agree to plead guilty.

Nixon saw no problem with Haldeman's suggestion. Rather, he viewed the potential payments to Liddy as a return favor; Liddy had, after all, only been trying to help the president secure reelection. This misplaced sense of guiltless loyalty, encouraged by Nixon's cohorts from the beginning of Watergate, led the president down a path toward inevitable self-destruction.

Presley's entourage performed in similar fashion. By refusing to confront their boss regarding his drug use and, in some cases, even encouraging it, Elvis' buddies were effectively supporting his habit. Like the president's men, they stood to lose a great deal should their leader realize the extent of his deeds. If Presley faced his addiction, those among him who used drugs would have to face theirs; those who did not would be accused of turning the other cheek in order to save their jobs. Either way, they were certain to lose the financial security Presley's fame afforded them. What they either failed or refused to realize was the amount of damage their golden goose was sustaining in order to furnish that security. During the early days, when Elvis had used uppers to stay awake during all-night drives, the effect on his health had been minimal; he was a growing boy, full of energy and enthusiasm for life. In the years since Gladys's death, that youthful vitality had slowly eroded in the wake of a demanding career — so demanding that it could no longer be supported without an adequate supply of chemical stimulation. As his tolerance grew, "adequate" became a relative term. How much was enough? Whatever it took to provide the energy required to climb on the stage and perform for his fans.

For Nixon, it was the power of his office that fueled his desire. Without the presidency, he would be unable to see his journey through to the end. If the voters found him unworthy of another term because of his policies in Vietnam, he would have to accept their decision, but to allow what he viewed as a "third-rate burglary" to threaten the prospects of world peace was incomprehensible. He wanted Watergate behind him, the sooner the better.

The Justice Department, now free of Mitchell's friendship with the president, was not so inclined. Fueled by the outrage among Democrats, Patrick Gray, the acting director of the FBI, launched an investigation into the burglary. (Hoover had passed away in his sleep on May 2; a permanent replacement had not been chosen, though Gray was the leading candidate.) Although the bureau had not yet built a case against Howard Hunt or traced the money

10. The Cancer Within

found on the burglars to the CRP, Nixon knew it was only a matter of time. Due to Hunt's former CIA involvement, the president reasoned the agency would prefer to keep Hunt's name — and past activities — out of the headlines. Thus, on June 23, six days after the break-in, he suggested that Haldeman speak with Vernon Walters, the deputy director of the CIA. Nixon wanted Walters to persuade Gray to end the FBI investigation, on the grounds that exposing Hunt's activities would endanger national security. Later that afternoon, Haldeman reported that Walters had agreed to take care of it.

In view of Walters's cooperation, Nixon was confident that his Watergate troubles were over. In reality, they had only just begun. Hunt threatened to reveal that cash had been funneled through illegal contributions from the CRP if he were indicted in connection with Watergate. The burglars made it clear they expected a post-November pardon in exchange for their silence, a threat complicated by the fact that no one among the president's staff knew who the Cubans or McCord might implicate, though Nixon feared it could go all the way to Mitchell. Just when the FBI appeared to be backing off, a handgun belonging to Hunt was discovered in an office safe at the White House, prompting Gray to resume the investigation.

As events unfolded, John Mitchell became so distracted with his wife's condition, which had taken a noticeable turn for the worse amid media speculation about his involvement in Watergate, that he was forced to resign as head of the CRP. Suspicion that Liddy's boss, Magruder, may have known about the burglary beforehand resulted in a grand jury investigation. In addition to the five burglars who had been caught on the premises, Hunt and Liddy were indicted in September on charges of burglary, conspiracy, and wiretapping.

Whereas the Democrats and the media expressed outrage at the activities of the CRP, the general public showed little interest in the scandal that was unfolding, suggesting that Nixon was correct in assuming most people viewed the break-in as "no big deal," an acceptable result of politics as usual. Years would pass before he realized the significance of his activities during that summer. In *RN*, he admitted having done nothing at the time to discourage the various lies that were being considered to cover up the CRP's involvement in the break-in, and he admitted having personally authorized efforts to pressure the CIA into limiting the FBI's investigation. While he conceded that his actions and those of his staff would soon be viewed by the media as a cover-up, he himself did not see it that way. To Nixon, Watergate was solely a matter of politics.

What Watergate really boiled down to was poor political decisions. Nixon made a mistake in allowing the CRP a free hand, especially during Mitchell's troubled leadership, and some bad choices were made as a result of that mistake. Prior to his discussion with Haldeman and Ehrlichman on June 23, Nixon was not personally responsible for any of those decisions. Had he come forward, publicly admitted his mistake, and taken responsibility for it, Watergate would have stopped well short of the Oval Office. Because he did not, he became caught in a web of deceit so tangled that even the power of the presidency could not stop the hungry spider from devouring him.

Nixon gave several reasons for his failure to go public from the beginning. First and foremost, he did not believe Watergate was an event worthy of his personal attention; nothing had been accomplished by the burglary, and, furthermore, the culprits had been caught. He cited concern for John Mitchell's well-being, reasoning that if the CRP connection were revealed, Mitchell would be found guilty by association. Last, he did not want to give the Democrats the satisfaction of having caused him public embarrassment.

Nixon's talk of friendship and loyalty was no doubt sincere, but, in the end, it was the fear of embarrassment that sealed his fate. Washington was a long way from Whittier, but he had never forgotten the journey. Every successful step had been taken alone: the Hiss case, the Checkers Speech, renomination as his party's VP, and, finally, the White House. He had scratched and clawed his way to the top, and he had no intention of allowing his Ivy League rivals to take it away over something as petty as Watergate. If he admitted one mistake, they would look for another and another, not stopping until they had succeeded in stripping him of his justly earned rewards.

Richard Nixon had become the most popular president in modern history. The people supported his decisions. They expected him to make the right ones. By admitting he had not, he was no longer worthy of their support. He would lose his bid for reelection and, with it, the chance to fulfill his destiny.

Psychologists might argue that such a line of thinking proves Nixon had become paranoid, but when viewing it from a lay perspective, obsessed seems a better term. Nixon had become convinced that his goal was so important that he was willing to do anything to achieve it. He therefore rationalized his behavior by assuming that his popularity with the voters gave him a blank check to make whatever decisions he deemed necessary.

Elvis suffered the same dilemma in regards to admitting his drug problem. Unlike his rebel image of the fifties, he had become an example for young people to follow, a poor boy made good who had never lost sight of his roots. He took care of his family and friends. He gave expensive gifts to strangers. He supported his government, going so far as to have the IRS figure his taxes so there would be no question he paid his fair amount. While he was held in contempt by the counterculture, most Americans were convinced he lived a good, clean life. On a conscious level, Presley was convinced of it as well. As a child, he had been taught to respect all adults, especially authority figures such as police officers, doctors, and clergy. Following his break-up with Priscilla, Presley's health declined drastically, no doubt advanced by the ever-increasing amounts of pills he received from Dr. Nick and other physicians. Among the entertainer's more serious problems were stomach disorders, liver disease, and a recurring colon infection. Because the addictive pain killers, uppers, and sleeping pills came from the same source as the treatment for legitimate problems — a legitimate doctor — it is understandable how Elvis convinced himself they were all necessary medications, if only for the sake of argument when someone questioned him about it.

To suggest Presley was so naive that he did not realize he was addicted to prescription medication insults his intelligence, but there is a fine line between admitting a weakness and accepting it. Subconsciously, Elvis's mind was working to bridge the gap. His offer to assist the Nixon administration in its war against drugs may very well have stemmed from a nagging sense of guilt. Studies dealing with the age-old factor of shame have found that insecure patients often harbor self-doubts and unexamined shame wounds. By drawing attention away from themselves, they are able to make another person the problem and thus feel good about themselves.[3]

Psychologists who study personality disorders report that people react most negatively to others who display characteristics they despise, such as foul language, drinking, or losing their tempers too easily, when they themselves suffer from the same problem but cannot or will not admit it. Carl Jung, famous for his development of analytical psychology, called this the shadow archetype. According to Jung, the shadow represents a person's dark, repressed nature, the side of our character that we reject or deny because it conflicts with our conscious tendencies or our opinions about ourselves.

Participating in a public antidrug campaign such as the one suggested by Nixon aide Bud Krogh would have been the perfect way for Presley to contain his shadow. But the strategy was not without risk. If Presley's own habit was discovered by people outside of his entourage, people he respected, surely they would have confronted him with the unpleasant truth. Either he would have had to seek help or admit to being a hypocrite.

Subconsciously, Elvis wanted to face that truth. Whether the counsel would have given him enough self-confidence to actually do so is another matter. Like Nixon, Presley's image was extremely important to him. The love and devotion of his fans remained the main nourishment in his chaotic life. The pills allowed him to maintain that love, via a frantic schedule that would have been impossible without the aid of drug-induced energy. (Elvis performed more than 160 shows in 1972 alone.) Admitting that he was not the ageless fountain of youth his adoring public expected would have made him feel unworthy of their continued support. Presley thrived on that support, every bit as much as Nixon did on the power of his presidency.

Naturally, Presley's dedication was not lost on the Colonel, who continued to devise various means of exploiting it. Despite the back-breaking schedule, millions of fans were unable to see their idol live on stage, a fact that disturbed Elvis, particularly in regards to his devoted following outside the U.S. "Inwardly, Elvis felt guilty about having neglected his fans overseas," Ed

Parker noted in *Inside Elvis* (159). "He handed me some of the charts from England and other parts of the world that showed his records were on top. 'Ed, look at what these people are doing for me over there and I haven't even done a thing for them.' I've got to go over there and give something back to these people who've given so much to me.'"

The Colonel offered a compromise in 1970, with the release of *Elvis: That's the Way It Is*, an MGM movie featuring Presley's Las Vegas stage act. The project was a huge success, garnering critical acclaim throughout the world. Executives at RCA joined in the celebration, resuming their policy to forgo studio sessions in favor of live recordings. Citing impressive box office receipts, the Colonel secured a contract for a sequel; *Elvis on Tour* would be promoted as a semibiography, intertwining some of Presley's early television performances with up-to-date concert footage.

As MGM readied what would be Presley's thirty-third — and final — feature film, Nixon got on with the business of the presidency, convinced the worst of Watergate was behind him. In August, he accepted his party's nomination for reelection, pledging to see his goal of peace with honor in Vietnam through to the end. Late September saw the North Vietnamese return to the bargaining table, reportedly discouraged by recent polls expressing renewed support for the president's handling of the war; 75 percent of Americans thought it was imperative that South Vietnam not fall to Communist rule.

The September talks produced an outline for U.S. withdrawal, contingent on the return of all American prisoners of war. An agreement was reached on October 21, with a tentative signing date set for the thirty-first. All that remained was securing South Vietnamese president Nguyen Van Thieu's signature on the deal, and Nixon's quest to end the war on his terms would be complete. On the morning of October 22, Kissinger met with Thieu in Saigon and reported back to Nixon that the South Vietnamese leader had given his okay. By late afternoon, Thieu had done an abrupt about-face, slashing hopes that a settlement might be reached before the election.

Despite the breakdown in negotiations with Vietnam, the Watergate burglary, and ongoing rumors of corruption surrounding the CRP, Nixon went on to win reelection by the second-largest majority in history. McGovern snagged a mere 37.5 percent of the popular vote, compared with Nixon's 60.7 percent.

The numbers gave Nixon's sliding confidence a much-needed boost, but the victory proved semisweet; as with Johnson's trouncing of Goldwater in 1964, the partisan landslide did not carry over to Congress. Determined to end the war at any cost, Democrats were threatening to cut off all funding for Vietnam. While Nixon had become fed up with Thieu's lack of cooperation, he was not willing to allow the loss of so many American lives to have been in vain. He vowed to bring about a settlement before Congress returned in January, even if it included terms that Thieu would not accept.

10. The Cancer Within

Kissinger returned to Paris in late November, hoping to smooth out the differences, but North Vietnam, still fuming over Thieu's stonewalling, wanted nothing to do with any new give-and-take. The talks ended with Hanoi reneging on several major issues they had agreed to in October. A meeting on December 4 produced such irate demands from the Communists that Kissinger contemplated resigning. As Nixon saw it, only two options were available: abandon Thieu and strike his own deal with Hanoi or launch an offensive equal to that of the previous May. His decision to carry out the latter became known as the "Christmas bombing," an attack so devastating that the North Vietnamese came running back to the table, anxious to resume talks.

On January 22, Lyndon Johnson died of heart-related problems, marking the first time in modern history that the nation was without a living former president. The following evening, Nixon went on national television to announce that a settlement had been reached: all U.S. troops would be withdrawn and the POWs returned. Afterward, he wrote a personal note to Johnson's widow, expressing regret that her husband had not lived to hear the announcement of the peace settlement.

With the war finally behind him, Nixon pledged to concentrate more heavily on his domestic agenda. Among his goals were to reform the budget, reduce federal bureaucracy, and revitalize the Republican party along what he called "New Majority" lines.

The Democratic Congress had other priorities, namely, convincing the voters that there was much more to Watergate than met the eye. Judge John Sirica, who was presiding over the trial of the Watergate Seven, substantiated the Democrats' argument. In January, the judge found all of the defendants guilty and urged that a more thorough investigation be conducted on the basis of "intriguing" testimony that had been heard throughout the trial. The Senate responded by establishing a special committee headed by Sam Ervin, a Democratic senator from North Carolina.

As members of Nixon's staff continued to come under fire, those highest on the totem pole scurried for position. Haldeman and Ehrlichman insisted Colson knew a lot more about the burglary than he was willing to admit and lobbied for his removal. Colson charged it was Haldeman and Ehrlichman who were covering up. On February 28, in an attempt to sort out the confusion, Nixon met with John Dean, the White House chief counsel who had been assigned damage control over Watergate. Nixon hoped by consulting a neutral source (he had no personal relationship with Dean), he would gain a clearer view of who had known what and when. What he had yet to realize was the extent to which Dean himself was involved in the cover-up.

Dean's association with the White House dated back to May 1970, when Bud Krogh had recommended him for a job there. It had taken some high-level maneuvering before Mitchell, then Dean's boss at the Justice Department, had agreed to the transfer. Recalling the event, Dean admitted, "I liked the notion of these powerful men negotiating for my talents."⁴ He liked it so much, in fact, that once inside, he was willing to do whatever it took to get noticed by the higher-ups. Years later, when asked how he had gotten so far in his career at such a young age (he was 31 when hired by Nixon), Dean calmly replied, "I kissed a lot of ass."⁵

During his testimony at the Watergate hearings, Dean would claim he had not realized the illegality of his acts, but his revelations in his 1976 book, *Blind Ambition*, prove otherwise. Not only was he well aware of his crimes long before his infamous March 21 comment to Nixon, "We have a cancer within, close to the Presidency, that is growing,"⁶ but he had been personally responsible for the largest obstruction of justice to date: removing documents from Hunt's safe and passing them along to FBI director Gray with the suggestion that Gray dispose of them. In addition, Dean had counseled Magruder to lie to the grand jury regarding the content and number of meetings the two had had concerning Watergate.

In late March, as his meetings with the president became more routine, Dean began suspecting that their conversations were being taped. The text of the *White House Transcripts* clearly shows him attempting to direct his own guilt toward others, in particular Mitchell, Haldeman, and Ehrlichman. He repeatedly raised the possibility of the president granting him immunity from testifying before the grand jury. Nixon soundly rejected the idea, a decision, he later acknowledged, that caused his eventual resignation.

On March 23, as Judge Sirica prepared to hand down sentences to the Watergate Seven, a new bomb exploded. McCord presented the judge with a letter stating that political pressure had been applied to keep him quiet, perjury had been committed at the trial, and clemency had been offered in return for silence. Sirica read the letter in open court. McCord was freed on bail, while the others received sentences ranging from six and a half to 40 years. McCord then met with the chief counsel of the Ervin committee. Among the highlights of his testimony was a claim that both Magruder and Dean had had advance knowledge of the break-in.

Dean was fired by Nixon on April 29, after continually refusing to provide the president with a thorough written report of his knowledge and involvement in the cover-up. In a decision that Nixon called one of the most difficult of his career, he also asked Haldeman and Ehrlichman to submit their resignations. Haldeman's problem related to his authority to distribute funds for the CRP, some of which had been approved as hush money for Howard Hunt. Ehrlichman had been directly responsible for hiring Liddy and Hunt. In addition, he appeared to have had prior knowledge of both the plot to burglarize Ellsberg's psychiatrist and the Watergate break-in.

Too late, Nixon had concluded that a housecleaning was in order. Although he would manage to hang on for another 16 agonizing months, his effectiveness as president would continue to erode with each passing day.

10. The Cancer Within

On April 30, Nixon laid the groundwork for impeachment hearings during a televised address to the nation. Faced with a second chance to acknowledge responsibility for the decisions that had led to Watergate, he opted to shelter himself with another lie, vowing that he had had no personal knowledge of a cover-up prior to his March 21 conversation with Dean. By this point, Nixon had convinced himself that continuing the investigation would impair his ability to lead, both at home and abroad. Given the importance he placed on his position as peace negotiator, it is comprehensible that he could have overlooked the impact his initial denial would have on future events. Once the decision had been put into motion, he could no more admit to having made a fateful error in judgment than could Elvis acknowledge his prescriptions as dangerous drugs. Both were heroes with images to maintain, images that did not afford the luxury of such crucial mistakes.

Arguably the highest elected official in the world, Nixon represented strength of character, a man willing to fight for what he believed in, regardless of cost. An admission that he had lied about Watergate would have violated the nation's trust, not only in the man they had elected but in the office of the presidency itself.

Elvis was more of a spiritual symbol, personifying eternal youth. When the 38-year-old Presley stepped up to the microphone, curled his lip, and cranked out the raunchy lyrics from "Hound Dog," the fans saw the hip-swiveling boy of 1956 and became convinced of their own immortality. Accepting Presley as a flawed human being would have defeated the very purpose of idolizing him.

Not everyone was thrilled with Presley's music or his style of presenting it, but who could deny his astounding, universal appeal? Like Nixon, he had entered 1973 riding an unprecedented wave of popularity. First, *On Tour* captured a Golden Globe Award for best documentary. Then, on January 14, *Elvis: Aloha from Hawaii*, a benefit concert performed at the Honolulu International Center Arena, became the first program to be broadcast live, via satellite, across the world. The breakthrough in technology put Presley's televised audience at a billion people — more than had witnessed the moon landing of Apollo 13. In Japan, the broadcast captured an amazing 98 percent of the evening's television audience. (Ironically, America had to wait until April 14 to view the concert, as it was first and foremost geared toward Asia and Europe. The U.S. version aired on NBC and went on to become the highest-rated program of the week.) Viewers expecting to witness a piece of America were not disappointed. Elvis was a picture of patriotism, dressed in a white jumpsuit and matching cape, both of which sported sequined red and blue eagles. The Colonel beamed from the sidelines as fans were moved to tears by the entertainer's powerful rendition of "American Trilogy," a medley of southern gospel tunes.

By now, Presley no longer represented the American Dream, he had become it. Drawing on the energy of his admirers, he continued his fervid pace, performing over 100 shows from January to June. An additional 28 were canceled, due to poor health, causing rumors of drug abuse to creep into the headlines. Elvis dismissed the stories as "junk." His entourage defended him, and his fans believed.

Nixon managed to retain his public's support as well, despite growing evidence of his involvement in the cover-up. Although he remained hopeful that severing ties with his guilty friends would bring closure to Watergate, he had begun to contemplate an ace in the hole: his tapes. The president was well aware that some of the material could be incriminating, but because the public did not know the tapes existed, he reasoned that he could submit excerpts — in the form of written transcripts — as evidence to support his innocence.

Nixon's view that the tapes would be beneficial in the long run is a strong indication of how deeply he believed he was innocent of any wrongdoing. While it is true the tapes supported his claim that he had had no prior knowledge of the break-in, they also contained proof he had participated in the cover-up from the beginning. His suggestion to Haldeman the previous June — that they use the CIA to squelch an FBI investigation — laid him open to charges of conspiracy and obstruction of justice. In the March 21 conversation with Dean, the two had discussed whether to continue paying hush money to Hunt. Still, the president believed that the good outweighed the bad, that once people understood the reasons behind his actions, they would agree he had made the right decisions.

Polls supported his theory as late as April 1973, when he still enjoyed a 60 percent approval rating. The numbers dropped substantially in May, however, when Dean, in a last-ditch attempt to gain immunity from prosecution, told all to the Ervin committee. By month's end, the former White House counsel had revealed the 1969 wiretappings, the Huston Plan, the existence of the Plumbers, and the break-in at the office of Ellsberg's psychiatrist.

Nixon issued a statement admitting he had authorized the wiretaps and the Plumbers but insisted his actions were justified because he believed national security had been at risk. Convinced of the excuse himself, he began listening to the March tapes in order to prepare his defense. Even hearing himself talk of raising $1 million in hush money was dismissed as inconsequential on the assumption that it could be explained with regard to motive.

Presley used similar logic to justify his drug abuse. Recent bouts with flu and exhaustion had given him a legitimate reason to up his intake of prescription medication. Rather than see his failing health as a consequence of the pills he regularly consumed, he used it as an excuse to take more. On stage, he continued to deliver what his trusting fans expected. The few — but slowly increasing — occasions when he did not were attributed to his not-so-fairy-tale life behind the scenes. Any hope that Priscilla might return had long since faded. As if the humiliation of losing her to Stone were not enough, four-year-old Lisa had begun to call mommy's new boyfriend "Daddy." The back-breaker came when Priscilla informed Elvis she would not allow Lisa to visit him at Graceland anymore until he stopped taking pills. Wrote Billy Stanley, "The situation helped lead Elvis into two obsessions that would dog him for the rest of his life: prescription drugs and overeating. Of course he'd already been using drugs and he'd had weight problems. But they were nothing compared to what was to come."[7]

Like Presley, Nixon continued to battle his problems by ignoring them. In mid-June, Brezhnev arrived in Washington for Summit II. An intense week of meetings produced no new breakthroughs on arms limitations, but progress was made in joint energy, transportation, and trade agreements. Overall, Nixon felt he had gained a greater understanding of the Soviet leader as a person, leaving him hopeful that Summit III, tentatively scheduled for 1974 in Moscow, would result in further progress.

On June 25, Dean began the first of five days of testimony at the televised Watergate hearings, negating the positive publicity Nixon had derived from the summit. Among the most damaging statements was Dean's accusation that he had personally discussed the cover-up with Nixon as early as September 1972.

The president responded to the charges by granting the Ervin committee open access to his staff. While assuring the public he had nothing to hide, he began to contemplate the possibility of destroying all tapes except those that dealt with national security regarding Vietnam.

Nixon still believed the tapes would exonerate him in the end, but the idea of sorting through them was overwhelming; he would need to listen to hundreds of conversations, many of such poor sound quality that some of the voices could not be positively identified. Because most of his trusted advisors had left the White House, he would have to take on the job himself or risk getting new people involved. The latter would, of course, defeat the purpose of the April housecleaning, in which he had vowed to make a fresh start by surrounding himself with aides untouched by the ugliness of Watergate. Stress continued to build as Nixon pondered the pros and cons of destroying his tapes until finally, on July 12, he was admitted to the hospital with viral pneumonia. While recovering, the decision became clear when Alex Butterfield, one of Haldeman's former aides, revealed the existence of the White House taping system during questioning by the Ervin committee. While technically the tapes were still Nixon's property, opting to dispose of them in light of Butterfield's bombshell would have created an irreversible impression of guilt, a scenario Nixon was unwilling to seriously consider.

Butterfield's disclosure prompted demands from Sam Ervin and Special Prosecutor Archibald Cox, requesting immediate access to the tapes. When Nixon refused, Cox countered with a subpoena for nine of the tapes, making Nixon the first president to test the power of executive privilege in the courts.

Nixon claimed he was well aware that most people thought he was using executive privilege as a shield to keep from disclosing his wrongdoing but insisted that wanting to protect himself did not change the fact that he believed in the ideals he was fighting for. The right of executive privilege, as he saw it, went to the very "heart" of the presidency. Nixon had become so caught up in fighting for what he believed was right that he was weakening the very principle he sought to protect.

Presley faced a similar quandary regarding his fans; the same pills that allowed him to maintain his superhuman schedule had also begun to diminish the quality of his performances. In addition to giving his fans less than his best, his progressive dependency on prescription drugs was shortening the time they would be able to spend together.

With an occasional exception, by mid-1973 Presley's shows had become humdrum, the repertoire predictable. Sadly, because neither factor affected ticket sales, Elvis had little incentive to change his ways. While critics may attribute the entertainer's endless appeal to blind loyalty, fans who witnessed him on stage offer a more convincing argument: even operating at a percentage of his once-brilliant self, Presley remained by far the best act in town. And he knew it. For better or worse, the King's audience remained in the palm of his hand.

Nixon's popularity had dipped steadily since the April poll, but he still maintained a substantial, loyal following at the time the Ervin committee hearings ended on August 7. (The committee had compiled an astounding 325 hours of televised hearings over 37 days.) The following week, he made his second Watergate-related speech to the nation, repeating his earlier denial of any wrongdoing and urging that the matter be turned over to the courts so he could get on with "the urgent business of our nation." Voters responded with a flood of supportive telegrams and phone calls.

The president's bolstered self-confidence took a major hit on August 29, when Judge Sirica ruled that he must surrender the nine subpoenaed tapes to the special prosecutor. Nixon appealed the decision, buying time to examine the conversations in question. The task of transcribing them fell to his trusted personal secretary, Rose Woods.

With Watergate on temporary hiatus, the media zeroed in on Vice President Agnew, who was accused of having accepted bribes in return for granting state contracts while governor of Maryland. The evidence was so striking that even Nixon could not defend him. Agnew resigned on October 10, after pleading guilty to tax evasion, and was sentenced to three years' probation and a $10,000 fine.

As Nixon weighed the options for Agnew's successor, he was scrambling to avert all-out war in the Middle East. On October 6, Egypt and Syria had launched a joint attack on Israel. Nixon countered with a massive airlift of military weapons to aid Israel's cause, infuriating the Soviets. Kissinger was

10. The Cancer Within

dispatched to Moscow to work with Brezhnev on negotiating a ceasefire that both sides could live with. In the meantime, the president nominated Gerald Ford, a middle-of-the-road Republican senator from Michigan, to become his new VP. Congress would approve Ford's nomination on December 6, 479–38.

Watergate returned on October 12, when the court of appeals ruled against the president, 5–2. He had one week to decide whether to comply or appeal to the Supreme Court. Hoping to avoid becoming the first president to have the right of executive privilege challenged in the Supreme Court, Nixon offered a compromise: he would forgo another delay via appeal if Cox would accept the transcripts Rose Woods had prepared instead of the actual tapes.

A liberal Democrat with ties to the Kennedy family, Cox had never fit the bill of a neutral observer in most Republicans' minds — thus it came as no surprise when he refused Nixon's offer. Frustrated by the special prosecutor's determination to prolong the Watergate investigation, Nixon ordered Attorney General Elliot Richardson to fire him. Richardson, who had been responsible for hiring Cox the previous May, resigned rather than carry out Nixon's request. His deputy, William Ruckelshaus, also refused and was promptly fired. Solicitor General Robert Bork, next in line at the Justice Department, carried out the president's order. The October 20 firings, dubbed the "Saturday Night Massacre" by the media, caused a burst of activity on Capitol Hill, resulting in 21 separate resolutions calling for Nixon's impeachment.

Nixon was shocked at how few people viewed the situation from his perspective. Small wonder, since by now he had isolated himself to such an extent that there were no colleagues left to observe it from his perspective. His policy of not discussing Watergate with his family effectively eliminated the possibility of his decisions being questioned. In effect, the only person left to argue with Richard Nixon was Richard Nixon — and even this occurred behind closed doors, via written entries in his diary.

While critics denounced him as a tyrant and a madman, Nixon focused on securing peace in the Middle East. On October 24, a ceasefire drafted by Kissinger and Brezhnev went into effect, but the prospects for lasting peace did not look promising. Caught in the middle, Egyptian president Anwar Sadat contacted American and Soviet leaders, requesting that military forces be sent to the area to police the agreement. Brezhnev quickly agreed, but Nixon refused, fearing the action might lead to nuclear war. When the Soviets threatened to send troops regardless, Nixon responded by ordering all U.S. forces placed on military alert. Brezhnev backed down, allowing Kissinger to proceed with negotiations. Rather than praise Nixon's efforts to stabilize a volatile situation, the media speculated that he had intentionally provoked the Mideast war in order to draw attention away from Watergate and to demonstrate that he was still capable of leading the country. Questions of his mental stability began to circulate through the political grapevine.

October was a stressful month for Presley as well. On the ninth, his divorce became final, splattering the details of his failed relationship over the front pages of every tabloid on the newsstands. Six days later, he checked into Baptist Memorial Hospital, reportedly suffering from what doctors called a "persistent case of recurrent pneumonia."[8] Later accounts attributed it to exhaustion.

Initially, fans reacted with shock and surprise; afterward, they were simply relieved. The exhaustion story made sense. Elvis's body had finally caved in to the stress, just as Nixon's had done that past July. All he needed was some time to relax. Presley's entourage agreed, publicly insisting there was nothing wrong with their boss that a few good nights' sleep could not fix.

Years later, a more likely scenario surfaced: Presley's three-week hospital stay was his first — and perhaps only — serious attempt to kick his prescription drug habit. "We tried to detoxify him from everything he was taking," Dr. Nick would later insist, when testifying before the Tennessee Board of Medical Examiners in 1979.[9] Details of the time frame support Nichopoulos's claim. Prior to his admission, Elvis had spent two weeks at his home in Palm Springs. Looking ahead, his concert schedule was empty for the remainder of the year. Why now, of all times, would he be suffering from burnout?

Hospital reports confirmed another bed was set up in Presley's room for Linda Thompson, who remained at his side throughout the ordeal. Given her outspoken manner, it is probable that she was the driving force behind the plan, which had likely been arranged during their stay in Palm Springs. Linda's support and encouragement, combined with Priscilla's earlier ultimatum — that he would have to give up the pills before Lisa could visit him at Graceland — may have nudged Elvis into facing his problem. Taking the entertainer's stubborn "I know what I'm doing" mentality into account, however, it is also possible that his apparent cooperation was a conscious attempt to prove both Linda and Priscilla wrong. By agreeing to undergo treatment, he may have been implying, "I'll show you I'm right and you're wrong. I'm not hooked. I can quit anytime I feel like it."

If Presley truly believed he was in control of his habit, it is no wonder he became depressed after his discharge from the hospital. "After Elvis came home again, he seemed to feel better for a while," recalled Mary Jenkins, Presley's cook at Graceland.[10] But she soon noticed Presley's mood swings had returned, worse than ever. According to Jenkins, even Linda Thompson's attempts to cheer him up with funny gifts proved unsuccessful.

Presley's failure to kick his habit was most certainly linked to the guilt he felt regarding his divorce. If he were to acknowledge the pills as the core of the problem, he would also have to accept that they had been responsible for his break-up with Priscilla. Denying his addiction allowed him to continue blaming outside factors, in this case Mike Stone, for his troubles.

10. The Cancer Within

In similar fashion, Nixon's bloated self-confidence overshadowed any guilt he might have felt regarding his actions in the cover-up. He realized he had technically broken the law, but he viewed it as a necessary means to the all-important end: world peace, which could only be brought about by his remaining in office. In Nixon's mind, firing Cox — and those who had defended him — had been the only logical solution. He was convinced Cox would not stop short of securing every tape, Watergate-related or not, and allowing him to do so would set a dangerous precedent that would permanently cripple the presidency.

Exercising the right to remove Cox, for whatever reason, proved another costly error in judgment. Like the two-bit burglary that had started it all, nothing was gained, but much was lost. People were asking, why fire Cox if the president had nothing to hide? The atmosphere of suspicion left Nixon with little choice but to appoint a new special prosecutor. The job went to Leon Jaworski, a prominent Texas Democrat and former president of the American Bar Association.

As calls for Nixon's resignation continued to be heard from Congress, another bomb fell from the cloudy December skies. While an index of the tapes to be turned over to Jaworski was being prepared, Nixon was told of an 18.5-minute gap that existed during a conversation between himself and Haldeman from June 20, 1972. Predictably, Rose Woods's explanation — that she had inadvertently pushed the record instead of the pause button while stopping to answer the phone — was dismissed as another lie to protect the president.

Meanwhile, a new fund scandal was picking up steam. The previous May, a report had appeared in a California newspaper speculating that Nixon may have used campaign money to buy his home in San Clemente. In truth, the cash had come from Abplanalp and Rebozo, via a personal loan. Cox had picked up on the story and vowed to investigate the matter. New rumors erupted shortly thereafter, claiming that Nixon had used government money to make home improvements, a charge that overlooked the fact that all such "improvements" had been security measures ordered by the secret service.

Nixon was disgusted by the renewed personal attacks. During a press conference on the evening of November 17, he finally allowed his frustrations to seep through amid reporters' questions regarding his finances. Ironically, while attempting to defend himself, he inadvertently provided the media with a fresh round of ammunition.

> In all of my years of public life, I have never obstructed justice. And I think, too, that I could say that in my years of public life, that I welcome this kind of examination, because people have got to know whether or not their President is a crook. Well, I am not a crook.[11]

The "I am not a crook" phrase stuck with him for the remainder of his lifetime, proving a constant source of embarrassment for himself and his family.

Nixon's determination to "tell all" via his tax returns proved an even bigger mistake. In 1969, he had taken a substantial deduction for donating his vice presidential papers to the National Archives, a move he said was suggested to him by President Johnson. In December of that year, Congress had passed a law disallowing such deductions, retroactive to July 25. While reviewing Nixon's returns, the IRS determined that one of his lawyers had backdated the deed for the papers in order to take advantage of the defunct allowance. The attorney responsible challenged the ruling, insisting that because the deal with the National Archives had been made three months *prior* to the deadline and a full eight months before Congress had enacted the legislation, the president was still entitled to the deduction. The IRS said no, but the GSA (Government Service Administration, in charge of handling government buildings and properties) agreed; thus Nixon lost both the deduction and his papers.

The IRS also determined that the president owed capital gains tax for selling off part of his San Clemente property to his friends Rebozo and Abplanalp. Nixon's accountant insisted he had not benefited from the sale (which was likely true, since Rebozo and Abplanalp had loaned him the money to buy the property in the first place). Nixon's lawyers urged him to challenge both decisions in court, but he declined, reasoning that he had already lost the case where it mattered — in the public's eyes.

The tax disclosures brought a wave of new and, in most cases, ridiculous allegations. Among the silliest was an argument that Nixon should not be allowed to claim a tax deduction for his home office in Florida because he had chosen to use his own money, rather than appropriated government funds, to pay for it.

As had been the case in 1952, critics were not content to confine their attacks to Nixon. Brothers Don and Ed were called on to disclose their personal finances. A gossip columnist accused Pat of keeping jewelry that had been given to her as state gifts. The IRS and the Ervin committee staff harassed Bebe Rebozo for some 18 months, determined to prove he had been illegally funneling cash to Nixon's campaign. (He was eventually found innocent of any wrongdoing.)

The most telling revelation of this period in Nixon's life was his determination to continue going it alone at a time when he so desperately needed guidance from family and friends. In *RN*, he admitted to rarely discussing any of the daily news reports about Watergate with Pat, saying only that she remained "magnificent" throughout the ordeal.

Clearly, Nixon knew how much his family cared. What he did not realize was to what extent his refusal to trust their judgment diminished the effectiveness of that love. Rather than help him find solutions to his problems, family members struggled to be who he wanted them to be. Of his daughters,

10. The Cancer Within

he found Tricia best equipped to communicate on his terms. In his memoirs, he spoke of her visiting him often throughout the Watergate scandal but never pressing him to talk about it. Rather, she would stay up late when he was working, just to be at his side. Nixon said he knew she "ached with concern" but was always careful not to let her feelings show. Julie, on the other hand, shared her father's combative spirit. When he suggested to her that she refrain from becoming personally involved in his troubles, she replied, "But Daddy, we have to fight."[12]

In the end, it was his family's ability to adapt to *his* needs that held them together throughout the ordeal. Nixon realized their desire to be a part of things, but he just could not bring himself to allow it. Watergate had become his own personal battle, and no one, not even those most dear to his heart, could deny him the right to fight it on his terms.

Presley, too, continued to go it alone. Although his relationship with Linda was evolving, he was still too busy trying to impress her to appreciate the wisdom of her advice. Since no one else was willing to confront him about his drug problem, he drifted even further into denial, continuing to fault others for behavior that mirrored his own. The harder he struggled to project his innocence, the deeper he sank into the valley of depression. The Christmas season, normally the highlight of the year, turned into a dreary affair of forced jubilation and plastic smiles. "The New Year's party was worse," recalled Billy Stanley. "Elvis and Linda made a fifteen minute appearance and then retreated to Elvis's room."[13] A thirty-ninth birthday celebration planned for January 8 was eliminated completely.

Nixon's holiday was nearly as gloomy, a mood in tune with the unseasonably dark, rainy weather at San Clemente, where he spent the first two weeks of the new year. Plagued by bouts of insomnia, he soothed his mind with music, spending many an early morning playing the piano. But mostly he thought about his options, which he had narrowed to two: resign or fight certain impeachment. Outrage over the content of the subpoenaed tapes had far exceeded his worst expectations. Critics charged his preoccupation with Watergate was responsible for the nation's current domestic woes — of which there were many. OPEC's oil embargo, in place since the Mideast crisis had erupted in October, had resulted in long lines at gas stations and cutbacks in heating oil. The stock market had tumbled. Inflation was skyrocketing.

Members of Congress were quick to point fingers at the White House, conveniently disregarding the fact that, prior to the Middle East conflict, they had shown little interest in acting on the president's requests for money for research and development of alternative fuel sources and his calls for voluntary cutbacks of energy consumption. In its determination to make Watergate an issue, Congress was just as guilty as Nixon of allowing the scandal to take precedence over the business of running the country.

Nevertheless, as commander-in-chief, Nixon bore full responsibility for the situation. If he resigned because of Watergate, he would have to live with the fact that he had abandoned the job his fellow Americans had elected him to do. The idea was unthinkable. Hannah and Francis had not raised a quitter. Twisted as Nixon's principles may have become, they remained the driving force behind his decision, as the following excerpt from his diary clearly illustrates.

> The answer—fight. Fight because if I am forced to resign the press will become a much too dominant force in the nation, not only in this administration but for years to come. Fight because resignation would set a precedent and result in a permanent and very destructive change in our whole constitutional system. Fight because resignation could lead to a collapse of our foreign policy initiatives.[14]

As had been the case so many times before, Nixon entered the ring poised but alone. Former allies, concerned with damaging their chances for reelection in November, were quietly distancing themselves from the Oval Office. Nixon did not blame them nor was he surprised. Most likely, he found the scenario quite fitting. Saving his presidency was not dependent on his political colleagues but on his loyal, silent majority, the blue-collar voters who had put him in the White House.

The president's strategy was simple: prove he was worthy of remaining in office by performing his duties to the best of his ability. He was convinced that once people saw how minute Watergate was in relation to the issues of domestic and foreign affairs they would pressure Congress to end the investigation. The idea was nothing new; he had been using similar tactics since the break-in, with mixed results. But the release of the subpoenaed tapes had changed everything; Nixon was no longer in control of what material would be released. His naive belief, that the average voter would filter out the straightforward, often appalling content in order to evaluate the underlying substance of what was being said, or not said, proved his worst miscalculation to date.

By April, the president had complied with the special prosecutor's request for access to Watergate-related conversations, including 25 tapes and some 700 documents, but, as he had feared, it was never enough. Jaworski's demand for an additional 42 tapes prompted the creation of the "Blue Book," a massive 1,300-page document containing verbatim transcripts of Watergate material.

Any hope Nixon had that the compromise would satisfy the House Judiciary Committee, which was currently deciding whether grounds for impeachment existed, vanished in the face of the public response. Between the Blue Book's abrasive covers lay solid proof that Dean had lied about how much Nixon had known, and when, but the evidence proved far less important than the way in which it was presented: rough language amid talk of paying hush money and bribes. Americans were so shocked by what their president had said, let alone considered doing, that they no longer cared whether he had had advance knowledge of the break-in (which the transcripts clearly showed that he had not).

Far too late, Nixon realized the consequences of admitting his imperfections. He wrote in *RN*:

> The American myth that Presidents are always presidential, that they sit in the Oval Office talking in lofty and quotable phrases, will probably never die — and probably never should, because it reflects an important aspect of the American character. With the Blue Book transcripts, as with so many other Watergate revelations, I was in the position of telling the American people things that they did not want to know.[15]

In the end, it was not the actual content of the transcripts that cost Nixon his presidency as much as the message behind them. A president did not consider doing such human things, much less have the audacity to admit them. Nixon's sudden fallibility revoked his hero status, and nothing he could say or do thereafter would restore it.

Since Presley was an avid supporter of Nixon, it stands to reason that he followed the Watergate saga. If America could turn on its president, what would happen to Elvis if his fans learned the truth? More than ever, it became imperative to deny his addiction to prescription drugs. And deny it he did, to whomever dared to question him about it. "I mentioned something in a guarded moment," recalled guitarist John Wilkinson. "He patted me on the back and said, 'It'll be all right, don't you worry about it.'"[16] In *Life with Elvis*, David Stanley contends he once approached Dr. Nick about the number of prescriptions being given to Elvis. The discussion ended in a shouting match, which was later related to his famous stepbrother. "You were way out of line," Presley reportedly told David. "If anything like this ever happens again, you can start looking for another job!" (163).

"We [his entourage] told him," Presley's former bodyguard Dave Hebler insisted, "and his response was, 'I need this stuff, leave me alone.'"[17]

"Of course, protect," Hebler commented in a later interview. "How do you protect a man from himself?"[18]

Although Nixon remained every bit as determined as Presley to prove his critics wrong, the Blue Book disaster forced him to reevaluate his strategy. Every action he had taken to defend himself thus far had backfired, especially in regards to the tapes. What logic was there in complying with the latest demand for an additional 64? The material, sure to be every bit as forthright as the transcripts, would do nothing to turn public opinion back in his favor. Worse, it would send a message to Jaworski that he was free to keep subpoenaing material until he found what he wanted: direct evidence of an impeachable offense.

By now Nixon had reviewed the June 23 tape (in which he had advocated using the CIA to stop the FBI's initial investigation into Watergate) included in the latest subpoena and concluded that, although the content was damaging, it was no worse than some of the previously released material. His failure to see the tape for the smoking gun it was supports his claim that, at least in his own mind, he still believed whatever actions he had taken had been justified. Further, he was convinced that the fight to maintain control of his tapes — in effect, his own personal property — was imperative to protecting the office of the presidency, not only for himself but for those who would follow.

Convinced that only one course of action remained, Nixon sent a letter to the House Judiciary Committee on May 22, informing them that he would not supply Jaworski with any further material, subpoenaed or not. Jaworski argued that the president's normal route of appeal would involve costly delays, eventually resulting in a decision that would be appealed to the Supreme Court. He boldly suggested that the Court hear the case directly. Nixon was stunned when the special prosecutor's request was granted. The move meant a final decision could come as early as July.

Until that time arrived, Nixon determined his best course of action was to carry on, day by day. Maintaining a fit, healthy image was part of the plan. Despite a recurring case of phlebitis in his left leg, he opted to go ahead with his scheduled trip to the Mideast on June 10, in celebration of the disengagement agreement that had been signed by Israel and Syria on May 31. An enthusiastic welcome from the people of Cairo reinforced his belief that strong leadership was the key to lasting world peace. Similar crowds greeted him in Syria, Saudi Arabia, and Jordan, giving his spirits a much-needed, albeit temporary, lift.

The president's busy schedule left little time to treat his phlebitis, which worsened during scorching temperatures in the Middle East. By the time he arrived in Moscow for Summit III on June 27, news reports had broken about his condition. In *RN*, he said the break in the story only made him all the more determined to keep from showing any outward sign of pain. He strained to live up to an image that had widened to include the illusion that he, like Presley, possessed a perfectly fit, indestructible body. In his diary, he spoke of how imperative it was that the people not see their president as "crippled mentally as well as physically," and he believed that he could avoid any such notion with "proper handling."[19] The strategy for "proper handling" was to carry on as if the problem did not exist, just as he had done throughout the cover-up. "He's not getting advice," Senator Goldwater had reported in an interview with the *Christian Science Monitor* the previous December. "and when he gets it, he doesn't listen to it."[20]

Elvis had used the same procedure effectively for many years, but because the drugs had now begun to affect his physical condition, he was finding it increasingly difficult to stay on course. His depression over the 1973-74 holiday season had led to increased eating binges — pork chops, fried chicken, and banana pudding were among his latest favorites. Attempting to compensate for the weight gain, he took up racquetball, played touch football with his pals, and became more heavily involved in karate.

In addition to Ed Parker, Presley studied under Kang Rhee, who ran a karate school in Memphis. At Rhee's school, Elvis and his bodyguards put in countless hours perfecting their art. Despite the great respect Presley held for his teacher, even Rhee could not persuade him to let up on the pills. "I say, 'You should not depend on any pill or medicine to get well, you have to get well yourself,'" Rhee told Elvis as he prepared to present the entertainer with his sixth degree black belt. "I think he understood."[21] Rhee's optimism faded later that night when Elvis took him aside and presented his narcotics badge. The Beatles took drugs, he calmly explained to the karate master. Not Elvis Presley.

Had Presley given up the drugs, perhaps the increased physical activity would have helped put him back on track. As it was, it only served as an excuse to continue his unhealthy habits. The exercise made him hungry, so he ate larger meals. He was tired, so he popped more pills. Inevitably, the effects carried over to his performance on stage. If a song was not to his liking, he would stop in the middle and begin something else. Or he would talk to the audience about whatever happened to run through his mind at the moment.

During one such performance, Presley stopped the show to discuss at length his passion for karate: the history of the sport, the animal symbols (tiger, eagle, dragon, etc.) and what they represented, the number of degrees that a student needed to pass before obtaining a black belt. Most interesting was his emphasis that karate was founded as a means of self-defense, not aggression, and that it required deep concentration rather than physical strength. "The purpose is not to harm but to protect life, make it better."[22] Presley felt it imperative that his fans not view him as a bully but rather as a man concerned with protecting himself, family, and friends against would-be assailants.

This monologue stretches to more than seven minutes on the homemade recording, after which the tape was obviously stopped, then restarted after Elvis began to sing again. Whether the fan simply became bored with the discussion or worried she would run out of tape before the performance ended is unclear. Regardless, she remained in her seat, waiting for the show to go on.

It is clear testimony to Presley's greatness that his fans not only accepted this new, spontaneous behavior but embraced it. Noted Billy Stanley:

> He'd go on and on. I'd say to myself, "What's Elvis doing?" But when he finished one of his long speeches and started to sing, the audience went wild with applause. They loved it. I realized that the fans had a love for Elvis akin to what my brothers and I felt for

him. They didn't care when he rambled on about the various degrees of karate belts he'd acquired. They didn't care that he was overweight, didn't move as much on stage, and would rather talk than sing. They just wanted to be in his presence.[23]

Elvis was their hero. He could do no wrong.

Nixon, meanwhile, was no longer a hero, even to his most avid supporters, and thus could do little right. While the results of Summit III proved less successful than hoped, due mainly to U.S. support for Israel during the October crisis, much had still been accomplished. Among the major points agreed on were threshold test bans on nuclear weapons, further restrictions on ABMs, and additional cooperation in the fields of energy and medical research. All would have been considered major achievements under normal circumstances. Instead, the battered president returned home to the latest Watergate headlines, awaiting the Judiciary Committee's decision on impeachment.

The wait proved mercifully short. When the Supreme Court ruled against him in *The United States v. Nixon* on July 24, Nixon knew that the unanimous decision left no room for compromise: either he complied with the Court's ruling or face certain impeachment. His woes continued later that evening as the House committee began its televised hearings. The vote came three days later: 27–11 in favor of impeachment, on the grounds that Nixon had engaged in a "course of conduct" intended to obstruct the Watergate investigation.

Only after the committee's vote, which had included six of the 17 Republicans voting in favor, did Nixon finally ask his aides to review the June 23 tape. Much to his chagrin, they confirmed his worst-case scenario: it was the "smoking gun" that would end his presidency.

Once Nixon accepted that he would have to resign, he discussed the situation with Bebe Rebozo, who urged him to reconsider. Though Nixon was moved by his friend's loyalty, he realized how hopeless the situation had become. The next evening, he gathered his family together in the Lincoln Sitting Room to inform them of his decision.

In her diary, Tricia said her father spoke that night of how an impeachment trial would be a disaster for the country, that stepping down was the best thing he could do for the nation as a whole — all the while remaining in constant control of his emotions. When it was over, she and the rest of the family left him alone, sitting in a chair by the fire, and went upstairs to retire for the evening. It was there, away from Nixon's guarded control, that his family allowed themselves a small, much-needed release. "We all broke down together, and put our arms around each other in circular, huddle-style fashion," Tricia related. "Saying nothing."[24]

Nixon's family ended their evening with him the way they knew he expected them to, by remaining strong, supporting his decision whether they agreed with it or not. Only when they had left his presence were they able to

10. The Cancer Within

express their true feelings and emotions — and even that was done in a way Nixon would have approved: saying nothing.

The June 23 tape was released on Monday, August 5. As White House aides awaited the reaction by the media, Nixon watched the sunset from the deck of the *Sequoia*, where he had dinner with his family and Rose Woods. They talked about the weather, the movies, the good times. "Everything," as Nixon bluntly put it, "but what was on everyone's mind."[25]

Reaction to the tape ranged from feelings of betrayal to outrage. There was no longer any question in Nixon's mind that he would lose a Senate trial if he opted to go that route. Family members urged that he take more time before making a final decision, but, as always, once his mind was set, there could be no turning back. On Wednesday, he met with Kissinger and asked the secretary of state to inform the world leaders of his impending resignation. Special messages were designated for the Soviet Union, China, and the Middle East, assuring them that President Ford would continue the policies the Nixon administration had worked so hard to put into place.

That evening, Nixon invited Rose Woods to join him and his family for a final dinner at the residence. Pat, falling victim to her emotions at last, welcomed her beloved husband with a hug and a kiss when he entered the room. Julie cried. Only Tricia remained on a par with her father: disciplined, under control. When Nixon requested that Pat join him in the Rose Garden for a farewell photograph, she was unable to respond, but Tricia, forced smile in place, quickly offered to fill in.

Understandably, no one had much of an appetite. Following a light meal, Nixon said his goodnights and retreated to the Lincoln Sitting Room to work on his resignation speech. Kissinger stopped by about nine. At the president's request, the two knelt together in the Lincoln bedroom and prayed.

Twenty-four hours later, Nixon sat behind his desk in the Oval Office, ready to address the country for the final time as president. Remaining in character to the end, he declined his family's request that they stand by his side while he delivered the speech. He had fought the battle his way, and he would accept responsibility for the defeat in the same manner. Alone.

He began by explaining the reason for his decision, that he no longer had enough support in Congress to effectively govern the nation. Still convinced he had done nothing to warrant removal from office, a full apology was not in order. Instead, he acknowledged what the people had already concluded: he was a human being, capable of making mistakes. "I regret deeply any injuries that may have been done in the course of the events that led to the decision. I would say only that if some of my judgments were wrong — and some were wrong — they were made in what I believed at the time to be in the best interest of the nation." In conclusion, he reminded the people of the goal he had outlined in his first inaugural address: to devote his energy to the cause of world peace.

> I have done my very best in all the days since to be true to that pledge. As a result of these efforts, I am confident that the world is a safer place today, not only for the people of America, but for the people of all nations, and that all of our children have a better chance than before of living in peace rather than dying in war.
>
> This, more than anything, is what I hoped to achieve when I sought the presidency. This, more than anything, is what I hope will be my legacy to you, to our country, as I leave the presidency.[26]

Back at the residence, his family awaited their broken hero with open arms. As crowds outside the White House chanted "Jail to the Chief," Nixon was finally free to display a hint of the human frailty that had caused his fall from grace. "Pat put her arms around me. Tricia. Julie. Ed. David. Slowly, instinctively, we embraced in a tender huddle, drawn together by love and faith."[27]

The mood carried over to the next morning, when Nixon bid his staff a final, emotional goodbye. Tricia described it as "not formal" and went on to say she felt good that her father had opted to show his more personal side and hoped such a glimpse into the man he really was would help others to get to know the "real" Nixon.

Years would pass before the real Nixon emerged to tell his story. In the meantime, he continued to wrestle with the perils of his own mortality.

On August 19, eleven days after seeing Nixon's presidency fall victim to Watergate, Presley returned to Las Vegas for 22 sold-out performances, intent on preserving his own cover-up. Of major interest during this engagement was the opening show, in which he not only shuffled the order of his songs but inserted several rare performances — from the bluesy "Down in the Alley," which had appeared as a bonus song on the *Spinout* soundtrack in 1966, to his upcoming single release, "Promised Land." Other surprises included "It's Midnight," I'm Leavin'," and "If You Talk In Your Sleep," all fairly recent recordings. Most shocking, however, was Presley's inclusion of "Good Time Charlie's Got the Blues," a song about a man lost amid sorrow and pills, searching for answers. The Danny O'Keefe tune, cut at Memphis's Stax studios in December 1973, had been included on Elvis' *Good Times* album, released in March 1974.

Presley's cover of O'Keefe's song was particularly interesting in that he both omitted and changed some lyrics. Among the most telling exclusions entailed phrasing in the third verse, which talks about taking pills to mask the pain, but finding no way to stop the rain. On the studio version, Presley simply hums through the section of the third verse where the pill lyrics would have appeared. During his live performance on the nineteenth, he attempted to make a joke of the obvious irony by adding several snide remarks. The first followed the song's lyrics that warned stepping out on his wife could lead to losing her. After singing the verse, Presley added "already did that." Moving on to the next line, which warns that playing around for too long could lead to losing one's life, Elvis quipped: "almost did that." The verse that referred to pills was omitted entirely.

The show was also unusual in that it contained very little dialogue between songs. Presley was in good voice, albeit somewhat nervous — as if he were worried about audience reaction to his updated repertoire. Tapes of the performance do suggest a less excited response from the crowd, though whether they were disappointed or merely surprised at the changes is hard to say. In any event, Elvis returned to his stable of old favorites, with a few exceptions per show, for the remainder of his engagement. "It was part of his own insecurity, not staying with it and keep on trying with it over a few nights," Presley's drummer, Ronnie Tutt, related in an interview. "That's just the way he was. If it felt wrong right then, the next show he'd say, 'Scrap that and go right back to what we used to do.'"[28]

Within a few nights, the speedy succession of one song to another had also been abandoned. By his closing show on September 2, the intermittent monologues had reached amazing heights. Noted a critic whose review of the show appeared in *Disc* on October 5, 1974:

> His last performance of the current stint — the midnight show — was one of the most remarkable I have ever seen on stage. He came on with a modest walk, a charming and decidedly evil grin, spread wide his hands and then got into it. All in all, he was mean, moody, witty and magnificent — in fact everything his legend says he should be.
>
> However, what made the performance extraordinary was not just the quality of the singing but the intensity of Presley's apparent need to communicate himself to his audience. Whether or not it was born out of some truth in the rumors of his ill-health, boozing, and so forth, he certainly did very much give the appearance of a man trying to expercise [sic] private demons. He was on stage for almost two hours, during which time he sang like an angel, moved like a dream, and gave an unprecedented view of himself and his current attitudes in some truly startling monologues....
>
> If it was frequently in bad taste, it was even more frequently hypnotizing — perhaps the nearest thing to a pure unveiling of troubled emotions since the days of Judy Garland.[29]

The show thus described exists in complete form on the bootleg circuit and includes all of Presley's monologues, which are every bit as remarkable as the unnamed critic reported. After introducing Priscilla, who was in the audience with Lisa Marie, Elvis went on to explain the details of his divorce and his reasons for doing it (he was gone too much, which was unfair to Priscilla). He insisted they had parted by mutual agreement and would remain close because they "had a daughter to raise." He spoke of the paternity suit that had been dismissed against him (blood tests proved Presley was not the father). Saving the most extraordinary for last, he related the following as his show wound down:

> I don't pay attention to rumors. I don't pay any attention to movie magazines. I don't read them because they're all junk. [*audience applause*] I'm talking about ... I don't mean to put anybody's job down. They have a job to do, they've got to write something. If they don't know anything, they make it up. In my case, they make it up. [*more applause*] I hear rumors flying around. I got sick in the hospital. In this day and time you can't even get sick. You are *strung out*. Well by God, I'll tell you something, friends: I have never been *strung out* in my life, except on music. [*long, loud applause*] When I got sick here in the hotel, when I got sick here that one night — I had 103 degree temperature, they wouldn't let me perform — from three different sources, I heard I was *strung out* on heroin. [*gasps from audience*] I swear to God. Hotel employees, Jack. Bellboys, freaks that carry your luggage up to the room, people working around, you know, talking maids. And I was sick, I was, you know. I had the doctor there, I had the flu. I got over it in one day, you know. But all across this town — strung out. But I told them earlier — and don't you get offended, ladies and gentlemen, because I'm talking to somebody else — if I find or hear the individual that has said that about me, I'm gonna break your neck, you goddamn son of a bitch! [*huge applause*] That is dangerous. That is damaging to myself, to my little daughter, to my father, to my friends, my doctor, to everybody, my relationship with you, my relationship with everyone up here on stage. It is dangerous. I will pull your goddamn tongue out by the roots! [*roaring approval and applause*][30]

As would be expected, Presley's tone of voice during the above comments varied from hurt to defensive to angry. Also predictable was the audience's response: they sided with their hero, refusing to believe their own eyes and ears. Clearly, Elvis was "strung out" throughout this performance. His obvious need to defend himself in front of his beloved fans only served to emphasize his guilt. The poor boy from Tupelo was in deep trouble, but no one close to him would admit it, least of all Presley himself.

Chapter 11

My Way: The Lonely Road to Recovery

Defeat doesn't finish a man — quit does.

— Richard Nixon

Sheltered by the devotion of his fans, Presley continued to teeter on the edge of the mountain as the president went tumbling by. Following the Vegas stint in September, Elvis hit the road for 15 shows in 10 cities over a period of 13 days. Forty-eight hours after the tour ended, he arrived in Lake Tahoe for a two-week engagement at the Sahara Hotel.

While the rigorous schedule afforded Presley little chance to process his fellow hero's fall from grace, Nixon had nothing but time to relive every tortured detail of the premature end to his dream. Returning his family to California did little to shelter them from the public humiliation that followed his resignation. Physically, he was anything but fit, having battled the phlebitis in his leg since early spring. Some three weeks after leaving Washington, he finally submitted to doctors' orders and checked into the hospital so his leg could be properly treated. About the same time, President Ford granted him a full pardon for whatever "crimes" he may have committed while in office.

Nixon accepted Ford's gesture — which the new president said he had done to hasten the country's healing from Watergate — with mixed emotions. While the pardon was certain to reduce his personal debts and legal battles in the months to come, it also carried with it the assumption that he was guilty of criminal wrongdoing, a scenario he refused to consider, let alone publicly admit.

The self-confidence that had seen Nixon through the worst summer of his life began to waver as he tried to adjust to forced seclusion in San Clemente. He had been wrong to resign, to give in to his enemies. He had helped them win. Thanks to his own weakness, the 30 years he had dedicated to serving his country would be erased overnight by an idiotic burglary that he had had nothing to do with. It wasn't fair. It wasn't right. Francis and Hannah would be ashamed and rightly so. He had failed them. He had failed his family and his supporters. Most of all, he had failed himself.

This second-guessing, combined with the shame that had become an everyday part of the former president's life, continued to fester throughout the following weeks until finally, in late October, he was readmitted to the hospital. The phlebitis, neglected again during his critical self-evaluation, had caused an 18-inch blood clot in his swollen leg. Surgery proved successful, but complications developed hours later when Nixon lapsed into sudden unconsciousness. His life hung in the balance for several hours before doctors stabilized his condition. Down, and definitely out, his recovery was further complicated by a lingering case of pneumonia. Considering all he had been through, it was a wonder he had not collapsed months, or even years, earlier. Beaten and stripped of his pride, who would have blamed him for giving up?

"The easiest period in a crisis situation is actually the battle itself," he had written in *Six Crises* 12 years earlier (xv). "The most difficult is the period of indecision — whether to fight or run away. And the most dangerous period is the aftermath. It is then, with all his resources spent and his guard down, that an individual must watch out for dulled reactions and faulty judgment."

At no other time in his life could Nixon's own words have proven more appropriate. Setting aside his self-pity, he sat up and looked around. His family remained at his side, after all he had put them through. Public support had waned but not vanished: thousands of cards and phone calls flooded into the hospital, wishing him a safe and speedy recovery. Among the more famous callers was none other than Elvis Presley.

For the 61-year-old Nixon, the moment of truth had arrived. Was he up for the ultimate challenge or ready to throw in the towel? His troubles would end if he never saw another sunrise, but what of Pat? Tricia and Julie? What of their children and their children's children? If he were not here, they would have to bear the shame he had caused them. Bear it alone. The very idea was disgusting. Immoral. He would not allow it to happen. He had weathered many a storm and returned to fight another day. Watergate would be no different. If achieving his goal was no longer possible from the White House, then he would find another way. Let Watergate have its place in history; Richard Milhous Nixon would be remembered, first and foremost, for his accomplishments as a messenger of peace.

While Nixon summoned the motivation necessary to work toward recovery, Presley had yet to find a reason to get himself back on track. He had acquired all the material possessions he could ever want but had no one whom he really cared for to share them with aside from his fans. And their love was exchanged from a distance. Out of the spotlight, he had failed as a husband to Priscilla and a father to Lisa; they would never be a family again.

11. My Way: The Lonely Road to Recovery

On the surface, Presley appeared to accept the inevitable, going so far as to joke about his divorce in song lyrics and during his Vegas monologues. Those who shared his private life saw another side to the story. Wrote his cook, Mary Jenkins, "Elvis told me more than once, 'Mary, if I ever marry again it will be to my daughter's mother.'"[1] Rick Stanley offered similar insight. "He's making a last ditch effort to get back with Priscilla," he informed his brother Billy in the late fall of 1974. "He wants it."[2]

Events at the time support the possibility. Elvis and Linda had been having problems since his unsuccessful attempt to dry out the previous September. On several occasions during his recent Vegas engagement, he had introduced model and up-and-coming actress Sheila Ryan to the audience as "my girlfriend." Ryan had appeared on the cover of *Playboy* in October 1973. The relationship proved little more than a temporary fling, however, as Sheila was far too Hollywood for Presley's taste. Linda returned shortly thereafter but left again after the Lake Tahoe engagement concluded in December. The proposed reconciliation with Priscilla, whether real or imaginary, never came to pass. Elvis spent his fortieth birthday holed up at Graceland, fueling the tabloids' rumors that he had become a fat, depressed, over-the-hill parody of himself.

Across the country in sunny California, Nixon ushered in his sixty-second year battling a similar depression. His acceptance of Ford's pardon, coupled with his refusal to offer a public apology for his Watergate-related crimes, sent Nixon's favorable rating in the polls crashing to new lows. He had lost nearly 20 pounds, giving his aging body a frail, somewhat shrunken appearance. There had been little to celebrate over the holidays. Bebe Rebozo continued to be hounded by the IRS, and the news that Haldeman, Ehrlichman, and Mitchell would be going to prison did little to lift anyone's spirits. Pat refused to leave the confines of their San Clemente estate. "Christmas 1974 was the lowest point in my father's life," daughter Julie would later recall.[3]

As upsetting as the personal attacks were — both to himself and his family — Nixon had more pressing troubles to address: back payments on his mortgage were stacking up; legal and medical bills continued to pour in. Lawsuits were dropping out of the ceiling, both from government and private sources. Nearly everyone, it seemed, wanted a piece of Richard Nixon. Complicating matters further, he was unemployed. Falling back on his law degree as he had done after his disastrous run for governor in 1962 was no longer an option. Aiming to further humiliate the disgraced ex-president, the New York Bar Association had disbarred him in public court.

Nixon had only two options: hit the lecture circuit and hope the proceeds would lift him out of the water or put the notes and tapes he had gathered over his White House years to pen and paper. The publishing world wanted to hear Richard Nixon's story and was willing to pay a hefty advance for the privilege. He discarded the first choice nearly out of hand, partly because he was not ready to face the outrage that was sure to follow him wherever he appeared but, more important, because he considered it morally wrong for a former president to accept paid speaking engagements.

Prior to Watergate, Nixon had had every intention of writing a book on his presidency, but he had intended to postpone it several years after leaving the White House. Since waiting was no longer an option, he set up an office on his San Clemente grounds and began the tedious task of organizing an outline. Warner Books won the bidding war for the rights to his upcoming work. (They later sold the rights to Grosset and Dunlap.) Despite his financial woes, Nixon gave each of his daughters $5,000 in anticipation of the advance.

Frank Gannon, Diane Sawyer, and Ken Khachigian, all prior members of Nixon's staff, were hired by the former president to assist on the project. Nixon implemented a strict routine that would be followed, with very few exceptions, for the next three years: work began at six or seven in the morning, and continued until five o'clock, seven days a week.

Aware of the importance his physical condition had on his mental state, Nixon also made time during his busy day for swimming, walking, and golfing. His interest in the latter led to a new friendship with a former military aide, Jack Brennan, who soon became his office administrator.

Presley would have done well to take a lesson from Nixon's self-discipline. While, consciously, he was every bit as determined as Nixon to retain the heroic image he had worked so hard to reach; subconsciously, he longed for a reason to maintain it. Every new day was the same day, over and over again; if he was not in the midst of a tour, he was preparing for one. The never-ending question remained: why? He had long since proven himself the top-drawing performer in America. What else could be accomplished?

It was not as if Presley himself were without ideas. A world tour had been at the top of his list for years. During a press conference prior to the first of four sold-out performances at Madison Square Garden in June 1972, Elvis had been asked if he would continue to do more concerts in the future. "I think so," he replied. "There's so many places that I haven't been yet. Like I've never played New York. I've never been to Britain yet, either."

"Would you like to go there, then?" another reporter inquired.

Presley responded, "I'd like to, yes sir. I'd like to very much. I'd like to go to Europe. I'd like to go to Japan and all those places. I've never been out of the country except in the service."

Later in the same interview, Elvis was asked, "How about doing a world tour?"

The entertainer quickly answered, "I think they're planning one now, they're talking about one now."[4]

Ever since Presley's triumphant return to Vegas, booking agents from Japan to England had been phoning the Colonel's office, wanting to know what it would take to bring the King to their home town. And always, Parker had some reason why their proposals were not feasible: Elvis's safety could not be guaranteed; he was already booked that day, and, the most questionable of all excuses, it would be far too expensive to take Presley's show on the road.

In 1974, Elvis had been offered $1.7 million to perform *one* concert in London. The offer was refused. The following year, promoter Arthur Howes upped his offer to $3.5 million.[5] Sorry, no thanks, came the Colonel's response.

Part of the trouble supposedly stemmed from Elvis's reluctance to play outdoor stadiums, which, at the time, would have been the only available facilities in Europe equipped to handle the huge crowds he would have drawn. Additionally, both Presley and his manager were committed to keeping ticket prices affordable, a practice that would have been more difficult, considering the added expenses involved with overseas travel. Difficult, perhaps, but certainly not impossible for an artist of Presley's stature.

Several authors have speculated that the real reason Parker refused these offers stemmed from the fact that he was not a U.S. citizen, and therefore he might not have been allowed back into the country once he left. While, as previously noted, much speculation surrounds this contention, realistically, if Elvis wanted to take his show on the road, surely he had the connections to bring it about, regardless of the Colonel's citizenship status.

Why, then, did Presley's manager turn down such lucrative offers? Elvis himself offered the most likely scenario. "I think the Colonel's afraid he'll lose control of the money if it goes out of the United States," he confided to Ed Parker. "That's the only reason I can see why we're not going."[6]

It is also quite possible that the Colonel had a verbal agreement with the Hilton management to keep Elvis stateside. When Presley's contract had expired in 1973, the Colonel had promptly negotiated a new, two-year deal. If Presley had been given the opportunity to take his show worldwide, it is unlikely that he would have continued to return to Las Vegas, as by now the main reason for doing so was to provide a forum for his overseas fans.

Presley hated the desert heat and feared the dry air would lead to chronic problems with his throat. "Hell, all the entertainers talk about Las Vegas throat, and here I am coming down with it," he complained during one engagement. "I don't think I'm going to work here a week at a time anymore. When they build that new hotel, three days, that's all I'm going to give them, three days; and then I'm cutting out."

"It wasn't a passing concern on his part," Ed Parker related. "He was deathly afraid of the possibility that he might lose his voice."[7]

Whatever the reason, Elvis never left American soil after his return from Germany in 1960. His amazing resurrection from the beach-blanket movie era nine years later had gone on to surpass everyone's expectations. He had risen to the challenge and proven his critics wrong along the way.

Presley had conquered his past. He was ready to attack the future.

Unfortunately, the Colonel was quite satisfied with the present. Elvis sold out every concert Parker could book and still had them begging for more. A copy of the entertainer's tax return for 1974 showed gross earnings of $7,273,622. The IRS bill came to $1,484,867. After deducting $4,295,372 in operating expenses, and the Colonel's take of $1,720,067, Elvis' lavish spending (on gifts for himself and others) left him with a year-end *deficit* of more than $700,000.[8]

Obviously, Presley paid far more than his fair share to the IRS. As previously mentioned, this was due in part to his sense of patriotism: he felt obligated to repay Uncle Sam for his overwhelming success. Another factor, which proved far more important in the long run, was his misguided sense of loyalty. Vernon felt money issues were private affairs to be kept within the family. Elvis agreed, which is how he had come to put his father in charge of his personal finances. The trouble was that Vernon knew nothing about tax shelters and investments nor did he want to learn. Recalled Larry Geller:

> One day in 1973 I was talking to Vernon about how the price of gold had reached unprecedented heights, and why it was such a good investment. Vernon listened, nodding his head, and promised he'd think about it. Six months later he said, "Larry, I took your advice. Come here, I want to show you something." With a flourish he produced a single gold piece, worth not more than one hundred dollars. Vernon was so proud of himself. He had made an "investment."[9]

Vernon's lack of education and business savvy proved a constant thorn in Elvis's side. Presley's earnings should have ensured him an early, comfortable retirement, with enough capital left over to pursue other ventures. Instead, he was working more than ever, trying to make ends meet.

Parker, meanwhile, lived more than comfortably off his share of the earnings. Although proceeds from Presley's concerts accounted for the majority of the Colonel's income, they did not represent the only source of cash derived from his lucrative client. For example, Parker had struck a deal with RCA, selling the rights to all of Elvis's recordings up to March 1973, for a flat fee of $5.4 million. The deal assured RCA endless, royalty-free profits from all of Presley's early — and most popular — recordings. Elvis received $2.8 million for his signature on the deal, along with a record company inclined to be less concerned with obtaining new, quality material for him to record. The Colonel pocketed a cool $2.6 million for conjuring up the agreement. Parker also controlled 40 percent of the profits from Boxcar Enterprises, Inc., a merchandising company he had set up to handle sales of "official" Elvis products. Presley received 15 percent.

As those around him battled over finances, Elvis was trying to shift his attention to new directions. In addition to the prospects for a world tour, which the Colonel continued to dangle in front of him, Presley was particularly excited about a visit from fellow superstar Barbra Streisand, who had approached him during his Vegas engagement in September, proposing that he costar with her in an upcoming remake of *A Star Is Born*. Presley was thrilled by the prospect. The character — a washed-up, alcoholic manager/husband who self-destructs in light of his famous wife's career — was the role he had been searching for. Streisand's proven box office draw was an added bonus. The film was certain to be a major success, providing the perfect catalyst for Presley's return to Hollywood as a serious actor. After giving Streisand a tentative thumbs up, he had contacted the Colonel and asked that Parker set to work on the particulars. So sure was Presley of the project that he phoned Priscilla, anxious to share the good news. "It looks like a sure thing," he told her. "Just the details have to be worked out."[10]

Even an inexperienced manager should have realized the potential of Streisand's offer, yet, to Colonel Parker, the negatives still outweighed the positives. Rather than share Elvis's vision, he warned him about the effect such a role might have on his fans. He played on Presley's sense of family values; what would Lisa think if her father made an R-rated movie? Most of all, he objected to the idea of his boy having to share top billing with another star, even one of Streisand's caliber. As always, Vernon kept insisting that the Colonel knew best. Elvis passed on the film, which went on to become one of the biggest hits of 1975.

During this same time frame, Uncle Sam had a change of heart regarding Presley's offer to assist the government with its drug war, calling on Elvis to allow the Bureau of Alcohol, Tobacco, and Firearms to place an undercover agent within his traveling band. Presley okayed the deal. No other details of the entertainer's involvement are available, other than confirmation from the bureau that the agent remained within Presley's group until 1976. That year, the bureau awarded Elvis a Certificate of Appreciation for his assistance.

Spurred on in part, perhaps, by his new undercover role, Elvis's interest in self-defense continued to soar. His passion for karate had drawn him into serious discussions with Ed Parker regarding two independently produced martial arts films. The first, a documentary, was to deal with the history of the sport and how it had been founded on spiritual principles. As executive producer, Elvis would do the voice narrative — to be written by Larry Geller — which would be dubbed over footage of various karate tournaments from across the country. "I felt that if there was anything that would wrest him away from his depression and his medication," Geller recalled, "this was it."[11]

The second project called for Elvis to star in a Chuck Norris–type action movie. "I want to be able to use my abilities in the martial arts and I want to show everybody that I can do a straight dramatic part," he told Ed.[12]

Obviously, the benefit to Presley was not contingent on the films' potential success at the box office. What would have breathed new life into him was the day-to-day involvement with people outside of his regular group: businesspeople, producers, karate experts. *Educated* people. To Colonel Parker, of course, such outsiders were anything but a plus. According to Larry and Ed, once the Colonel got wind of the movies, and the fact that his only part would be to help with their distribution, he went to Vernon complaining about how expensive they would be to produce and how Elvis was sure to fall victim to unscrupulous Hollywood types whose only concern would be what was in it for them.

Vernon went for the Colonel's spiel hook, line, and sinker. In addition to pressing his son to drop the film projects, he whined to Elvis about his impending break-up with Dee and the costly divorce settlement that was sure to follow. The couple had split several times over the past year, due mainly to Vernon's extramarital fling with Sandy Miller, a nurse some 20 years his junior. Dee had finally called him on it and was threatening to sue for divorce.

Elvis drew a short reprieve from the in-house bickering after the holidays, when Linda Thompson returned, willing to give things another try. Presley responded by checking himself into the hospital in late January for a much-needed rest. By now the drugs were affecting his liver and colon; the latter was responsible for considerable swelling, which made him appear heavier than he was. The downturn in his appearance, hammered on and exaggerated by the tabloids, was certainly motivation for change. Moreover, he was excited about the karate movies, and a possible reconciliation with Linda waited in the wings. For the first time since his break-up with Priscilla, Elvis saw a tomorrow worth waiting for.

Nixon had faced his ultimate challenge with courage and determination only three months earlier. Now the moment of truth hovered at Presley's door.

As Elvis lay in bed mulling over the possibilities, Vernon arrived as a patient — the victim of a heart attack. Elvis immediately blamed himself. If he had not insisted on pursuing the film projects; if he had not spent so much money on jewelry, cars, and strangers; if he had been more sympathetic about Vernon's troubles with Dee. If, if, if. His career had destroyed his mother and his marriage. Now it wanted to claim his father, the only tie that remained to his cherished boyhood past. The link to his true, imperfect self.

Movie discussions were put on hold while Vernon recovered. According to Geller, the documentary was never mentioned again in any serious manner. Discussions regarding the action movie continued, on and off, for the next two years, though Presley's hectic tour schedule and declining health kept him from firming up the deal. Two weeks later, Elvis emerged from the hospital, reportedly rested and fit — well enough, at least, that on March 10 he reported to RCA's Hollywood studio for a four-day recording session (his last session in an actual studio). Ten songs were cut, destined for his upcoming album *Elvis Today*. On the eighteenth, he was back in Las Vegas for 29 shows. Tours followed in April, May, June, and July, as he zigzagged across the country from Massachusetts to Indiana to Texas.

11. My Way: The Lonely Road to Recovery

Exhausted, overweight, and ill, Elvis finally succumbed to the pressure, displaying erratic behavior, both on and off stage. Band members and backup singers who had been with him for the better part of five years were publicly embarrassed by comments Presley directed toward them while performing. It got so bad in Norfolk, Virginia, that a harmony singer, soprano Kathy Westmoreland, walked out in the middle of a show. Two members of his female backup group, the Sweet Inspirations, followed suit.

Elvis later apologized, claiming he had not realized his comments were being taken to heart. In all fairness, he probably had not. To Presley, it was just another in the line of practical jokes, a way to combat boredom, a means of changing the routine. Considering the numerous drugs in his system, it is not hard to understand how things got out of control. Mercifully, a break was at hand. The last summer tour wrapped up on July 24, leaving Presley a full month to rest before he returned to Las Vegas.

Unable to escape his fate through creativity and perhaps in part to strike back at Vernon, Elvis went on a spending spree. On July 27, he purchased 14 new cars from a local Cadillac dealer, including one for a total stranger who happened to be in the showroom, admiring luxurious automobiles far beyond her pocketbook. But the sticker prices for the caravan amounted to a pack of gum when compared to his next acquisitions.

With his return to the concert circuit, Elvis had finally conquered his fear of flying and had, in fact, come to enjoy it. The hectic schedule made booking commercial flights next to impossible. On occasion, he had borrowed other celebrities' jets (Howard Hughes's, in particular) to use while touring; most of the time he chartered a plane, an increasingly expensive practice. The solution was obvious: Elvis needed his own wings. After scouting around, he decided on a Convair 880. The former Delta Airlines jet, purchased from a dealer in Florida, cost a cool million. Because the plane would become his home away from home, he opted to invest another $750,000 customizing it. In order to commute from Memphis to Forth Worth, where the airplane was to receive its makeover, he bought a Lockheed Jet Star. The four-engine plane set Presley back another $850,000. But he was not finished yet. Now that he would be traveling in style, it seemed fair that his musicians and backup singers should do the same. And what about the Colonel? The Elvis Presley show had an image to maintain. Elvis bought two more airplanes to the tune of $1 million.

Once the bills found their way into Vernon's office, the elder Presley nearly had another heart attack. What did his son think he was doing? Had he lost his mind? When the screaming was over, two of the planes were put up for sale in the *Wall Street Journal*. Elvis kept the Jet Star and went ahead with his plans to customize the Convair, which he proudly dubbed the *Lisa Marie*.

The buying binge might have emptied Presley's bank account, but, clearly, it had lifted his spirits. By the time his August engagement got underway, the offensive behavior that had plagued the summer tours was a thing of the past. Elvis played up to his audience more than ever, going so far as to place a "request box" on stage. Fans dropped song titles into the box prior to show time, and Elvis did his best to accommodate their wishes.

Of particular interest during this period was a song Presley had added to his repertoire during the summer months. "Fairytale" was among those recorded the previous March. Whether its inclusion was an attempt to get a point across or simply a song he enjoyed performing, the irony of the lyrics cannot be denied. The song relates the story of a man who, finally free of his "fairytale" dream state regarding his girlfriend, is able to see her for what she is — a user who has been deceiving him. Obviously in Presley's case, this girlfriend figurehead could have related to most everyone within his tightly-knit circle of friends and family.

Good quality audio and video recordings of these Vegas shows exist. Contrary to some reports, Presley was in good voice for these performances. His words were not slurred, nor did he stumble over song lyrics — except when he drew some titles from the request box, many of which he had not performed since the fifties. (Presley laughed off a request for "Old Shep" but crooned out a short version of "Young and Beautiful.")

Physically, he appeared quite top heavy — at least 30 pounds heavier than he had been a year earlier — but the padding did not prevent him from moving on stage. His legs still kept time to the beat, his arm and hand movements remained precise. He joked with the audience, at one point taking a frog hand puppet from a fan and using it to mimic his backup singers during their part in the song — all while wearing a huge pair of sunglasses (also given to him by a fan). Particularly noticeable, however, was the increasing effort needed to continue as the show wore on. Elvis clearly appeared tired, sweating profusely, resting on a stool between songs. His choice of stage costumes — by now quite gaudy, with loud colors and very wide belts — definitely added to his bloated look, making one wonder if, subconsciously, he was testing his fans' devotion. Judging by the wild applause and the continual stream of women rushing the stage for a scarf or a kiss, nothing had changed in their minds since he had opened in the show room of the International Hotel, slim and sassy in 1969.

Regardless of his improved mental state, further exhibited by the notable lack of the previous summer's endless monologues, the scheduled two-week stint ended after only five shows in three days, when it became obvious Presley was simply too ill to perform. He was whisked away to Baptist Memorial in Memphis, where he spent the next two and a half weeks. Doctors focused on his colon problem, which had worsened substantially over the past few months. Word of the singer's plight soon reached Nixon in San Clemente. Recalling Elvis' kind gesture during his post–Watergate bout with phlebitis, the former president phoned to wish Presley his best.

At his doctors' urging, Elvis okayed a plan for Marian Cocke, the head nurse on his floor, to accompany him to Graceland after his discharge. She and another caretaker, Kathy Seamon, alternated shifts at Graceland during the entertainer's recovery. Their major duty was to monitor Presley's numerous medications. Doctors had prescribed several for his colon problem. He was also receiving treatment for hypertension and an irregular heartbeat. Another pill was meant to counteract the abundance of salt he piled onto his food (the sodium contributed to his bloated look). Sleeping tablets remained a staple every night, rounding out the official packet.[13]

Cocke and Seamon also tried — for the most part, unsuccessfully — to keep an eye on his diet. Presley's domestic employees were extremely loyal. Their underlying motive was to please their boss, and they did so in the way they knew best, by bowing to his whims. Elvis loved rich, fried foods. The nurses' argument, that a lack of nutrition was hurting the beloved Mr. P, as his household staff affectionately called him, was not enough to counteract the pleasure they took in making Elvis happy.

Presley's domestic employees were not the only ones affected by his irresistible charm. Cocke insisted that, in all the time she spent with Elvis, she never saw him take any medication other than the above-noted prescriptions. She did concede, however, that such prescriptions could have been acquired, via other doctors, and passed along to Presley without her knowledge.

In any event, the next three months proved among the most relaxing of Presley's career since the film era of the sixties. In spite of the Colonel's claim to the media that his boy was in good health, Elvis remained at Graceland until his scheduled make-up engagement in Las Vegas, which began on December 2.

The usual lull that plagued the Desert City during the holiday season proved a thing of the past for 1975. Presley sold out every show and was in excellent form — laughing, singing, having fun again. He had dropped weight since his heavy point in August, looking at least 15 pounds lighter. His jubilant mood continued through the holidays, giving Christmas a much different look than the year before. Graceland was alive with celebration. Lisa was there, Linda was back. Things were finally looking up.

The holiday season was a marked improvement over the previous year for Nixon as well. Physically, he had never felt better. In addition to maintaining his exercise routine, he had altered his diet, eating much lighter foods: fruits, vegetables, and fish. Work on his memoirs, though slow and tedious, was progressing on schedule. Although his bank account was hardly bursting at the seams, new buddy Jack Brennan was in the midst of putting together several foreign business deals that would lessen the Nixons' financial difficulties. Watergate had proven far less damaging overseas, where the former president's assistance as a consultant and advisor remained in high demand.

Socially, Nixon had begun to venture beyond the walls of San Clemente, only to find things were not quite as bad as he had envisioned. People approached him on the golf course to shake his hand; cheers erupted when he was recognized at baseball games; he hosted dinner parties and people came — old friends and new. One such event resulted in a joking exchange with John Wayne, one of the former president's strongest supporters. After the Duke had presented Nixon with a Boehm horse sculpture, the ex-president held it up and said with a smile, "You never know, one day this horse may gallop again."[14]

Meanwhile, management at the MGM Grand (formerly the Hilton) had been so pleased with Presley's draw in December that they wanted their winning horse back on the track for New Year's Eve. The Colonel smiled and politely declined, having already planned Elvis's celebration at the Silver Dome in Pontiac, Michigan, where he could collect admission from 60,000 fans.

"It was so cold our strings kept changing key," Elvis's rhythm guitarist, John Wilkinson, recalled.[15] The temperature was not the only problem. Presley's center stage was a good four to five feet *above* the platform where the band, orchestra, and backup singers were positioned. Elvis could not see or hear them, let alone interact with them. After numerous trips to the stairs, where he repeatedly bent over to retrieve items from his stage assistant, things went from bad to worse. "I just ripped the seat of my pants," he said, turning to his audience. "Do you believe it?"[16] He left the stage briefly to change his outfit, then joked about it on his return and went on with the show, making certain his fans got their money's worth. "The show wasn't exactly like he wanted it or I wanted it," concluded J. D. Sumner, bass singer for Elvis's backup group, the Stamps Quartet, "but it was a good show nonetheless, and the fans were happy."[17]

Once Presley left the stage, the biggest smile came from the Colonel, who danced happily off to the bank. His boy had broken Led Zeppelin's box office record for a one-night gig at an indoor stadium, grossing a hefty $800,000.

Elvis spent his forty-first birthday snowmobiling with Linda and his friends in Vail, Colorado, leaving the Pontiac experience behind him. In February, RCA crews set up shop in Presley's den at Graceland, where Elvis recorded his first studio material in 11 months. Twelve new songs were cut in seven days, resulting in the ingeniously titled album *From Elvis Presley Boulevard*, released in May. Graceland may not have been the ideal place, but the material itself, a mixture of heartbreaking love songs — by far his most depressing collection of material to date — proved solid enough to reach the top spot on Billboard's country album chart, selling in excess of a half million copies.

Nixon, too, continued to defy his critics. Indeed, he had won the first round of the post-Watergate battle, no longer feeling the need to hide behind the walls of his San Clemente retreat. But the war had only begun; his efforts to reestablish contact with the White House were met with cool restraint. It was an election year: neither Ford nor Republican party leaders wanted the albatross of Watergate dangling around their necks for all the voters to see.

Pushing senior citizen status at age 62, Nixon knew he could not afford to delay his political resurrection until Washington chose to offer an invitation.

11. My Way: The Lonely Road to Recovery

Since Watergate had done little to erode his reputation abroad, Nixon found himself wondering whether it was imperative that he continue to represent his country in an official capacity in order to advance his quest. Were there, perhaps, similar opportunities awaiting him as a private citizen?

The answer came in February, when he accepted an invitation to return to Beijing in commemoration of his landmark visit four years earlier. As far as the Chinese were concerned, nothing had changed. Nixon received the red carpet treatment for the extent of his visit, which included a meeting with the aging Chairman Mao Tse-tung. Mao had been stricken with a stroke, robbing him of some of his verbal abilities, but the two men conversed via a translator. The gist of their discussion was not surprising. "I said that we must continue to cooperate in seeking peace, not only between our two countries but among all the nations of the world," Nixon recalled.[18]

The resulting publicity upon Nixon's return further strained his relationship with President Ford, but all in all, the good had far outweighed the bad. Nixon's confidence was returning, his goal once again within reach.

Presley, meanwhile, could barely keep pace on the treadmill. March 17 marked the first of more than 90 concerts he would perform on the road in 1976 (in addition to 30 appearances in Las Vegas and Lake Tahoe), ensuring that his bicentennial year would be a rerun of years gone by. As the weeks progressed, it became obvious the star of the show was not the only one who had tired of the routine. Several of Elvis's musicians left for greener pastures — less pressure and more money. Longtime pals Red and Sonny West, reportedly fed up with Presley's drug habit, had begun to take out their frustration on the fans; several incidents resulted in lawsuits that charged that Elvis's bodyguards had used unnecessary roughness when protecting their boss.

Still battling the fat-and-forty headlines, Presley could not afford the additional negative publicity brought on by his bodyguards' antics, not to mention the extra cash required to settle the suits out of court. The solution seemed painfully obvious, at least to the Colonel: Red and Sonny would have to go. Guilty by association, Dave Hebler, a former student of Ed Parker's who had worked his way into the entourage via his friendship with Red and Sonny, was added to the spring cleaning list.

Elated at a new excuse to reduce the payroll, Vernon jumped on the idea. His son was not so sure. Firing Dave was one thing; he had known the man for only a few years. But Red. The guy had bailed him out of trouble many times during their days at Humes High, when Presley had been too small and shy to stick up for himself. Sonny was Red's cousin. They were family. *Were* was the key, Vernon insisted. If they truly valued Elvis's friendship, why did they continue to cause him such trouble?

Unable to fight both Vernon and the Colonel, Elvis finally gave in. The elder Presley agreed to break the news while Elvis dashed off to Palm Springs for a much-needed rest between tours.

Sonny, Red, and Dave were officially cut from the payroll on July 13. Each made a point of denouncing Elvis as gutless for assigning the task to his father. They were "hurt" that Presley had not informed them of the decision personally — an action that they most certainly realized would have been impossible for their boss to undertake, given his personal feelings toward them. Bottom line, if Elvis had been left to do the job, it would not have gotten done. The Colonel and Vernon knew as much as, very likely, did Elvis.

Whether the former bodyguards were more upset over the actual termination of their employment or that Elvis had left the duty to his father remains in question to this day, but one thing is certain: their subsequent actions assured Presley that he had made the right decision. While no one had been seriously injured as a result of the Wests' or Hebler's actions, the potential would have existed as long as they remained on the payroll. Eager to point fingers at their famous boss, each nursed a similar drug problem of his own. Their jobs permitted them to carry concealed weapons. All were short-tempered and proficient in karate. Any of these factors in itself was cause for concern; the combination was a disaster waiting to happen.

Parker showed solid judgment in advising Elvis to fire the Wests and Hebler, but his future vision left much to be desired. Watergate had spawned a list of tell-all books by Nixon's former cronies, none of whom were concerned about the effect their half-truths would have on the former president's reputation. "Those by critics I understood," Nixon later wrote of the attacks in his 1990 offering, *In the Arena* (20). "Those by friends I found a bit hard to take." Did Parker really expect any different from the likes of Red and Sonny, not to mention newcomer Dave Hebler? Or was he simply convinced that his boy was untouchable in the eyes of the fans?

Considering that he could not have helped but witness Presley's physical decline over the past couple of years — and the lack of effect it had on ticket sales — the latter is the most likely scenario. Surely Parker knew his golden goose was on a downhill slide and that drastic measures would be needed to put him back on track. If those efforts proved unsuccessful, then it would matter little to Elvis, who would be in no condition to care about the ugly results of his former buddies' exposés. While on a personal front Parker may have been pulling for Elvis, the business end — always the Colonel's strong suit — dealt in cold, hard reality. Whether Elvis persevered or not, the bodyguards' rumors would sell copy, records, and any souvenir with his boy's face plastered on it. Thus, whichever way the wind decided to blow, Parker was covered. Why go out of his way to reach a compromise that had so little chance of succeeding?

Red and Sonny, meanwhile, cut off and set adrift after years of what they perceived as devoted service, had one thing on their minds: payback. Hebler, sensing the chance to make a quick buck off of the Wests' erratic emotional state, eagerly boarded the bandwagon. Together, these men had a story to tell.

A shocking tale of drugs and sex that would make peoples' heads spin. Attention, world: Elvis is a flawed human being, no longer worthy of his halo, and we're going to prove it. Several publishers who viewed the would-be authors' motives as questionable turned down their potential blockbuster. Realizing they would need an "in" to the business, the Wests contacted several tabloid reporters before reaching an agreement with Steve Dunleavy, formerly with the *Star*.

July proved an even more upsetting month for Nixon. As he sauntered into the kitchen for his usual cup of coffee on the morning of the eighth, he noticed Pat's hand shaking and the corner of her mouth drooping badly. Quickly determining that she had had a stroke, he phoned for an ambulance. By the time she reached the hospital, Mrs. Nixon's speech was slurred, her mouth contorted. The night before, she had just finished reading *The Final Days*, Woodward and Bernstein's sensationalized account of her husband's last days in office, which the former president described as "particularly vicious."[19]

The tragedy was a wake-up call for Nixon's emotions; most likely, his response surprised even him. For the next two weeks, he was at his beloved wife's side every day, reading her some of the thousands of get-well wishes that poured into the hospital, arranging the accompanying flowers, holding her hand, and assuring her that she would be her old self before long—all without the least bit of concern about whom might witness the out-of-character, warmhearted side of Richard Nixon. When he was not consoling Pat, he was a doting father, comforting Julie and Tricia in their time of need.

Months of extensive physical therapy lay ahead, but Pat would prove up to the challenge, just as her husband had so many times before. "Doctors did not do it for her," Nixon wrote years later. "Her family did not do it for her. Her friends did not do it for her. She did it by herself, which is characteristic of her whole life. My critics in the media called her 'Plastic Pat.' What they did not know was that her plastic was tougher than the finest steel."[20]

As the bicentennial summer wound down, Presley's ex-bodyguards began spinning yarns to Dunleavy—unbeknown to Elvis, who pressed on with his grueling schedule. Although his weight had ballooned once again, this time he did not allow the extra pounds to adversely affect his mood or performance. The insulting behavior he had directed toward his musicians the previous summer was replaced by genuine praise. An intimacy with his audience, previously reserved for the smaller crowds in Las Vegas, now also became a part of his normal routine while on tour. He played rhythm guitar during an occasional number midway through the shows, insulting himself jokingly in the process: "People say I can't play the guitar. And they're right."[21]

Several new songs had been added to the repertoire, the most powerful being the emotional ballad "Hurt." Presley's performance of this song alone should have refuted the contentions of some critics that he had lost his vocal ability along with his slim physique. Videotapes show an elated Elvis intent on proving himself worthy of the audience's enthusiastic reactions. Often, he would repeat the song's powerful ending — or the number in full — much to the delight of the spellbound crowd.

As Nixon had learned in the wake of Watergate, however, positive actions rarely overshadow the negative. "Fat and Forty — But Also Sold Out" read the headline in the *Memphis Press-Scimitar*. "He is so busy being an idol," wrote one critic, "that he barely concentrates on his singing."

"He's moving slowly," reported another. "He's got a paunch. He's not the fireball he was."[22]

Perhaps not. Still, with the pressures of Red and Sonny behind him, Elvis entered his October tour a noticeably slimmer, happier man. "He had lost a phenomenal amount of weight in a very short time," Ed Parker recalled after joining Presley on the road in Chicago. "He looked sharp."[23] Videotapes of these tours confirm Parker's assessment. While not the Greek God who had dazzled the world with his *Aloha* special, Presley looked thinner than he had in several years.

Hopeful, perhaps, that better times lay ahead for their top-selling artist, RCA crews returned to Graceland on October 29, intent on gathering enough material for another album. They left a few days later, a mere four songs in the can. Various factors were probably at fault, the most obvious being Presley's exhausted condition.

Although his personal life appeared to be edging back on track in many respects, all was not as it seemed. His on-again, off-again romance with Linda had finally hit a dead end.

There was not a member of Presley's inner circle who did not feel that Linda and Elvis genuinely loved each other; she had proven a trustworthy, fun, and loving companion for years. "We were lovers, we were friends, we were everything to each other," she related during an interview after the break-up. "It was an all-encompassing relationship for an awfully long time."[24]

In the end, it was the longevity of the relationship that caused it to falter. The couple had talked many times of tying the knot during their four-plus years together, yet on each occasion, Elvis had found some reason to put it off. Insecurity and fear of commitment were the most likely culprits. Still smarting from one failed marriage, he felt ill-equipped to deal with the prospects of another. In fairness, Presley had reason to be skeptical, having witnessed the recent break-up of Vernon and Dee. Most members of his entourage had suffered similar fates. The overall lesson seemed painfully clear: marriage and life on the road equaled a recipe for disaster.

Linda had proven far more liberal than Priscilla insofar as her expectations regarding Elvis's faithfulness; from the beginning, she had resigned herself to the fact that he would continue to have an occasional fling. Whether she would have retained this mindset as the second Mrs. Elvis Presley, however, was another question, as was Presley's own attitude toward the situation. Stepping out on a girlfriend, no matter how tasteless, did not compare with cheating on a spouse. Gladys had raised him to believe that marriage was a sacred vow to be honored and respected. He had failed to do so with Priscilla, and the Lord had punished him by taking her away. Why risk a similar fate with Linda?

Given the circumstances, Presley's attitude, while not commendable, does have its own logic. Thompson had left him many times, only to return, professing her love. To date, she had given no indication that the pattern would be altered, even when he persisted in his self-destructive behaviors. But, after all she had given of herself, Elvis was still not ready to return the commitment. Finally, even Linda proved to have her limits.

Following his break-up with Priscilla, Elvis had drowned his sorrows in the arms of new love. The only change to the pattern following Linda's exit was a shortened waiting period. Thompson left for good sometime in late October. (On May 5, 1981, Linda married Olympic decathlon star Bruce Jenner. The couple divorced in 1987.) Within two weeks of her departure, Elvis began to date another local beauty, 20-year-old Ginger Alden. Once again, fellow Humes High classmate George Klein was credited with the introductions.

When comparing a 1976 photo of Alden to that of a young Priscilla, the resemblance is striking. So, too, was the rate at which a romantic relationship developed. Ginger was invited along on the November tour and to Las Vegas for the December gig. She accompanied Elvis to Pittsburgh for his New Year's Eve show, which, unlike the fiasco in Pontiac a year earlier, ranks among Presley's best. Elvis made a point to introduce Ginger to the audience, looking truly enthralled as he asked her to stand so his fans could see her.[25]

According to several inside sources, Presley proposed to Alden in January. In his book, Larry Geller, who had received certification, via mail order, to perform marriage ceremonies, reported the wedding date was set for late summer and that Elvis asked him to perform the ceremony. Ginger claimed the marriage was to have occurred on Christmas and that Elvis planned to make the announcement during his Memphis concert on August 27.

Much speculation exists as to whether the marriage would have ever taken place. Geller felt it was a spontaneous act on Elvis's part, an action he had no intention of following through on. Most members of the entourage agreed, insisting that their boss was never that serious about Ginger. "We talked of his forthcoming marriage to her," Presley's nurse-friend Marian Cocke recalled, "and the main thing he said was, 'I'm engaged, but....'"[26]

When questioned about his son's supposed wedding plans after Elvis's death, Vernon said, "I knew he had gotten engaged, but to my knowledge no date had been set."[27] Presley's longtime friend and stagehand Charlie Hodge took things a step further, insisting that Elvis had made up his mind to end things with Ginger. "Do you remember that old song, 'One Sided Love Affair'?"

Presley reportedly asked as he and Hodge were going over music for what would be the singer's final tour. "I think that's what I've got on my hands with Ginger.... I dreamed I was singing the song on this tour that's coming up. That means I'm never going to marry her."[28]

Alden is the only person who knows the truth, but certainly Presley was a spur-of-the-moment guy, thinking nothing of taking off for a cross-country spin in the *Lisa Marie* at four in the morning because the mood struck him. He may very well have popped the question without having thought it through. If the Christmas date was correct, it left plenty of time for second thoughts. It is not unusual for a person on the rebound to engage in another relationship without stopping for a breath, determined not to make the same mistakes again. If Presley had been brooding over his break-up with Linda, his inability to offer her a commitment, he may have offered that same commitment to Ginger — first, to keep her from leaving him as Linda had done and, second, to prove to himself he was capable of giving what he expected in return.

If Presley had indeed been serious about the proposal, it is likely he began to have second thoughts shortly afterward. Unlike Linda, Ginger was not comfortable traveling with the Elvis Presley Show. Barely old enough to leave the nest, she remained close to her mother and sisters, reluctant to travel for extended periods of time. Insiders claim that the Alden family was a constant source of friction between Elvis and Ginger. This stands to reason, fitting neatly into the seams of Presley's past. Ginger's devotion to her family was probably one of the major qualities that had attracted him to her; on the other hand, he wanted to know he came first in her life.

He soon learned Ginger would not jump at his beck and call. When he requested that she accompany him to Nashville for a recording session in late January, she refused. Elvis went anyway but never left his hotel. Three days later, he returned to Memphis, having never once set foot in the studio.

Much of Presley's moodiness could be attributed to the worsening effects of the drugs circulating in his body. Certainly his ego was still smarting from the loss of Thompson, a feeling that no doubt intensified when he compared her with Ginger; there had been no question in his mind about his ranking in Linda's life. These factors combined with a new problem that had begun to weigh heavily on his mind. Friends and associates had informed him they were receiving phone calls from Red and Sonny, asking for clarification of dates and events. It did not take long to put two and two together. "They're writing a book about me," he told Billy. "And they can make me look bad. I don't care about myself. But if they tell all they know what's Lisa going to think?"[29]

Elvis tried several times to dissuade Red and Sonny from proceeding with the project, appealing to their sense of past friendship, to no avail. They did not want their jobs back, they did not want money. A late July publication was planned, and there was nothing Presley could do or say to stop it.

While the Wests' version of events may or may not have been the case — Elvis was, after all, *the* Elvis Presley, with friends and contacts from the powerful Vegas hotel chains to fellow entertainer Frank Sinatra — Presley decided to let the chips fall where they may. On February 12, he embarked on a tour through the South, performing nine shows in nine days. Several concerts equaled the quality of his October tour, while others were less than adequate. Elvis appeared bloated and ill regardless, the sparkle no longer present in his eyes or smile.

Upon returning home, he must have felt the change in himself. On March 3, he called Ginger Alden and Charlie Hodge up to his bedroom to witness the signing of his will. Vernon, Lisa Marie, and Elvis's grandmother, Minnie Mae, were named as the sole beneficiaries. This unpleasant task behind him, Presley invited Ginger and her sisters to join a caravan of friends and relatives on a spring vacation to Hawaii. In all, Elvis picked up the tab for 28 people. The days were "happy and relaxing," according to Ed Parker. Elvis spent time in the sun, sampled island delicacies, and went shopping: normal things that normal people do. "As the days progressed, I could see the color returning to Elvis' cheeks," Parker recalled. "His complexion had improved, and he had begun to regain some of his stamina.... He was at peace. And for the first time in many months he was thoroughly enjoying himself."[30]

Years later, Ed would speak of the Hawaiian vacation as Elvis's last chance to save himself and admitted that he said as much to Presley in a heart-to-heart talk. "I encouraged him to take a year off and get some rest. I told him he had to, or he'd be dead within a year. Elvis thanked me for being his friend, and promised he would talk to the Colonel about cutting back when they returned to the mainland."[31]

Despite Presley's assurances, Parker doubted that Elvis would follow through, regardless of his good intentions. It was a combination of many things: pressure from Vernon and the Colonel to keep the money rolling in, a feeling of responsibility for the entourage and their families (all of whom were dependent on his income), guilt over firing Red and Sonny, concern about the bodyguards' book, uncertainty over his relationship with Ginger. But most of all, it came down to the same thing that had kept him racing against the wind since he had signed his first recording contract with Sam all those years ago. Elvis was addicted to his fans' love and would not — *could* not — do anything to put their relationship in jeopardy.

And so, upon returning to the mainland, he picked up where he had left off. A concert in Tempe, Arizona, on March 23 kicked off what turned out to be an aborted tour through the Southwest. The energy he had stored up from his island vacation carried him through seven more concerts. The ninth show, set for March 31 in Baton Rouge, Louisiana, was canceled just moments before tip-off, when Presley deemed himself too weak to take the stage. He was flown to Baptist Memorial in Memphis, where he remained for the next four days.

Marian Cocke had stopped coming to Graceland on official nursing business in January 1976, although she had continued to make frequent visits as a friend. The mutual affection between the two probably accounted for her less-than-observant account of Presley's final hospital stay. "He checked into the hospital around 6 A.M. and looked good. I was happy to see him and was given the customary hug and got him settled."[32]

In her book, Cocke went into detail about the time she spent with Elvis during his stay, yet she failed to mention why he had entered the hospital or what treatment, if any, he received. As head nurse of her floor, surely Marian knew a sick person when she saw one, yet there was Elvis, having nearly collapsed on the road a few hours earlier but looking "good." That she could have been blind to what was obviously a very ill Presley clearly demonstrates the power of emotion over logic where the beloved entertainer was concerned. Unfortunately for Elvis, his friends and fans not only accepted *his* denial of the truth, they did everything in their power to perpetuate the fable that their hero was beyond human frailties and would thus live forever.

March had its ups and downs for Nixon as well. Although his book was proceeding on schedule, its completion was at least a year away, royalties even further. Meanwhile, bills continued to accumulate at a frantic pace. Lawyers handling his legal matters threatened to quit unless payment was rendered. Desperate for a quick burst of cash, Nixon found a most unlikely solution: television. British TV host David Frost agreed to pay $600,000 for 24 hours of interviews with the former President.

After viewing the taped results, Frost's producers concluded they had been duped: the interviews were "soft," Frost had not taken the initiative, allowing Nixon to come off smelling like a rose. Frost countered by requesting an additional four hours of interviews, tricking Nixon into believing the extra time would be devoted to his accomplishments in China. Instead, the hours were used to grill the former president almost exclusively on Watergate. Nixon fell on the defensive as Frost came out firing. Sweat dripped from his brow. He stuttered, shifting uneasily in his chair. It was the debate with Jack Kennedy all over again, Nixon versus the cameras. He looked like a beaten man.

Once Nixon acknowledged having made mistakes, Frost pressed him to elaborate. Would he agree that he had abused his power and, most important, would he offer the American people a sincere apology for all he had put them through?

Nixon admitted he had done things "not worthy" of a president. He conceded that he had lied about the cover-up. And for those things, yes, he felt "very deep regret." But beg for forgiveness? "People didn't think it was enough to admit mistakes. Fine. If they want me to get down and grovel on the floor, no. Never. Because I don't believe I should."[33]

What about his friends and associates? Was it fair that President Ford had granted him a pardon while they went off to jail? "I can only say that no one in the world, and no one in our history could know how I felt. No one can know how it feels to resign the Presidency of the United States."[34]

As the end drew near, Nixon turned his moist eyes away from the camera and remarked in a broken voice, "I let down my friends. I let down the country.... I let the American people down. And I have to carry that burden with me for the rest of my life."[35]

Frost had gotten much of what he had wanted. Though he did not realize it at the time, Nixon, too, had benefited from the emotional moment. Finally, he had exorcised the Watergate demons. He was free to move on.

Not as fortunate, Presley emerged from Baptist Memorial on April 4, looking every bit as ill as when he had checked in. Priscilla, at Graceland with Lisa visiting Grandma Dodger when Elvis returned, described a much different patient than Marian had seen. "He called me up to his room. He did not look himself; his face and body were bloated. He was wearing pajamas, which he seemed to prefer these days when at home." Elvis was very much into numerology at this point and, as usual, longed to share his interests. "That night he read to me, searching for answers," Priscilla recalled, "just as he had done the year before and the year before that and the years before that."[36]

Among the disturbing questions: how could Red and Sonny turn their backs on a lifetime of love and friendship? "He was visibly upset," guitarist John Wilkinson recalled during yet another canceled recording session. "He had big huge tears in his eyes behind his glasses. He said he loved [Red and Sonny] like brothers and he couldn't understand why they'd want to stab him in the back."[37] Indeed, if Red and Sonny could turn on him, who was next? Was Ginger in it for the money, too? How could he really know if anyone truly loved him for him?

Sadly, only one sure love came to mind. He took to the road, where he knew he was appreciated, night after night. To this love affair, the bodyguards' book was irrelevant. Elvis had been, and would always remain, a hero in the eyes of his adoring fans.

To RCA, of course, Presley's behavior was anything but heroic. Perhaps the company had forgotten the dismal way it had treated him during the static sixties, when it was content to turn out one meaningless soundtrack album after another, the only concern being dollars and cents. It is unlikely that Elvis forgot, though whether it factored into his reluctance to return to the studio in later years is mere speculation. In any event, it was obvious to RCA that Mohammed was not coming to the mountain — certainly not in time for a June release. Desperate for material, RCA had no choice but to fill the empty slots on his upcoming album, *Moody Blue*, with live recordings. Four such tracks, coupled with the songs that had been recorded at Graceland the previous October (two from February and one reprise from an earlier LP), filled the slots for Presley's seventieth LP (total number of LPs refers to *official* U.S. releases only, and includes several multiple album sets), which was pressed on "limited edition" blue vinyl to draw attention to the title tune. Copies were rushed to stores in June. Meanwhile, camera crews tagged along to Omaha and Rapid City, collecting footage for the Colonel's latest venture, *Elvis in Concert*, a television special set to air on CBS in the fall.

The month of July gave Presley his first extended break since January but, rather than enjoy the peace and quiet, he tangled with another round of stress. On August 1, initial copies of *Elvis: What Happened?* hit bookshelves across the nation. Supermarket tabloids featured excerpts from the sure-to-be bestseller, spicing up their copy with recent photos of a very fatigued, overweight Elvis. "The book was a distortion," noted Jerry Hopkins, rock critic and author of the 1971 best-selling Presley biography *Elvis*. "A bitter diatribe without perspective or compassion, motivated by a wish to get even and rich. It was perfect for its gossipy time and perfect in its timing."[38]

Not so, claimed the Wests and Hebler, who insisted they were not out for revenge. Rather, just the opposite was true. By bringing Presley's weaknesses to the surface, flaunting them for all to see, they were, in effect, helping Elvis face his problem — the first step toward healing. "He will read and he will get hopping mad at us because he will know that every word is the truth," Sonny West said when questions arose regarding the motive behind the book. "Maybe, just maybe, it will do some good."[39]

Not a bad idea in theory, perhaps. The trouble was that the writers had blended so much fiction into their facts it was impossible to distinguish where one left off and the other began. Numerous contradictions crept into the text. The authors complained about how poorly Elvis had paid them over the years, then went on to describe the lavish gifts they had received while in his employ. Presley was described as cold and uncaring yet thoughtful enough to pay the living expenses of his employees and their families with no questions asked. Professing their devotion, Red, Sonny, and Dave spoke of listening intently while their boss discussed his religious and philosophical beliefs, only to admit they would gather together later and share a good laugh about how they had fooled him into believing they were actually interested. In the ultimate show of hypocrisy, they blasted Presley for his drug addiction while admitting their own. "We were there, right in with him," Sonny said. "Don't get the idea we're angels."[40] Indeed. Nor was the good Dr. Nick, whom the Wests patted on the back throughout their text for the outstanding job he did, keeping a watchful, caring eye on Presley's habit. The same good doctor who had prescribed more than 5,000 pills for Elvis and his traveling entourage from January 1977 through August 15.[41]

The lone bright spot during Presley's summer vacation was a visit from Lisa, her first extended stay at Graceland without her mother since the divorce. Priscilla, well aware of the betrayal by Elvis's friends, had agreed to the proposed three-week visit, hoping it would raise his spirits. The strategy proved successful. Elvis played with his nine-year-old daughter every day, raced around with her in golf carts, and took her shopping, to the movies, and to the amusement park.

As the mid–August tour approached — the first time Presley would face his fans since the release of the bodyguards' book — he felt up to the challenge. "We'll just have to show 'em how wrong they are," he told his security man, Dick Grob, referring to critics' reaction toward the expose. His remarks came amid-last minute instructions to locate the words and music to several new songs Presley planned to add to his upcoming concerts. With a confident smile, he assured Grob, "We'll make this the best tour ever."[42]

Whether Presley would have made good on his pledge, no one will ever know. Unable to sleep, he bid Ginger goodnight and retired to his lounge chair in the bathroom to explore Larry Geller's latest gift, *The Scientific Search for the Face of Jesus*. The time, according to Ginger, was about 9 A.M. Some four hours later, Alden found him lying face down on the carpeted floor, Geller's open book at his side. After frantic attempts to revive him failed, Presley was rushed to Baptist Memorial, where doctors worked for an additional 30 minutes to bring the hero back to life. But it was all too little — and much too late.

Elvis was pronounced dead on August 16 about 3:30 P.M. Memphis time, the victim of "cardiac arrhythmia," a result of erratic breathing. In lay terms, he had had a heart attack, came the official word from Jerry Francisco, chief medical examiner at the coroner's office. Francisco stressed that no illegal drugs had been found in Presley's system.

Dr. Nick seconded the coroner's assessment, which came as little surprise considering he had been responsible for all of the "legal" drugs that were found in the singer's body. If it had not been for the eerily timed release of *Elvis: What Happened?* chances are that the extent of Presley's drug problem would never have seen the light of day. As it was, the sad truth unfolded, albeit slowly.

But first, the nation and the world went into mourning. As word of the entertainer's death spread, Graceland was swamped with some 3,100 floral arrangements. Locals wanting to convey their condolences in similar fashion were soon turned away, as every flower shop in Memphis sold out. People flocked to the fallen hero's mansion in droves and stood outside the famed musical gates in mid-nineties heat to pay their respects. Touched by the tremendous outpouring of grief, Vernon opted to permit public viewing of his son's body.

Presley's death was the lead story on two of the three major U.S. television networks during their prime-time news broadcasts that evening. (Only CBS chose to give it second billing.) Tribute shows monopolized the world's airwaves well into the next week, while magazines and newspapers scrapped their regular copy in favor of Presley-related articles. Meanwhile, Elvis's records disappeared from music shops at such a frantic pace that RCA's main plant in Indianapolis, as well as its European factories, went on around-the-clock production to meet the demand.

"Elvis Presley was the greatest legend of the modern entertainment world," proclaimed the president of RCA records. "The legend is lost to us, and all the millions of people around the world whose lives were in some way touched by his music can only be saddened by his death."[43]

Noted fellow entertainer Bing Crosby, "What he did and created was a part of history and it's something wonderful that he's left behind."[44]

From the White House, a somber President Jimmy Carter remarked, "Elvis Presley's death deprives the country of a part of itself. His music and his personality, fusing the styles of white country and black rhythm and blues, permanently changed the face of American popular music."[45]

What the country was not to be deprived of, people soon learned, was the hype surrounding the *image* of Elvis Presley. Hucksters set up shops across the street from Graceland, selling tee shirts, mugs, and just about anything else that could be decorated with the entertainer's likeness to thousands of eager takers. Colonel Parker, working with his new associate, Harry Geissler of Factors Etc. in New York, wasted no time in launching a series of lawsuits to keep such "unauthorized" Presley products off the streets, contending that they demeaned Elvis's memory. Meanwhile, Parker's own company, Boxcar Enterprises, announced a new slogan — "Always Elvis" — promising the fans that, although the beloved entertainer was no longer with them, he would never be forgotten. "Elvis didn't die," he would calmly explain to those who phoned his office in the weeks to follow. "The body did."[46]

The Colonel had never been more astute. The atmosphere of the tragic and bizarre that had surrounded Presley in life showed no sign of letting up. In the early morning hours of August 18, a drunken driver plowed into the crowd gathered outside the mansion gates, killing two fans and injuring several others. Weeks later, Memphis police thwarted an attempt to steal Presley's body from the cemetery, where it was entombed in a white marble mausoleum. The kidnappers had planned to ask $10 million in ransom. Vernon had his son's remains moved to Graceland soon afterward, where it remained under 24-hour guard. Gladys Presley's remains were also moved from the cemetery to Graceland and buried beside Elvis in the Meditation Garden.

As the shock of Presley's death wore off, questions regarding the allegations that had been raised in *Elvis: What Happened?* began to dominate the tabloids. Every soul who had ever known Elvis — or claimed to have known him — was asked about the singer's possible drug usage. Some said yes, while others insisted Presley had never taken a pill in his life. Charging that a cover-up was taking place, ABC news called for an investigation into the circumstances surrounding Presley's death. In keeping with Tennessee law, Baptist Memorial Hospital refused to release the official autopsy, further increasing speculation that all was not as it seemed.

Indeed, it was not. Although Presley may not have died from a direct result of any one drug in his body or even from a combination of prescription medications, all but the most fanatical of his fans have since come to accept that his heart attack, while in itself a "natural" cause, was at least in part the result of years and years of abuse — abuse that could have been prevented, had either Presley or his friends been willing or able to make the necessary effort.

Nixon was not only willing *and* able, he was driven. Even in his darkest hours, "quit" had never been an option. He had noted in his diary on December 7, 1974:

> I simply have to pull myself together and start the long journey back — live through the agony of the balance of the tapes whatever they are; fight over the papers, whatever comes at the trial, and do the only creative thing that perhaps I have left to do which is to write a book — maybe one, maybe more — and to follow it with speeches, television of course where possible, which will maybe put some of these things in perspective.[47]

His memoirs did just that. After he finished the proofs in March 1978, he watched *RN: The Memoirs of Richard Nixon* go on to sell an amazing 330,000 hardcover copies in six months, making it the best-selling presidential autobiography of the twentieth century. Not bad for the "disgraced" president, as he had come to be known around Washington.

Nixon's comeback continued with a trip to Britain that same year, where the "Iron Lady," Margaret Thatcher, welcomed him with open arms, despite the serious misgivings of many of her colleagues. The most notable of four scheduled speaking engagements during this trip occurred at Oxford Union, where the former president was met by an angry throng of 150 demonstrators chanting "Jail to the Chief." Undaunted, Nixon proceeded to deliver one of the most well received speeches of his political career. Two hours later, the once-skeptical crowd rose to its feet, cheering and applauding. For Nixon, the message was nothing new. "So long as I have a breath in my body I am going to talk about the great issues that affect the world. I am not going to keep my mouth shut. I am going to speak out for peace and freedom."[48]

Nixon's momentum could not be stopped, despite efforts by the Carter administration to limit his influence abroad. An eventual truce was brought about by the administration's decision to normalize diplomatic relations with China. Following Carter's public announcement on December 15, 1978, Nixon sent the president a letter, agreeing fully with the decision and outlining possible strategies for dealing with whatever backlash might crop up from overseas friends and foes as a result of pending U.S. action. Carter was impressed — so much so that he invited Nixon to attend a White House dinner for the P.R.C.'s vice premier, Deng Xiaoping, on January 29.

The domestic recovery was further hastened by Pat's insistence that they return to the East Coast so they could be near their new grandchild, Christopher Nixon Cox, born on March 14, 1979. By February 1980, the Nixons were living in New York, a mere seven blocks from the home of Tricia, Ed, and Christopher.

Nixon's next book, *Real War*, became a global and domestic bestseller that summer. The tough-talk policies discussed in the text — a reaction on Nixon's part to the continual build-up of Soviet arms — formed the basis of Ronald Reagan's foreign policy, for which Nixon would serve as an "unofficial" advisor for the next eight years.

In 1982, the Nixons sold their Manhattan townhouse and moved to Saddle River, New Jersey. The new home's price tag of $950,000 served as testimony to his success as an author. While people may have shunned him as a President, they could not seem to get enough of Nixon, the writer. His next offering, *Leaders*, shot to the bestseller list in 1982. The book, which many critics laud as his best, offered the former president's views on the many great leaders he had met throughout his political career. Noticeably absent was any inclusion of Eisenhower.

The following year, Nixon was so anxious to get out his latest ideas that he self-published his next offering, *Real Peace*, and sent copies to various leaders and journalists throughout the world so as to avoid the normal delay involved with a large publishing house. The book, a short 107 pages, advocated updating of the tough policies outlined in *Real War* for the fast-changing times, including a somewhat softer realigning with détente. The New York Times Syndication Sales Corporation picked up the newspaper rights at a book auction. Little, Brown acquired publishing rights to the reprint, which went on to become yet another bestseller.

Between books, Nixon continued his travels abroad: two more visits to China, four to Europe, and two to the Far East. He shared his observations via columns published in such media giants as *Time*, *Newsweek*, the *Wall Street Journal*, and the *New York Times*. His literary success continued in 1985 with *No More Vietnams*, a subjective study of the war. A solid readership kept it on the bestseller lists for eighteen weeks.

In April of the following year, Nixon was invited to address the American Newspaper Publishers Association on world affairs. His speech drew a standing ovation. Afterward, cameras caught him shaking hands with Katharine Graham, publisher of his longtime nemesis, the *Washington Post*. His domestic recovery was complete in May, when his smiling face appeared on the cover of *Newsweek*. "He's Back" the accompanying headline crowed.

Back, and on a roll. *1999: Victory without War* his first book for Simon & Schuster, was published on April 10, 1988. In it, Nixon discussed what he thought future presidents might be able to learn from the positive and negative aspects of his experience in foreign policy. To promote the work, he appeared in an hour-long segment of NBC's *Meet the Press*, then took to the road for a national book tour.

Responding to a new and obviously more receptive public, Nixon turned personal with *In the Arena*. Dedicated to his family, the fascinating collection of essays covered his thoughts on everything from Watergate to his grandchildren (of whom there now were four). "Intensely personal," proclaimed the *Washington Times*. "Perhaps even more than his autobiography, this book invites the reader to get to know Richard Nixon."[49]

Those who made the effort to discover Nixon unmasked liked what they saw. On July 19, 1990, a crowd of 50,000 braved sunny, mid-nineties heat to attend the dedication ceremony of the Richard Nixon Library and Birthplace in Yorba Linda. Nixon had spent some $2 million of his own money to have the home his father had built turned into a museum; the remaining $23 million needed to complete the project had been donated by private funds. Notably absent from the library were Nixon's presidential papers, which were stored in a vault at the National Archives as he continued his battle in the courts to obtain control of their contents.

On hand to witness the historic event were former presidents Bush, Reagan, and Ford, each in the company of their wives. The occasion marked the first time that four presidents — and four first ladies — had appeared together in public. Many of Nixon's former associates were also in attendance, among them Kissinger, Al Haig, and William Rogers. Evangelist Billy Graham and numerous other celebrities rounded out the guest list. "It's a long way from Yorba Linda to the White House," Nixon told the captive audience. "I believe in the American Dream because I have seen it come true in my own life."[50]

Free of the unreasonable hero aspirations that had plagued him for most of his life, Nixon continued to pursue that dream as a much-respected, but notably flawed, human being. Through sheer willpower and determination, he lived to see the result of his struggles to end Communist rule in Russia when the Soviet Union's government collapsed in August 1991. In *Seize the Moment: America's Challenge in a One-Superpower World*, published the following year, Nixon urged that the U.S. make the most of the extraordinary opportunity by supporting Boris Yeltsin's reforms to ensure democracy was firmly established.

"Richard Nixon helped change the course not only of America but of the entire world," George Bush had proclaimed at the dedication ceremony in Yorba Linda. "As the movement towards democracy sweeps our globe, you can take great personal pride that history will say of you, 'Here was a true architect of peace.'"[51]

Nixon never stopped drafting plans for his vision of the future. *Beyond Peace*, completed shortly before he suffered a stroke on April 18, 1994, addressed the major issues facing America in its ongoing role of world leader, both at home and abroad. "We have to build a society that the world can continue to admire," he had related to William Safire, his former speechwriter turned columnist for the *New York Times*, in an interview several weeks earlier. "That's the message I would like to leave for the kids."[52]

Richard Nixon died on April 22, 1994, at the age of 81, having made great strides in relaying that message. Upon hearing of Nixon's death, President Bill Clinton ordered the White House flag lowered to half-mast; the former president received an all-services honor guard funeral five days later.

"He achieved greatly and he suffered deeply, but he never gave up," Henry Kissinger told the prominent crowd, which included presidents and first ladies Clinton, Bush, Reagan, Carter, and Ford. "He loved his country and he considered service his honor. It was a privilege to help him."[53]

Each former commander-in-chief had something positive to relate in his eulogy, but it was President Clinton — leader of the party who had forced Nixon's removal from office — who extended the final olive branch as he stood over his predecessor's flag-draped coffin. "May the day of judging President Nixon on anything less than his entire life and career come to a close."[54]

CONCLUSION
Let the Record Show

One must wait until the evening to see how splendid the day has been.

— Sophocles

    Emotions seal the fate of every character, be it the courageous heroine of a bestseller or the night shift janitor struggling to make ends meet. Nixon's final comeback succeeded because Francis and Hannah had taught him to control his feelings. Presley failed because Gladys encouraged him to cater to his.

    Unable to contemplate life without the love of his adoring fans, Presley relied on chemical stimulation to provide what he thought was expected of him. "There's no place in the world I'd rather be than up here on this stage, performing for you," he said many times during his final years of touring.[1] By then, it was true. Keeping their love had become his only aspiration.

    Losing the presidency to Watergate forced Nixon to search for alternative methods to chase his dream. Had Presley been removed from his protective environment, he, too, would have had to adjust.

    As difficult as life had been for Elvis as a child, once success arrived, his security was never seriously threatened again. Regardless of how bad the movie, his fans paid to see it. No matter how awful the soundtrack, they bought it. His concerts sold out whether he put his heart and soul into the performance or spent 20 minutes talking about karate. If the faithful had stopped turning out when his performance diminished, he would have realized something was wrong and done whatever necessary to correct it. Instead they continued to pledge undying loyalty, granting unconditional approval for his actions.

    Although voters had done the same for Nixon during much of his presidency, the crushing defeats he had suffered throughout his career left him prepared to deal with the negative outcome of Watergate. "Greatness comes not when things go always good for you," he told his associates as he prepared to leave office after announcing his resignation, "but the greatness comes and you are really tested when you take some knocks, some disappointments, when sadness comes, because only if you have been in the deepest valley can you ever know how magnificent it is to be on the highest mountain."[2]

Presley remained on top for so long that he never saw what the bottom looked like. And he was terrified of finding out. As it was, his fears proved well-founded. "This doesn't change a thing," the Colonel said upon hearing the news of his client's death.[3] From a business standpoint, he was absolutely correct: Elvis-as-merchandise became hotter than ever. So it remains today. In the more than 20 years since Presley's passing, nearly every spider has crawled out of its hole to tell his version of what life was like with the King. In death, as in life, Elvis continues to provide.

While the tabloid exposes are likely to continue indefinitely, time has afforded a more positive scenario in regards to Presley's career. As the turn of the century nears, critics have begun to judge Elvis for the legacy he left behind: his music. Remastered boxed sets of his recordings, each spanning a separate decade, have met with rave reviews. An icon of American pop culture, he will go down in history as having reshaped the form of popular music. And rightfully so, for as John Lennon once said, "Before Elvis, there was nothing."[4]

Nixon's long-sought acknowledgment of forgiveness began on the day of his funeral, when President Clinton asked that his predecessor be judged on the basis of his entire career. Whether the media and general public will heed Clinton's call remains to be seen, but history suggests that future generations, free of any direct emotional involvement, tend to judge an individual more on the basis of accomplishments than failures. JFK's decisive action during the Cuban Missile Crisis is given far more space in history books than the Bay of Pigs disaster. Recent evidence proving that Lyndon Johnson supported the Vietnam War not because he believed in the cause, but because he feared Congress would remove him from office if he did not, has failed to diminish his reputation as a leader in civil rights.

Regardless of the negative impact inflicted by the media over the years — or perhaps in part because of it — the phenomena of Presley's and Nixon's popularity continue to expand. The initial release of the photographs and documents provided in the appendix of this book drew an unprecedented 12,000 orders within a few days' time. The "Presley File" has since become the bestselling official document in U.S. history.

A recent Internet search of "Elvis" turned up 96,479 sites, while "Nixon" produced 51,749. A search of the "Beatles" turned up 86,047. Modern-day artists pale in comparison. Michael Jackson pulled up 19,274, while one of today's most popular American rock groups, Smashing Pumpkins, managed only 14,688. On the political end, former president Bush (searching under

"George Bush") pulled up 17,101 sites. "Clinton" netted a massive 1,024,472 hits, though many proved unrelated to the president. When entering "Bill Clinton," a separate search brought up 80,123 sites.[5] (A year earlier, prior to the Monica Lewinsky scandal, the figures for Clinton were 220,944 and 43,649, respectively.)

On January 8, 1993, the United States celebrated the country's first National Elvis Presley Day, which coincided with the official launch of a commemorative U.S. postage stamp that sold out a print run of 500 million copies in just a few months. Presley's stately Graceland mansion, granted a place in the National Register of Historic Places in late 1991, ranks among the top ten museum draws in the country. Attendance has soared from 100,000 visitors during its first year of operation in 1982 to more than 700,000 each year since 1996.

In April 1995, the U.S. Postal Service issued a commemorative stamp for President Nixon, ignoring critics who claimed Watergate should have excluded him from such an honor. The general public appears to agree: the Richard Nixon Library and Birthplace boasts the highest attendance figures of any presidential library, upwards of 500,000 per year. Initially owned and operated by Nixon's family, the historic landmark will eventually fall under the control of the National Archives (as are other presidential libraries) due to an agreement with the U.S. government.[6]

Nixon's museum is also one of the largest presidential libraries to date, containing 22 rooms of permanent exhibits amid its nine-acre spread of galleries, theaters, and gardens. The National Archives plans further expansion. According to the public relations staff in Yorba Linda, one of the library's most popular attractions is none other than a videotape of Nixon talking about Elvis. "Well, he was very flamboyant," the former president admitted. "But as I talked to him, I sensed that basically he was a very shy man."

Presley now rests beside his mother, father, and grandmother in the Meditation Garden at Graceland, the home that epitomized his life's journey. Nixon lies beside his beloved Pat (she died of lung cancer on June 22, 1993) in Yorba Linda, on the grounds where he played as a boy, dreaming of a bigger and better world.

Appendix: Documents and Photographs Pertaining to the Presley-Nixon Meeting

Within this appendix are a number of letters and memos from the days leading up to and following the Presley-Nixon meeting on December 21, 1970. Several photographs taken at the meeting are also included. Unless otherwise noted, all documents and photographs are courtesy of the Nixon Presidential Materials Project, National Archives.

AmericanAirlines

In Flight...

Altitude:

Location:

Dear Mr. President.

First I would like to introduce myself. I am Elvis Presley and admire you and Have Great Respect for your office. I talked to Vice President Agnew in Palm Springs 3 weeks and expressed my concern for our country. The Drug Culture, the Hippie Elements, The SDS, Black Panthers, etc do not consider me as their enemy or as they call it the Establishment. I call it America and

Above and on following five pages: Presley's letter to President Nixon, was composed en route to Washington, D.C., in the early morning hours of December 21, 1970. Note Presley's mention of his meeting with Vice President Agnew three weeks earlier, perhaps the only documented proof that such a meeting took place. Also note Presley's spelling of his alias, Jon Burrows, not "John Burroughs" as later reported in Jack Anderson's column in the *Washington Post* and other secondary sources.

AmericanAirlines

In Flight...

Altitude: ②

Location:

I love it. Sir I can and will be of any service that I can to help the country out. I have no concern or motives other than helping the country out. So I wish not to be given a title or an appointed position, I can and will do more good if I were made a Federal agent at large, and I will help out by doing it my way through my communications with people of all ages. First and Foremost I am an entertainer but all I need is the Federal credentials. I am on this Plane with

AmericanAirlines

In Flight…

Altitude:

③

Location:

Sen. George Murphy and We have been discussing the problems that our Country is faced with. So I am Staying at the Washington hotel Room 505-506-507 - I have 2 men who work with me by the name of Jerry Schilling and Sonny West. I am regestered under the name of Jon Burrows. I will be here for as long as it takes to get the credentials of a Federal agent. I have done an in depth study of Drug abuse and Communist Brainwashing

AmericanAirlines

In Flight...
Altitude:
Location:

4

techniques and I am right in the middle of the whole thing, where I can and will do the most good I am Glad to help just so long as it is kept very Private. You can have your staff or whomever call me anytime today tonight or Tomorrow I was nominated the coming year one of America's Ten most outstanding young men. That will be in January 18 in my Home Town of Memphis Tenn. I am sending you the short autobiography about myself so you can better understand This

AmericanAirlines

In Flight...

Altitude;

Location; 5

~~approach~~ approach. I would love to meet you just to say hello if you're not to Busy.

Respectfully

Elvis Presley

P.S. I believe that you Sir were one of the Top Ten outstanding men of America also.

I have a personal gift for you also which I would like to present to you and you can accept it or I will keep it for you until you can take it.

Mr. President NUMBERS
These are all my PVT NUMBER

BEVERLY HILL	278-3496
	278-5935
PALM SPRINGS PVT #	325-3241
Memphis	392-4427
	398-4832
	398-9722
PVT. #	
Col. P.S. #	325-4781
Col. R.H. #	274-8498
Col. OFF. M.&M	870-0370

WASHINGTON HOTEL) PHONE ME 85900
RM 505-506.
PRIVATE   UNDER THE NAME
AND CONFIDENTIAL   OF JON BURROWS
Atten, President Nixon
Via Sen George Murphy
from
Elvis Presley

MEMORANDUM

THE WHITE HOUSE
WASHINGTON

December 21, 1970

MEMORANDUM FOR: MR. H. R. HALDEMAN

FROM: DWIGHT L. CHAPIN

SUBJECT: Elvis Presley

Attached you will find a letter to the President from Elvis Presley. As you are aware, Presley showed up here this morning and has requested an appointment with the President. He states that he knows the President is very busy, but he would just like to say hello and present the President with a gift.

As you are well aware, Presley was voted one of the ten outstanding young men for next year and this was based upon his work in the field of drugs. The thrust of Presley's letter is that he wants to become a "Federal agent at large" to work against the drug problem by communicating with people of all ages. He says that he is not a member of the establishment and that drug culture types, the hippie elements, the SDS, and the Black Panthers are people with whom he can communicate since he is not part of the establishment.

I suggest that we do the following:

> This morning Bud Krogh will have Mr. Presley in and talk to him about drugs and about what Presley can do. Bud will also check to see if there is some kind of an honorary agent at large or credential of some sort that we can provide for Presley. After Bud has met with Presley, it is recommended that we have Bud bring Presley in during the Open Hour to meet briefly with the President. You know that several people have mentioned over the past few months that Presley is very pro the President. He wants to keep everything private and I think we should honor his request.

Above and on following page: The initial White House "contact" memo, advising Haldeman, Nixon's chief of staff, of Presley's presence in Washington, his request to meet with the president, and his wish to keep the meeting private. Note Haldeman's handwritten remark on the second page.

2.

I have talked to Bud Korgh about this whole matter, and we both think that it would be wrong to push Presley off on the Vice President since it will take very little of the President's time and it can be extremely beneficial for the President to build some rapport with Presley. *You must be kidding*

In addition, if the President wants to meet with some bright young people outside of the Government, Presley might be a perfect one to start with.

Approve Presley coming in at end of Open Hour *H.*

Disapprove _____

December 21, 1970

MEMORANDUM FOR: MR. H. R. HALDEMAN

FROM: DWIGHT L. CHAPIN

SUBJECT: Elvis Presley

[handwritten note: Dep" 21 Butterfield / Presley is / coming in / about / 12:15 PM / today / NEJ]

Attached you will find a letter to the President from Elvis Presley. As you are aware, Presley showed up here this morning and has requested an appointment with the President. He states that he knows the President is very busy, but he would just like to say hello and present the President with a gift.

As you are well aware, Presley was voted one of the ten outstanding young men for next year and this was based upon his work in the field of drugs. The thrust of Presley's letter is that he wants to become a "Federal agent at large" to work against the drug problem by communicating with people of all ages. He says that he is not a member of the establishment and that drug culture types, the hippie elements, the SDS, and the Black Panthers are people with whom he can communicate since he is not part of the establishment.

I suggest that we do the following:

> This morning Bud Krogh will have Mr. Presley in and talk to him about drugs and about what Presley can do. Bud will also check to see if there is some kind of an honorary agent at large or credential of some sort that we can provide for Presley. After Bud has met with Presley, it is recommended that we have Bud bring Presley in during the Open Hour to meet briefly with the President. You know that several people have mentioned over the past few months that Presley is very pro the President. He wants to keep everything private and I think we should honor his request.

A copy of the above memo from Chapin to Haldeman was sent to Alexander Butterfield, an assistant to Haldeman, informing Butterfield that Presley's visit had been approved for 12:15 that afternoon.

THE WHITE HOUSE

December 21, 1970

MEMORANDUM FOR: THE PRESIDENT

SUBJECT: Meeting with Elvis Presley
December 21, 1970
12:30 p.m.

I. PURPOSE

To thank Elvis Presley for his offer to help in trying to stop the drug epidemic in the country, and to ask him to work with us in bringing a more positive attitude to young people throughout the country.

In his letter to you, Elvis Presley offered to help as much as possible with the growing drug problem. He requested the meeting with you this morning when he presented himself to the guard at the Northwest Gate bearing a letter.

II. PARTICIPANTS

Elvis Presley

Bud Krogh (staff)

III. TALKING POINTS

A. We have asked the entertainment industry - both television and radio - to assist us in our drug fight.

B. You are aware that the average American family has 4 radio sets; 98% of the young people between 12 and 17 listen to radio. Between the time a child is born and he leaves high school, it is estimated he watches between 15,000 and 20,000 hours of television. That is more time than he spends in the classroom.

Above and on following page: Bud Krogh's suggested agenda for Nixon during the meeting with Presley. While it appears from Krogh's report on the actual meeting that most of the topics under "Talking Points" were indeed discussed by Presley and the president (see next memo), there is nothing to indicate that any of the "Suggestions for Presley Activities" were ever mentioned during the actual meeting.

Appendix

-2-

C. The problem is critical: As of December 14, 1970, 1,022 people died this year in New York alone from just narcotic related deaths. 208 of these were teenagers.

D. Two of youth's folk heroes, Jimi Hendrix and Janis Joplin, recently died within a period of two weeks reportedly from drug-related causes. Their deaths are a sharp reminder of how the rock music culture has been linked to the drug sub-culture. If our youth are going to emulate the rock music stars, from now on let those stars affirm their conviction that true and lasting talent is the result of self motivation and discipline and not artificial chemical euphoria.

E. Suggestions for Presley activities:

1. Work with White House Staff

2. Cooperate with and encourage the creation of an hour Television Special in which Presley narrates as stars such as himself sing popular songs and interpret them for parents in order to show drug and other anti-establishment themes in rock music.

3. Encourage fellow artists to develop a new rock musical theme, "Get High on Life."

4. Record an album with the theme "Get High on Life" at the federal narcotic rehabilitation and research facility at Lexington, Kentucky.

5. Be a consultant to the Advertising Council on how to communicate anti-drug messages to youth.

THE WHITE HOUSE
WASHINGTON
December 21, 1970

MEMORANDUM FOR: THE PRESIDENT'S FILE

SUBJECT: Meeting with Elvis Presley
                    Monday, December 21, 1970
                    12:30 p. m.

The meeting opened with pictures taken of the President and Elvis Presley.

Presley immediately began showing the President his law enforcement paraphernalia including badges from police departments in California, Colorado and Tennessee. Presley indicated that he had been playing Las Vegas and the President indicated that he was aware of how difficult it is to perform in Las Vegas.

The President mentioned that he thought Presley could reach young people, and that it was important for Presley to retain his credibility. Presley responded that he did his thing by "just singing." He said that he could not get to the kids if he made a speech on the stage, that he had to reach them in his own way. The President nodded in agreement.

Presley indicated that he thought the Beatles had been a real force for anti-American spirit. He said that the Beatles came to this country, made their money, and then returned to England where they promoted an anti-American theme. The President nodded in agreement and expressed some surprise. The President then indicated that those who use drugs are also those in the vanguard of anti-American protest. Violence, drug usage, dissent, protest all seem to merge in generally the same group of young people.

Presley indicated to the President in a very emotional manner that he was "on your side." Presley kept repeating that he wanted to be helpful, that he wanted to restore some respect for the flag which was being lost. He mentioned that he was just a poor boy from Tennessee who had gotten a lot from his country, which in some way he wanted to repay. He also mentioned that he is studying Communist brainwashing and the drug culture for over ten years. He mentioned that he knew a lot about this and was accepted by the hippies. He said he could go right into a group of young people or hippies and be accepted which he felt could be helpful to him in his drug drive. The President indicated again his concern that Presley retain his credibility.

Above and on following page: Overview of the meeting between Presley and the president, as observed by Bud Krogh.

Appendix

-2-

At the conclusion of the meeting, Presley again told the President how much he supported him, and then, in a surprising, spontaneous gesture, put his left arm around the President and hugged him.

In going out, Presley asked the President if he would see his two associates. The President agreed and they came over and shook hands with the President briefly. At this meeting, the President thanked them for their efforts and again mentioned his concern for Presley's credibility.

Bud Krogh

Bud Krogh

Lucy:

Elvis Presley (believe it or not) was granted an appointment with the President on Monday, Dec. 21. He left these autographed photos with the President. I don't think any acknowledgment would be necessary. For your good disposition!

Bev.

Recd. gun previously –

The author of this note is unknown. Lucy is obviously a secretary to the president. It seems likely the photos mentioned are the same ones Presley showed Nixon during their visit; several Presley family photos (Elvis, Lisa, and Priscilla) autographed by Elvis are presently on display at the Richard Nixon Library and Birthplace in Yorba Linda, California.

UNITED STATES GOVERNMENT

Memorandum

TO: Mr. Bishop

FROM: M. A. Jones

DATE: 12-22-70

SUBJECT: ELVIS PRESLEY

Senator George Murphy (R-California) telephoned your office late yesterday to advise that captioned individual who is, of course, the prominent entertainer and motion picture personality, had accompanied him to Washington on a flight from Los Angeles and expressed interest in meeting the Director during his stay in Washington.

According to Senator Murphy, Presley, whom he described as being a very sincere young man, is deeply concerned over the narcotics problem in this country and is interested in becoming active in the drive against the use of narcotics, particularly by young people.

According to Senator Murphy in response to Presley's request, he Murphy, has arranged an appointment for Presley with John Ingersoll, Director of the Bureau of Narcotics and Dangerous Drugs. Senator Murphy advised that he was aware that the FBI has no jurisdiction in narcotics matters but wished to pass Presley's request to see Mr. Hoover along to the Director.

Senator Murphy was advised that the Director was out of the City and not expected to return until around the first of the year. Thereupon Senator Murphy requested that someone from the Bureau get in touch with Presley and express the Director's regrets.

This has been done and Presley expressed appreciation for the call noting that as he had advised Senator Murphy, he was becoming increasingly concerned with the dissident activities and use of narcotics by young people in this country and was desirous of doing whatever he could to be of service in alleviating this problem. Presley noted that his rise to prominence in the entertainment field is evidence of what can be accomplished in this country by the poor and the deprived. He said that his relative youth and his background in the entertainment industry has helped him establish rapport with the younger generation and that in gratitude for all this country has done for him he would like to be of service. In this regard he indicated that should the Bureau

1 - Mr. Sullivan
1 - Mr. Bishop
1 - Miss Gandy
1 - Miss Holmes

GTQ:ksf
(6)

CONTINUED - OVER

Above and on following page: FBI memo from Jones to Bishop, informing Bishop of Senator Murphy's phone call, in which Murphy expressed his impressions of Presley as a "sincere young man." Note the concluding paragraph, "Information in Bufiles," which dredged up the bureau's past information on Presley, all of it negative.

M. A. Jones to Bishop Memo
RE: ELVIS PRESLEY

ever have need of his services he can be reached under the pseudonym of ~~Jon Burrows~~, 3764 Highway 51, South, Memphis, Tennessee, telephone number ~~[redacted]~~

INFORMATION IN BUFILES:

Bufiles reflect that Presley has been the victim in a number of extortion attempts which have been referred to the Bureau. Our files also reflect that he is presently involved in a paternity suit pending in Los Angeles, California, and that during the height of his popularity during the latter part of the 1950's and early 1960's his gyrations while performing were the subject of considerable criticism by the public and comment in the press.

RECOMMENDATION:

For information.

UNITED STATES GOVERNMENT

Memorandum

TO : Mr. Bishop
FROM : M. A. Jones
DATE: 12-30-70

SUBJECT: WILLIAM N. MORRIS
FORMER SHERIFF, SHELBY COUNTY, TENNESSEE
ELVIS PRESLEY
REQUEST FOR BUREAU TOUR AND MEET WITH
THE DIRECTOR

Mr. William N. Morris, former Sheriff, Shelby County, Memphis, Tennessee, telephoned Assistant Director Casper from the Washington Hotel today and advised that he was in town with the well-known entertainer Elvis Presley and six other people in Presley's party and inquired concerning the possibility of a tour of our facilities and an opportunity to meet and shake hands with the Director tomorrow, 12-31-70. Morris indicated to Mr. Casper that Presley had just received an award from the President for his work in discouraging the use of narcotics among young people and for his assistance in connection with other youth problems in the Beverly Hills, California, area.

Mr. Casper advised Morris that the Director was out of the city, however, that he, Casper, would see what could be done to arrange a tour for Morris, Presley and party. Morris advised that he could be reached at Room 702, Washington Hotel, telephone number 638-5900.

BACKGROUND:

By memorandum dated 12-22-70, which is attached, you will recall that Senator George Murphy (Republican-California) telephoned your office on 12-21-70 and advised that Presley had accompanied him, Murphy, to Washington on a flight from Los Angeles and expressed interest in meeting the Director during his stay in Washington.

Murphy described Presley as a very sincere young man who was interested in becoming active in the drive against the use of narcotics, particularly by young people. Murphy indicated that he had arranged an appointment for Presley with John Ingersoll, Director of the Bureau of Narcotics and Dangerous Drugs.

Murphy was advised that the Director was out of the city and not expected to return until around the first of the year at which point he requested that someone from the Bureau get in touch with Presley and express the Director's regrets. This was done.

Enclosures (2)

1 - Mr. Sullivan   1 - Mr. Casper   1 - Miss Holmes   1 - Tour Room
1 - Mr. Bishop   1 - Miss Gandy   1 - Mr. Malmfeldt 1 - M. A. Jones
1 - Mr. Mohr

GTQ:cf (10)

CONTINUED - OVER

Above and on following page: Second memo from Jones to Bishop, advising Bishop of Presley's request to meet with Hoover and tour the FBI headquarters with a party of friends, including Memphis's former sheriff, William Morris. An overview of Murphy's phone call from the previous week is included, along with background from the "Bufiles" on both Presley and Morris. Presley's manner of dress appears to be the main reason his request to meet Hoover was denied.

M. A. Jones to Mr. Bishop Memo
RE: WILLIAM N. MORRIS AND ELVIS PRESLEY

INFORMATION IN BUFILES:

Bufiles reflect that Presley has been the victim in a number of extortion attempts which have been referred to the Bureau. Our files also reflect that he is presently involved in a paternity suit pending in Los Angeles, California and that during the height of his popularity during the latter part of the 1950's and early 1960's his gyrations while performing were the subject of considerable criticism by the public and comment in the press. The files of the Identification Division fail to reflect any arrest record for Presley.

Our Memphis Office advised that relations with former Sheriff Morris were excellent during the period he was in office, and that several men from his department were accepted for attendance at the FBI National Academy while he was Sheriff. According to Memphis, Morris is now associated with a public relations firm in that city, but that he has political ambitions and it is anticipated that he will eventually run for Mayor of Memphis.

Our files and the files of the Director's Office fail to reflect that the Director has ever met Presley or Morris.

OBSERVATIONS:

Presley's sincerity and good intentions notwithstanding he is certainly not the type of individual whom the Director would wish to meet. It is noted at the present time he is wearing his hair down to his shoulders and indulges in the wearing of all sorts of exotic dress. A photograph of Presley clipped from today's "Washington Post" is attached and indicates Presley's personal appearance and manner of dress.

RECOMMENDATION:

That the Director permit someone from your office to return former Sheriff Morris' call and advise him that while we will be pleased to afford him, Presley and their party a special tour of our facilities tomorrow, 12-31-70, that it will **not** be possible for the Director to see them.

December 31, 1970

Dear Mr. Presley:

It was a pleasure to meet with you in my office recently, and I want you to know once again how much I appreciate your thoughtfulness in giving me the commemorative World War II Colt 45 pistol, encased in the handsome wooden chest. You were particularly kind to remember me with this impressive gift, as well as your family photographs, and I am delighted to have them for my collection of special mementos.

With my best wishes to you, Mrs. Presley, and to your daughter, Lisa, for a happy and peaceful 1971,

Sincerely,

RICHARD NIXON

Mr. Elvis Presley
Box 417
Madison, Tennessee 37115

RN/lf/cf/cf

gift

Personal thank you note from Nixon to Presley. The word "gift" in the bottom right corner suggests the president may have sent Elvis something in return.

UNITED STATES GOVERNMENT

Memorandum

TO : Mr. Bishop

FROM : M. A. Jones

DATE: 1-4-71

SUBJECT: ELVIS PRESLEY
WILLIAM N. MORRIS
FORMER SHERIFF, SHELBY COUNTY, TENNESSEE
BUREAU TOUR 12-31-70

        Presley and Morris and six individuals who provide security for Presley visited FBI Headquarters and were afforded a very special tour of our facilities in accordance with plans approved by the Director.

        Regrets were expressed to Presley and his party in connection with their request to meet the Director. Presley indicated that he has long been an admirer of Mr. Hoover, and has read material prepared by the Director including "Masters of Deceit," "A Study of Communism" as well as "J. Edgar Hoover on Communism." Presley noted that in his opinion no one has ever done as much for his country as has Mr. Hoover, and that he, Presley, considers the Director the "greatest living American." He also spoke most favorably of the Bureau.

        Despite his rather bizarre personal appearance, Presley seemed a sincere, serious minded individual who expressed concern over some of the problems confronting our country, particularly those involving young people. In this regard, in private comments made following his tour, he indicated that he, Presley, is the "living proof that America is the land of opportunity" since he rose from truck driver to prominent entertainer almost overnight. He said that he spends as much time as his schedule permits informally talking to young people and discussing what they consider to be their problems with them. Presley stated that his long hair and unusual apparel were merely tools of his trade and afforded him access to and rapport with many people particularly on college campuses who considered themselves "anti-establishment." Presley said that while he has a limited education, he has been able to command a certain amount of respect and attention from this segment of the population and in an informal way point out the errors of their ways. He advised that he does not consider himself

Enclosure 1-4-71
1 - Mr. Sullivan - Enclosure
1 - Mr. Bishop - Enclosure
1 - C. D. Brennan - Enclosure
GTQ:dkg (9)

1 - Miss Gandy - Enclosure
1 - Miss Holmes - Enclosure
1 - M. A. Jones - Enclosure
(CONTINUED - OVER)

Above and on following two pages: Yet another memo from Jones to Bishop, this time reporting on Presley's tour of FBI headquarters. Elvis appears to have convinced Jones of his sincerity, albeit too late.

M. A. Jones to Bishop Memo
RE: ELVIS PRESLEY

competent to address large groups but much rather prefers small gatherings in community centers and the like, where he makes himself accessible for talks and discussions regarding the evils of narcotics and other problems of concern to teenagers and other young people.

Following their tour, Presley privately advised that he has volunteered his services to the President in connection with the narcotics problem and that Mr. Nixon had responded by furnishing him an Agent's badge of the Bureau of Narcotics and Dangerous Drugs. Presley was carrying this badge in his pocket and displayed it.

Presley advised that he wished the Director to be aware that he, Presley, from time to time is approached by individuals and groups in and outside of the entertainment business whose motives and goals he is convinced are not in the best interests of this country and who seek to have him to lend his name to their questionable activities. In this regard, he volunteered to make such information available to the Bureau on a confidential basis whenever it came to his attention. He further indicated that he wanted the Director to know that should the Bureau ever have any need of his services in any way that he would be delighted to be of assistance.

Presley indicated that he is of the opinion that the Beatles laid the groundwork for many of the problems we are having with young people by their filthy unkempt appearances and suggestive music while entertaining in this country during the early and middle 1960's. He advised that the Smothers Brothers, Jane Fonda, and other persons in the entertainment industry of their ilk have a lot to answer for in the hereafter for the way they have poisoned young minds by disparaging the United States in their public statements and unsavory activities.

Presley advised that he resides at 3764 Highway 51, South, Memphis, Tennessee, but that he spends a substantial portion of his time in the Beverly Hills, California - Las Vegas, Nevada, areas fulfilling motion picture assignments and singing commitments.

He noted that he can be contacted anytime through his Memphis address and that because of problems he has had with people tampering with his mail, such correspondence should be addressed to him under the pseudonym, Colonel Jon Burro

- 2 -

CONTINUED - OVER

M. A. Jones to Bishop Memo
RE: ELVIS PRESLEY

        It should be here noted following their tour and prior to their departure from the building, Mr. Morris indicated that Presley had been recentl selected by the Junior Chamber of Commerce as one of the "ten outstanding men' in the United States and that of these ten in a ceremony to be held in Memphis sometime in January, 1971, Presley would be named as the "most outstanding" of the ten. According to Morris, similar recognition was afforded President Nixon some 25 years ago and the late President Kennedy was also a recipient of this award.

        Morris observed that he has known Presley for many years, that despite his manner of dress, he is a sober, clean minded young man who is good to his family and his friends and who is very well regarded by all, including the law enforcement community in the Memphis Tennessee, area where he was raise and still resides.

        Presley, Morris, and their party expressed appreciation for the courtesies extended them.

OBSERVATION:

        Presley did give the impression of being a sincere, young man who is conscious of the many problems confronting this country. In view of his unique position in the entertainment business, his favorable comments concernin the Director and the Bureau, and his offer to be of assistance as well as the fact he has been recognized by the Junior Chamber of Commerce and the President, it is felt that a letter from the Director would be in order.

RECOMMENDATION:

        That the attached letter to Presley be approved and sent.

ST 1171

REC 85

January 4, 1971

Mr. Elvis Presley
3764 Highway 51, South
Memphis, Tennessee 38101

Dear Mr. Presley:

    I regret that it was not possible for me to see you and your party during your visit to FBI Headquarters; however, I do hope you enjoyed your tour of our facilities.

    Your generous comments concerning this Bureau and me are appreciated, and you may be sure we will keep in mind your offer to be of assistance.

                      Sincerely yours,

                        J. Edgar Hoover

1 - Memphis
1 - Las Vegas
1 - Los Angeles

PERSONAL ATTENTION SAC'S: For your information, Presley, accompanied by Mr. William N. Morris, former Sheriff of Shelby County, Tennessee, and a party of six other individuals visited FBI Headquarters on 12-31-70. Presley offered to be of assistance on a confidential basis should there ever be need of his services.

MAILED 3
JAN 4 1971
COMM-FBI

1 - Mr. Sullivan (detached)
1 - Mr. Bishop (detached)
1 - Mr. C. D. Brennan (detached)
1 - Miss Gandy (detached)
1 - Miss Holmes (detached)
1 - Mr. M. A. Jones (detached)

NOTE: See M. A. Jones to Mr. Bishop Memo dated 1-4-71, captioned "Elvis Presley, William N. Morris, Former Sheriff, Shelby County, Tennessee, Bureau Tour 12-31-70."

GTQ:dkg/cl
(12)

A note from Director Hoover to Presley, acknowledging his offer of assistance.

The Washington Merry-Go-Round
THE WASHINGTON POST Thursday, Jan. 27, 1972 D 23

Presley Gets Narcotics Bureau Badge

By Jack Anderson

By presidential dictum, Elvis Presley, the swivel-hipped singer, has been issued a federal narcotics badge.

The emotional Presley was so overwhelmed at getting his own genuine, gold-plated badge that tears sprang from his eyes, and he grabbed President Nixon in a Hollywood bear hug.

The rock 'n' roll star is a police buff who collects law enforcement badges and donates thousands of dollars to police charities. Hearing of this, Deputy Narcotics Director John Finlator a few months ago sought to enlist Presley in the anti-drug fight.

Finlator invited the singer to the Narcotics Bureau for a quiet visit and arranged for the guards to admit him under the pseudonym "John Burroughs."

Presley played the part of the anonymous John Burroughs like he does all his movie roles. He pulled up in front of the Narcotics Bureau in a gaudy Cadillac. Resplendent in purple suit and cloak, with a gold belt buckle and amber sunglasses, he sashayed through the door.

En route to Finlator's office, the elegant Elvis, alias John Burroughs, had half the secretaries in the building oohing and aahing.

Presley readily agreed to cooperate with the anti-drug campaign and offered on the spot to donate $5,000 to the Narcotics Bureau. Finlator gently declined the money, explaining that the Bureau isn't permitted to accept donations.

Then Presley showed Finlator some police badges and asked whether he could have one from the Narcotics Bureau. Finlator suggested diplomatically that he try the FBI. But Elvis insisted he wanted a narcotics badge.

"I can't," said Finlator apologetically. "I absolutely can't let you have one."

Presley's face fell, then brightened again. He said he had an appointment at the White House. "Would you mind," he asked, "if I asked President Nixon for a narcotics badge?"

"That's the only way you'll ever get it, Elvis," replied Finlator good humoredly.

At the White House, Presley was ushered in to see the President. They chatted briefly, then Presley raised the question of the badge.

"See that he gets it," the President directed his top enforcement adviser, Egil (Bud) Krogh. Unable to suppress his excitement, Elvis hugged the startled Nixon.

Krogh immediately called Finlator and asked him to bring a badge to the White House.

"You know how it is, John," Krogh greeted Finlator later at the White House. "I hear you turned him down."

"I sure as hell did," said Finlator, smiling. "Okay, I've been reversed."

When Finlator finally handed Presley the badge and promised to issue him "consultant" credentials, the singer was overcome with emotion, and his eyes became misty.

It was another happy ending for the swivel 'n' sway idol.

Footnote: Finlator recently retired from the Narcotics Bureau to write a book about his experiences.

The Labor Department has refused to allow the son of murdered United Mine Workers insurgent Jock Yablonski to speak to a group of department employees who asked to hear him.

The son, Joseph (Chip) Yablonski, is a Washington attorney who specializes in labor law. He had been invited to appear by the department's management interns. Previously, they had been allowed to hear whomever they wanted.

The young Yablonski was expected to discuss the Labor Department's refusal to intervene when his father begged for help in his campaign against UMW President Tony Boyle in 1969.

When Labor Under Secretary Laurence Silberman heard of Yablonski's invitation he was apoplectic. He ordered that Yablonski be un-invited.

The labor official won't discuss the episode. His reticence is easy to understand. He is the architect of the department's disastrous "boys-will-be-boys" approach to the Boyle machine's crude and corrupt suppression of the reformers who, under the late Yablonski, tried to clean up the union.

Silberman, then the department's general counsel, advised against an investigation of the union election despite repeated documented pleas for action from the Yablonski camp.

Only after Yablonski, his wife and daughter were murdered in their beds did he consent that the department begin an investigation. The probe, of course, quickly turned up evidence of massive corruption and led to a lawsuit by the department to set the election aside. By then, however, it was too late for Yablonski.

© 1972 Bell-McClure Syndicate

Jack Anderson's column, as it originally appeared in the *Washington Post* on January 27, 1972, over a year after Presley's meeting with Nixon. This is believed to be the first public report on the meeting. Note how Anderson's account makes it appear as if the meeting occurred only a few months earlier and as if the idea that Presley become involved in the administration's war on drugs was initiated by Finlator. (Reprinted by permission of UFS, Inc.).

Appendix

January 27, 1972

Washington Post

MEMORANDUM FOR NEAL BALL

SUBJECT: GUIDANCE ON JACK ANDERSON COLUMN - ELVIS PRESLEY

Elvis Presley came to the White House on December 21, 1970. He had informed certain White House Staff members that he wanted to report to the President on some of the activities (this includes financial support and public statements and appearances on behalf of law enforcement) he had undertaken in support of law enforcement throughout the country and of his efforts to fight drug abuse through his public performances.

He briefly sketched for the President his activities and then pointed out how much he loved his country, always felt that he had to do his duty for his country, his friends, and his family. The President expressed appreciation for the efforts which Presley had made and encouraged him to do more. When Presley asked the President for a Bureau of Narcotics and Dangerous Drugs badge, Krogh was asked to look into it. Presley collects badges. An arrangement was worked out where Presley would receive a specially prepared badge from BNDD, with his name on it. (Refer questions on specifics to Justice.)

A few weeks earlier, Elvis Presley had been announced by the Chamber of Commerce as one of the top ten outstanding young Americans, a distinction which was concurrently bestowed on the President's Press Secretary.

Bud Krogh

This appears to be a public relations memo in response to an inquiry concerning Nixon's meeting with Presley. It arrived right after publication of Anderson's column.

DEPARTMENT OF THE TREASURY
BUREAU OF ALCOHOL, TOBACCO AND FIREARMS
WASHINGTON, D.C. 20226

NOV 2 9 1982

Refer To
822255

This is in response to your undated request for information concerning the Certificate of Appreciation awarded to Elvis Presley in 1976 by the Bureau of Alcohol, Tobacco and Firearms.

During the period of 1974 through 1976, Mr. Presley provided one of our undercover agents, who was a musician, a job cover. Mr. Presley confirmed to anyone inquiring that the agent/musician was a member of one of his traveling bands. Although Mr. Presley was not actively involved in any of the investigations, his assistance in this regard made it possible for our agent to develop a number of quality investigations. The certificate was presented to Mr. Presley by the Regional Director of BATF, Mr. William Griffin.

Mr. Presley's visit to the White House in 1970, was not related to his assistance to this Bureau. Although I am not sure, I believe that President Nixon recognized Mr. Presley's contribution and assistance to the Drug Enforcement Agency.

Sincerely yours,

Bob Pritchett
Chief, Disclosure Branch

Letter from Bob Pritchett in response to the inquiry of an Elvis fan. (Courtesy U.S. Department of the Treasury.)

DEPARTMENT OF THE TREASURY
Bureau of Alcohol, Tobacco and Firearms
Washington, D.C. 20226

DEC 22 1982

Refer To
822314

This is in response to your letter, dated December 7, 1982, in which you asked for additional information about Elvis Presley. There were no photographs taken; nor are there any materials available that you could see

We are unable to comment on any of the many rumors, and obviously we cannot identify the agent involved, who is not willing to elaborate on his undercover role. Most of the files are Criminal Investigative files and do not mention or involve Mr. Presley. The fact is Mr. Presley was not aware of these investigations. All he knew was that our agent needed a cover story.

I am sorry I cannot be of further assistance to you in this matter.

Sincerely yours,

Bob Pritchett
Chief, Disclosure Branch

Pritchett's refusal to elaborate on the details of Presley's undercover work. (Courtesy U.S. Department of the Treasury.)

DEPARTMENT OF THE TREASURY
BUREAU OF ALCOHOL, TOBACCO AND FIREARMS
WASHINGTON, D.C. 20226

JUN -9 1994

REFER TO: CM:D:AG
M060794

Ms. Connie Kirchberg
32400 51st Avenue SW
Federal Way, Washington 98023-1936

Dear Ms. Kirchberg:

This is in response to your inquiry dated May 16, 1994, for information maintained by the Bureau of Alcohol, Tobacco and Firearms (ATF) relative to a meeting between Mr. Elvis Presley and President Nixon in the Oval Office.

Since 1982, there has been **no** changes regarding information about Mr. Elvis Presley and/or the meeting in the Oval Office.

The Bureau of ATF has no objections to the republication of Mr. Pritchett's letters of 1982, or the publication of this correspondence with you.

I regret we cannot be of more help to you in this matter. If we can be of assistance in the future do not hesitate to write, or call at (202) 927-8480.

Sincerely yours

Averill P. Graham

Averill P. Graham
Disclosure Specialist

Continued lack of disclosure from the Treasury Department (see paragraph 2). (Courtesy U.S. Department of the Treasury.)

DEPARTMENT OF THE TREASURY
BUREAU OF ALCOHOL, TOBACCO AND FIREARMS

REFER TO: D:LP:D:AG
M102194

Ms. Connie Kirchberg
32400 51st Street Avenue SW
Federal Way, Washington 98023-1936

Dear Ms. Kirchberg:

This is in response to your letter of October 15, 1994 wherein you request information you perceive is maintained by the Bureau of Alcohol, Tobacco and Firearms (ATF).

I regret there is no copy of the certificate of appreciation that was given to Elvis Presley.

We wish you the best in your writings.

Sincerely yours,

Averill P. Graham
Disclosure Specialist

Confirmation that no copy of Presley's certificate is available. (Courtesy U.S. Department of the Treasury.)

Appendix 203

Top: The Oval Office. *Bottom:* Nixon and Presley. (Photograph by Ollie Atlans.)

Top: Nixon and Presley. *Bottom:* Presley and the president with Nixon aide Bud Krogh. (Photographs by Ollie Atkins.)

Top: Nixon, Presley and Bud Krogh. *Bottom:* Presley's bodyguards, Sonny West (center) and Jerry Schilling (right), meet Nixon. (Photographs by Ollie Atkins.)

Notes

Chapter 1

1. Monologue interview, *Elvis Aron Presley* (RCA, 1980).
2. Richard Nixon, *In the Arena* (Simon & Schuster, 1990), 79.
3. Peter Guralnick, *Last Train to Memphis* (Little, Brown, 1994), 14.
4. Elaine Dundy, *Elvis and Gladys* (Dell, 1986); 80.
5. *In the Arena*, 86.
6. Roger Barr, *The Importance of Richard M. Nixon* (Lucent, 1992), 16.
7. *Elvis and Gladys,* 144.
8. *Elvis Presley: The Fifties Interviews* (Magnum Music Group, 1990).
9. *In the Arena*, 86–89.

Chapter 2

1. Richard Nixon, *RN: The Memoirs of Richard Nixon* (Touchstone, 1990), 6.
2. *In the Arena*, 103.
3. *The Importance of Richard M. Nixon*, 9.
4. *RN*, 9.
5. *The Importance of Richard M. Nixon*, 9.

Chapter 3

1. Tom Wicker, *One of Us: Richard Nixon and the American Dream* (Random House, 1991), 16.
2. *In the Arena*, 80–81.
3. *One of Us: Richard Nixon and the American Dream*, 9.
4. *One of Us: Richard Nixon and the American Dream*, 8–9.
5. *The Importance of Richard M. Nixon*, 14.
6. *In the Arena*, 109.
7. *In the Arena*, 97.

8. Jonathan Aitken, *Nixon: A Life* (Regnery, 1993), 88.
9. *Last Train to Memphis*, 19.
10. *Elvis and Gladys*, 105.
11. *Ibid.*
12. Terry Hopkins, *Elvis* (NY: Warner paperback library edition, 1972), 33.
13. *Last Train to Memphis*, 35.
14. *Last Train to Memphis*, 37.
15. *Last Train to Memphis*, 38.
16. *Last Train to Memphis*, 53.
17. *David Halberstam's the Fifties, Volume 5: The Beat*–A&E home video, 1997.
18. George Klein, "Growing Up with Elvis," *Goldmine* (Aug. 7, 1992).
19. *Elvis Presley: The Fifties Interviews.*
20. *Ibid.*

Chapter 4

1. *RN*, 43.
2. *RN*, 69.
3. *One of Us: Richard Nixon and the American Dream*, 61.
4. *RN*, 76–77.
5. *One of Us: Richard Nixon and the American Dream*, 80.
6. *RN*, 103.
7. Roger Morris, *Richard Milhous Nixon: The Rise and Fall of an American Politician* (Henry Holt, 1990), 827.
8. *One of Us: Richard Nixon and the American Dream*, 99.
9. *One of Us: Richard Nixon and the American Dream*, 98.
10. *Last Train to Memphis*, 96.
11. *Last Train to Memphis*, 114.
12. *Elvis Presley: The Fifties Interviews.*
13. Marc Hendrickx, *Muziek Mens Mythe* (Antwerpen: Coda, 1994), 107.
14. *Last Train to Memphis*, 182.
15. *Last Train to Memphis*, 111.
16. *Last Train to Memphis*, 285.

Chapter 5

1. *Elvis: Songs & Statements* (SPA, n.d.).
2. *Last Train to Memphis*, 133.
3. *Last Train to Memphis*, 109.
4. Notes from author interview.
5. *Last Train to Memphis*, 200.
6. *Elvis and Gladys*, 283.
7. *Last Train to Memphis*, 285.
8. *Elvis and Gladys*, 254.
9. *RN*, 146.
10. *RN*, 163.
11. *Last Train to Memphis*, 327.
12. *RN*, 176.
13. Stephen E. Ambrose, *Nixon: Ruin and Recovery, 1973–1990* (Simon & Schuster, 1991), 582.

Chapter 6

1. *Toronto Star*, Oct. 29, 1956.
2. Louis Weber, ed., *Elvis Album* (Beekman House, 1991), 114–16.
3. *Last Train to Memphis*, 474.
4. *Last Train to Memphis*, 427.
5. *Last Train to Memphis*, 446.
6. *Elvis and Gladys*, 326.
7. *Beatles Anthology* (ABC, Nov. 1995).
8. Andreas Schroer, Michael Knorr, and Oskar Hentschel, *Private Elvis* (London: Boxtree, 1993), 37.
9. J. D. Considine, "Elvis Presley: A Look Back," *The Baltimore Sun*, August 16, 1987.
10. *Great Performances, Volume 2* (Buena Vista Home Video, 1990).
11. *Last Train to Memphis*, 437.
12. *Elvis Album*, 139.
13. *Elvis Aron Presley* (RCA, 1980).
14. *Last Train to Memphis*, 448–49.
15. *Beatles Anthology*.
16. Priscilla Beaulieu Presley (with Sandra Harmon), *Elvis and Me* (Putnam, 1985), 187–88.
17. Peter Haning ed., *Elvis in Private* (St. Martin's, 1987), 47.
18. *Elvis in Private*, 127.
19. *Ibid.*, 127.
20. *One of Us*, 178.
21. *RN*, 209.
22. *Simpson's Contemporary Quotations* (Mindscape Complete Reference Library, 1995).
23. *Nixon: A Life*, 284.
24. *The American Experience: Nixon* (PBS, 1997).
25. Billy Stanley, with George Erikson, *Elvis, My Brother* (St. Martin's, 1989), 63.
26. *Nixon: A Life*, 321.
27. *Nixon: A Life*, 340.
28. *From Nashville to Memphis: The Essential 60's Masters, Vol. 1* (RCA/BMG, 1993), liner notes.
29. *Elvis Album*, 232–33.

Chapter 7

1. *RN*, 320.
2. Joan Hoff, *Nixon Reconsidered* (Basic, 1994), 283.
3. *RN*, 493.
4. *Elvis, My Brother*, 42.
5. *Ibid.*
6. Larry Geller (and Joel Specter with Patricia Romanowski), *If I Can Dream* (Arrow, 1990), 132.
7. *Elvis and Me*, 214.
8. David Stanley, *Life with Elvis* (Fleming H. Revell, 1986), 88–89.
9. Proof of this comes from the entertainer's own words, taken from an audience recording of his closing show in Las Vegas on September 2, 1974. After introducing

O'Grady and plugging O'Grady's upcoming book, *O'Grady — 26 Years in Hollywood's Narcotics Department*, to be released later that month, Elvis said, "John just came back from New York, where he had a meeting on this. I have been a member of this organization for five years, the International Narcotics Enforcement Officers Association." He continues, apparently reading from the proclamation he'd been given: "In recognition to the outstanding loyalty and contribution to the support of narcotic law enforcement, this award is a special honor bestowed upon Elvis Presley, a lifetime member of the International Narcotics Enforcement Officers Association. I just got that."

    10. Red West, Sonny West and Dave Hebler, *Elvis: What Happened?*, 313.

Chapter 8

    1. Red West, Sonny West and Dave Hebler (as told to Steve Dunleavy), *Elvis: What Happened?* (Ballantine, 1977), 234.
    2. *Elvis: The Final Years*, 11.
    3. In his book, *Elvis: The Inside Files*, author John Parker claims Presley later assisted Hoover in his frantic attempts to have John Lennon deported from the U.S. Parker theorized that Presley was on a mission to "pay back" Lennon for the Beatles having bumped him off the top of the charts in the mid-sixties. As previously mentioned, Presley joined the group for an enthusiastic jam session in 1965 at his home in California. During the seventies, he cut several Beatles tunes, including "Yesterday" and "Hey Jude."
    4. *Elvis, My Brother*, 108.
    5. *RN*, 389.
    6. *RN*, 476.

Chapter 9

    1. Elvis: His first and only press conference, *Current Audio Magazine*, vol. 1, no. 1.
    2. *One of Us*, 651.
    3. *Nixon: A Life*, 342.
    4. *Nixon: Ruin and Recovery*, 265.
    5. *RN*, 434.
    6. Ed Parker, *Inside Elvis* (Rampart House, 1978), 164.
    7. *Beatles Anthology*.
    8. Trevor Cajiao, "So That's Tutt and That's Scheff — That's Tutt Scheff Anyway You Look at It, Part One," *Elvis: The Man and His Music* (Mar. 1989).
    9. *Inside Elvis*, 28.
    10. *Ibid*.
    11. *If I Can Dream*, 176–77.
    12. *In the Arena*, 18.
    13. *Elvis, My Brother*, 138.
    14. *Inside Elvis*, 83.
    15. Marty Lacker, Patsy Lacker, and Leslie S. Smith, *Elvis: Portrait of a Friend* (Wimmer Brothers, 1979), 172–73.
    16. *Elvis, My Brother*, 231.

Chapter 10

1. H.R. Haldeman (with Joseph D. Mona), *The Ends of Power* (New York Times Books, 1978), 5.
2. *The Ends of Power*, 10.
3. Robert Karen, "Shame," *Atlantic Monthly* (Feb. 1992).
4. John W. Dean, *Blind Ambition: The White House Years* (Simon & Schuster, 1976), 12.
5. *Blind Ambition*, cover flap.
6. *The White House Transcripts* (Bantam, 1974), 134.
7. *Elvis, My Brother*, 182.
8. *Elvis Album*, 259.
9. *Elvis: The Final Years*, 111.
10. Mary Jenkins, as told to Beth Pease, *Memories beyond Graceland Gates* (West Coast, 1989), 52.
11. Bob Woodward and Carl Bernstein, *The Final Days* (Avon, 1977), 89.
12. *RN*, 964.
13. *Elvis, My Brother*, 193.
14. *RN*, 970.
15. *RN*, 996.
16. *Elvis: The Final Years*, 136.
17. Linda Jones, "An Interview with Dave Hebler," *Elvis: The Man and His Music* (June 1995).
18. *This Is Elvis* (Warner Bros., 1981).
19. *RN*, 1027.
20. *Nixon: Ruin and Recovery*, 284.
21. *Elvis: The Final Years*, 95.
22. Audiotape from authors' private collection.
23. *Elvis, My Brother*, 208.
24. *RN*, 1061.
25. *RN*, 1063.
26. *Nixon: A Life*, 522.
27. *RN*, 1084.
28. Trevor Cajiao, "So That's Tutt and That's Scheff—That's Tutt Scheff Anyway You Look at It, Part Two," *Elvis: The Man and His Music* (June 1989).
29. *Kickin' Back* (Live Archives, 1974); liner notes.
30. Audiotape from authors' private collection.

Chapter 11

1. *Memories beyond Graceland Gates*, 52.
2. *Elvis, My Brother*, 215.
3. Julie Nixon Eisenhower, *Pat Nixon: The Untold Story* (Simon & Schuster, 1982), 437.
4. Interview disc from authors' private collection.
5. *Elvis Album*, 270.
6. *Inside Elvis*, 159.
7. *Inside Elvis*, 162.
8. *Elvis: The Final Years*, 137–38.

9. *If I Can Dream*, 198.
10. *Elvis and Me*, 306.
11. *If I Can Dream*, 195.
12. *Inside Elvis*, 158.
13. Marian J. Cocke, *I Called Him Babe: Elvis Presley's Nurse Remembers* (Memphis State University Press, 1979), 143–44.
14. *Nixon: A Life*, 537.
15. *Elvis: The Final Years*, 175.
16. Videotape from authors' private collection.
17. Notes from author interview.
18. Richard Nixon, *Beyond Peace* (Random House, 1994), 4.
19. *In the Arena*, 234.
20. *In the Arena*, 235.
21. Videotapes from author's private collection.
22. *Elvis Album*, 275–76.
23. *Inside Elvis*, 167.
24. *Elvis: The Final Years*, 200.
25. Videotape from authors' private collection.
26. *I Called Him Babe*, 133.
27. "Worldwide Tributes Serve to Lighten Father's Grief," *Commercial Appeal* (Aug. 21, 1977).
28. Charlie Hodge, with Charles Goodman, *Me 'n Elvis* (Castle, 1984), 189.
29. *Elvis, My Brother*, 244.
30. *Inside Elvis*, 185–86.
31. Notes from author interview.
32. *I Called Him Babe*, 127.
33. *The Nixon Interviews with David Frost, Vol. 1: Watergate,* MCI Universal Home Video, 1992.
34. *The Nixon Interviews, Vol. 4: The Final Days.*
35. *Nixon Interviews, Vol. 1, Watergate.*
36. *Elvis and Me*, 310.
37. *Elvis: The Final Years*, 208.
38. *Elvis: The Final Years*, 232.
39. *Elvis: What Happened?* cover notes, introduction.
40. *Elvis: What Happened?* 189.
41. *Elvis: The Final Years*, 257.
42. *Elvis: The Final Years*, 235.
43. Anne E. Nixon, *Elvis 10 Years After* (Heanor Record Centre, 1986), 116.
44. "Elvis: Scrapbook of an Era," *Chicago Tribune* (Aug. 21, 1977).
45. AP news reports (August 16, 1977).
46. *Elvis: The Final Years*, 256.
47. *Nixon: A Life*, 535.
48. *Nixon: A Life*, 547.
49. *In the Arena* (Pocket Books, NY, 1991), n. p.
50. *Nixon: Ruin and Recovery*, 580.
51. *Nixon: A Life*, 567.
52. William Safire, "Richard M. Nixon on the Record: Now It Can Be Told," *Seattle Post-Intelligencer*, April 29, 1994.
53. CNN news broadcast (Apr. 27, 1994).
54. Ibid.

Conclusion

1. Audio tapes from author's private collection.
2. *Nixon: The American Experience* (PBS, 1997).
3. Jane and Michael Stern, *Elvis World* (New York: Alfred A. Knopf, 1987), 67.
4. Sid Shaw, *Elvis in Quotes* (Elvisly Yours LTD, London), 54.
5. Figures compiled on Oct. 12, 1998, using the popular InfoSeek search engine.
6. The deal, which affords Nixon's estate monetary compensation in exchange for relinquishing control of the library, stems from a 1992 U.S. Court of Appeals decision ruling that Nixon, "like every other President before him, has a compensable property interest in his presidential papers." Currently, Nixon's presidential papers are stored at the National Archives in College Park, Maryland. Dubbed the "Nixon Project," the catalog includes some 44 million pages of documents and 4,000 hours of the secretly recorded White House tapes. Kept on the grounds of the Nixon museum in Yorba Linda in a special archives building are Nixon's private pre- and post-presidential papers.

Select Bibliography

Books

Aitken, Jonathan. *Nixon: A Life*. Washington, D.C.: Regnery, 1993.
Ambrose, Stephen E. *Nixon: Ruin and Recovery, 1973–1990*. New York: Simon & Schuster, 1991.
_____. *Nixon: The Triumph of a Politician, 1962–72*. New York: Simon & Schuster, 1989.
Barr, Roger. *The Importance of Richard M. Nixon*. San Diego: Lucent, 1992.
Bly, Robert. *Iron John*. New York: Vintage, 1992.
Campbell, Joseph. *The Hero with a Thousand Faces*. 2d ed. Princeton: Princeton University Press, 3rd Printing, 1973 (paperback).
Cocke, Marian J. *I Called Him Babe*. Memphis: Memphis State University Press, 1979.
Dean, John W. *Blind Ambition: The White House Years*. New York: Simon & Schuster, 1976.
Dundy, Elaine. *Elvis and Gladys*. New York: Dell, 1995 (first paperback print, 1996).
Edwards, Michael. *Priscilla, Elvis, and Me*. New York: St. Martin's, 1988.
Ehrlichman, John. *Witness to Power: The Nixon Years*. New York: Simon & Schuster, 1982.
Eisenhower, Julie Nixon. *Pat Nixon: The Untold Story*. New York: Simon & Schuster, 1982.
Geller, Larry. *If I Can Dream*. London: Arrow, 1990.
Guralnick, Peter. *Last Train to Memphis*. New York: Little, Brown, 1994.
Haldeman, H. R. (with Joseph DiMona). *The Ends of Power*. New York: New York Times Books, 1978.
Haning, Peter, ed. *Elvis in Private*. New York: St. Martin's, 1987.
Hendrickx, Marc. *Muziek Mens Myth*. Antwerp: Coda, 1994.
Hodge, Charlie (with Charles Goodman). *Me 'n Elvis*. Memphis: Castle, 1984.
Hoff, Joan. *Nixon Reconsidered*. New York: Basic, 1994.
Hopkins, Jerry. *Elvis: A Biography*. New York: Warner, 1972.
_____. *Elvis: The Final Years*. London: W.H. Allen and Co., 1980.
Jenkins, Mary. *Memories Beyond Graceland Gates*. West Coast, 1989.
Kissinger, Henry. *White House Years*. New York: Little, Brown, 1979.
Krogh, Bud. *The Day Elvis Met Nixon*. Bellevue, WA: Pejama, 1994.
Lacker, Marty. *Elvis: Portrait of a Friend*. Memphis: Wimmer Brothers, 1979.
Morris, Roger. *Richard Milhous Nixon: The Rise and Fall of an American Politician*. New York: Henry Holt, 1990.

New York Times. *The White House Transcripts*. Gerald Gold, general ed. New York: Bantam, 1974.
Nixon, Anne E. *Elvis 10 Years After*. Heanor Record Centre, 1986.
Nixon, Richard. *Beyond Peace*. New York: Random House, 1994.
_____. *In the Arena*. New York: Simon & Schuster, 1990.
_____. *Leaders*. Warner, 1982.
_____. *RN: The Memoirs of Richard Nixon*. NY: First Touchtone Edition, New York, 1990.
_____. *Six Crises*. W. H. Allen, 1962.
Parker, Ed. *Inside Elvis*. Orange: Rampart House, 1978.
Presley, Dee, Billy Stanley, Rick Stanley and David Stanley (as told to Martin Torgoff). *Elvis, We Love You Tender*. New York: Delacorte, 1980.
Presley, Priscilla Beaulieu. *Elvis and Me*. New York: Putnam, 1985.
Safire, William. *Before the Fall: An Insider's View of the Pre-Watergate White House*. New York: Doubleday, 1975.
Schroer, Andreas, Michael Knorr, and Oskar Hentschel. *Private Elvis*. London: Boxtree, 1993.
Shaver, Sean. *Elvis in Focus*. Kansas City: Timur, 1982.
_____. *The Life of Elvis Presley*. Kansas City: Timur, 1979.
_____. *Photographing the King*. Kansas City: Timur, 1981.
Stanley, Billy (with George Erikson). *Elvis, My Brother*. New York: St. Martin's, 1989.
Stanley, David. *Life with Elvis*. Old Tappan: Fleming H. Revell, 1986.
Stern, Jane, and Michael Stern. *Elvis World*. New York: Alfred A. Knopf, 1987.
Tunzi, Joseph A. *Elvis Sessions*. Chicago: JAT, 1993.
Vellenga, Dirk (with Mick Farren). *Elvis and the Colonel*. New York: Delacorte, 1988.
Voorhis, Horace Jeremiah. *Confessions of a Congressman*. New York: Doubleday, 1947.
Weber, Louis, ed. *Elvis Album*. Lincolnwood, IL: Beekman House, 1991.
West, Red, Sonny West, and Dave Hebler. *Elvis: What Happened?* New York: Ballantine, 1977.
Westmoreland, Kathy (with William Quinn). *Elvis and Kathy*. Glendale, CA: Glendale House, 1987.
Wicker, Tom. *One of Us: Richard Nixon and the American Dream*. New York: Random House, 1991.
Woodward, Bob, and Carl Bernstein. *All the President's Men*. Warner, 1975.
_____. *The Final Days*. New York: Avon, 1976.
Worth, Fred L., and Steve D. Tamerius. *Elvis: His Life from A to Z*. Great Britain: Corgi, 1989.

Articles

Cajiao, Trevor. "So That's Tutt and That's Scheff—That's Tutt Scheff Anyway You Look at It, Part One." *Elvis: The Man and His Music*, March 1989.
_____. "So That's Tutt and That's Scheff—That's Tutt Scheff Anyway You Look at It, Part Two." *Elvis: The Man and His Music*, June 1989.
Chicago Tribune. "Elvis: Scrapbook of an Era." August 21, 1977.
Commercial Appeal. "Worldwide Tributes Serve to Lighten Father's Grief." August 21, 1977.
Jones, Linda. "An Interview with Dave Hebler." *Elvis: The Man and His Music*. June 1995.

Karen, Robert. "Shame." *Atlantic Monthly*, February 1992.
Klein, George. "Growing Up with Elvis." *Goldmine*, August 7, 1992.

Records, Tapes, Compact Discs

Beatles Anthology, Volume 1. Apple Corps, 1995.
Beatles Anthology, Volume 2. Apple Corps, 1996.
Beatles Anthology, Volume 3. Apple Corps, 1996.
Between Takes with Elvis. Creative Radio and Osborne Enterprises, 1989.
Elvis: Aloha from Hawaii via Satellite. RCA, 1972.
Elvis Aron Presley. RCA, 1980.
Elvis as Recorded at Madison Square Garden. RCA, 1972.
Elvis: Exclusive Live Press Conference. Green Valley Record Store, 1977.
Elvis in Concert. RCA, 1977.
Elvis Is Back. RCA Victor, 1960.
Elvis Tapes. Great Northwest Music, 1977.
Elvis: That's the Way It Is. RCA, 1970.
Elvis Presley: A Golden Celebration. RCA, 1984.
Elvis Presley: Interviews and Memories of the Sun Years. Sun International, 1977.
Elvis Presley Platinum: A Life in Music. RCA/BMG, 1997.
Elvis Presley: The Fifties Interviews. Magnum Music Group, 1990.
Elvis: Songs & Statements. SPA, n.d.
From Elvis in Memphis. RCA, 1969.
From Elvis Presley Boulevard, Memphis, Tennessee. RCA, 1976.
From Memphis to Vegas / From Vegas to Memphis. RCA, 1969.
From Nashville to Memphis: The Essential 60's Masters, Vol. 1. RCA/BMG, 1993.
G.I. Blues. RCA Victor, 1960.
Good Times. RCA, 1974.
Kickin' Back. Live Archives, 1974.
King of Rock and Roll: The Complete 50's Masters. RCA/BMG, 1992.
Moody Blue. RCA, 1977.
On Stage, February 1970. RCA, 1970.
Walk a Mile in My Shoes: The Essential 70's Masters. RCA/BMG, 1995.

> Various audiotapes recorded during Presley's concerts and distributed through private channels also contributed to the content of this book.

Videos, Movies, Television

Beatles Anthology. ABC, Nov. 1995.
Biography: Henry Kissinger: A Diplomat's Life. A & E.
Biography: John F. Kennedy: A Personal Story. A & E.
Biography: Richard Nixon: Man and President. A & E, 1996.
Blue Hawaii. Paramount, 1961.
Elvis 56. Music Media, 1987.
Elvis: 68 Comeback Special. Music Media, 1988.
Elvis: Aloha from Hawaii. Music Media, 1988 (original broadcast, NBC, Jan. 14, 1973).

Elvis Files. Anchor Bay Entertainment, 1990.
Elvis in Concert. CBS, Oct. 3, 1977.
Elvis Memories. Syndicated television broadcast, 1981.
Elvis: One Night with You. Music Media, 1985 (original broadcast; Showtime, Jan. 5, 1985).
Elvis on Tour. MGM, 1972.
Elvis Presley's Graceland. Showtime, Jan. 8, 1985.
Elvis: That's the Way It Is. MGM, 1970.
Elvis: The Echo Will Never Die. Syndicated television broadcast, Aug. 1985.
Elvis: The Hollywood Years. United American Video, 1993.
Follow that Dream. MGM/UA, 1962.
George Wallace. Turner Home Video, 1997.
G.I. Blues. Paramount, 1960.
Great Performances, Volume 1. Buena Vista Home Video, 1990.
Great Performances, Volume 2. Buena Vista Home Video, 1990.
Investigative Reports: The Secret White House Tapes. A & E.
Jailhouse Rock. MGM/UA, 1957.
John F. Kennedy. PBS, 1992.
Kennedys: The Later Years 1962–1980. Shanachie Video, 1992.
Kid Galahad. MGM/UA, 1962.
King Creole. Paramount, 1958.
Lost Elvis Found! The Milton Berle Show. Amvest Video, 1989.
Lost Performances. MGM/UA Home Video, 1992.
Love Me Tender. 20th Century–Fox, 1956.
Loving You. Paramount, 1957.
The Nixon Interviews with David Frost, volumes 1–5, MCI Universal Home Video, 1992.
David Halberstam's the Fifties, volume 5: The Beat. A&E Home Video, 1997.
Richard M. Nixon Remembered. CNN video, Turner Home Entertainment, 1996.
The American Experience: Nixon, PBS, 1997.
Private Elvis: Elvis in Germany — The Missing Years. Merline Group/Lumiere Pictures, 1993.
Rare Moments with the King. Goodtimes Home Video, 1987.
Real Richard Nixon. Monterey Home Video, 1994.
Richard Nixon Reflects. MPI Home Video, 1994.
This Is Elvis. Warner Brothers, 1981.
Wild in the Country. 20th Century–Fox, 1961.

> *Various videotapes recorded during Presley's concerts and distributed through private channels also contributed to the content of this book.*

Index

ABC 164
Abplanalp, Bob 99, 100, 106, 107, 114, 129, 130; history of 100
Agnew, Spiro 80, 81, 87, 88, 126; history 80; resigns 126
Aitken, Jonathan 108
Albrink, Fred 16
Alden, Ginger 157, 158, 159, 161, 163
"All Shook Up" 79
Allen, Steve 49
Aloha from Hawaii (television special) 123
Ambrose, Stephen 57
American Sound Studios 79
Annual Minstrel Show 24
"Are You Lonesome Tonight?" 64
Arnold, Eddy 45, 46, 47
Assembly of God 10, 19, 21
Atkins, Chet 38
Ausborn, Carvel Lee *see* Mississippi Slim
Ausborn, James 19
Austin, Gene 46
Avalon, Frankie 64

"Baby, Let's Play House" 25, 47
Baez, Joan 66
Banke, Bruce 46
Baptist Memorial Hospital 128, 150, 159, 161, 163, 164
"Bear Cat" 25
Beatles 61, 65, 66, 67, 68, 69, 73, 79, 82, 92, 135, 170; break up of band 79; effect on Presley's career 66; history of 65; meeting with Elvis 68
Beeson, Jane 10
Berle, Milton 49, 50
Bernstein, Carl 155
Best, Pete 65
Beyond Peace 167

Bienstock, Freddy 47
Billboard 38, 64, 66, 73, 79, 152
Binder, Steve 78, 79
Black, Bill 23, 37, 39, 40, 45, 47, 64, 65, 78
Black, Johnny 23, 24, 37
Black Panthers 96
Blackwood Brothers Quartet 24, 47
Blue Book Transcripts 132, 133
Blue Hawaii (movie) 66, 73
"Blue Moon of Kentucky" 38
Bonnie and Clyde (movie) 82
Boone, Pat 58, 95
Bork, Robert 127
Boxcar Enterprises 146, 164
Brennan, Jack 144, 151
Brezhnev, Leonid 112, 113, 125, 127
Brown, Pat 72, 74
Brownfield, Lyman 16
Bureau of Alcohol, Tobacco, and Firearms 147
Bureau of Narcotics and Dangerous Drugs 89
Bush, George 167, 168, 171
Butterfield, Alex 125

Cambodia 83
Camp, Mrs. (Presley's teacher) 21
Camp David 97
Capone, Al 96
Carter, Jimmy 164
Carter Sisters 49
CBS 39, 162, 163
Chambers, Whittaker 33
Chapin, Dwight L. 91, 94
CIA 97, 101, 102, 117, 124, 134
Clambake (LP) 73
Clement, Frank 46
Clinton, Bill 168, 170, 171
Cocke, Marian 150, 151, 157, 160

219

Cole, J.D. (Presley's grade school principal) 19
Colson, Chuck 115, 121
Committee to Reelect the President (CRP) 113, 115, 117, 118, 120, 122
Confessions of a Congressman 31
Counterculture 80, 82, 83, 84, 85, 86, 88, 95, 97, 99, 118
Cox, Archibald 125, 127, 129
Cox, Christopher (Nixon's grandson) 166
Cox, Edward (Nixon's son-in-law) 108, 166
Cox, Patricia Nixon ("Tricia," Nixon's daughter) 36, 71, 107, 108, 131, 136, 137, 138, 142, 155, 166
Crosby, Bing 59, 164
Crown Electric 25, 27, 39, 40
Cuban Missile Crisis 72

Dark Tower (play) 16
Dave Clark Five 66
Davis, Edward 88
Davis, Oscar 41, 42, 45, 46, 47
Dean, James 64, 82
Dean, John 115, 121, 122, 123, 124, 125, 132; career history 121; testifies to Ervin Committee 124
Democratic National Headquarters (DNC) 115
Deng Xiaoping 165
Dewey, Tom 33, 34, 35, 36
Dillinger, John 96
"Do the Clam" 68
"Don't Be Cruel" 79
Dorsey Brothers Stage Show 14, 49
Douglas, Helen Gahagan 34
Douglas, Melvin 34
"Down in the Alley" 138
Downey, Sheridan 34
Duke University 15, 16, 20, 30
Dulles, Foster 33
Duncan, Bill 92
Dundy, Elaine 6, 21, 45
Dunleavy, Steve 155
Dylan, Bob 66, 73, 82

Eagle's Nest 38, 41, 45
Easy Rider (movie) 82
Ed Sullivan Show 37, 59, 67
Education and Labor Committee 31

Egan, Richard 59
Ehrlichman, John 116, 117, 121, 122, 143
Eisenhower, David (Nixon's son-in-law) 108
Eisenhower, Dwight 34, 35, 36, 37, 51, 52, 53, 54, 55, 56, 58, 70, 71, 78, 84, 99, 107, 166
Eisenhower, Julie Nixon (Nixon's daughter) 71, 100, 107, 108, 131, 137, 138, 142, 143, 155
Eisler, Gerhart 32, 33
"Eleanor Rigby" 73
Ellis Auditorium 24, 45, 66
Ellsberg, Daniel 101, 102, 111, 122, 124
Elvis and Gladys 6, 45
Elvis and Me 67, 73, 87
Elvis and the Colonel 45
Elvis' Christmas Album (LP), 74
Elvis in Concert (television special) 8, 162
Elvis Is Back (LP) 64
Elvis on Tour (movie) 73, 120, 123
Elvis: The Final Years 89
Elvis: What Happened? 87, 89, 162, 163, 164
Emerson, Ralph Waldo 2
Epstein, Brian 66
Ervin, Sam 121, 122, 124, 125, 126, 130

"Fairytale" 150
"Fame and Fortune" 63, 64
Father of Country Music Festival 24
FBI 89, 91, 94, 95, 97, 102, 103, 116, 117, 122, 124, 134
Fielding, Lewis 102
Fike, Lamar 62
Finlator, John 92, 93, 94
Fitzgerald, F. Scott 3
Flaming Star (movie) 59, 64
Follow That Dream (movie) 66
Fonda, Jane 85
Fontana, D.J. 67, 78
Forbess, Buzzy 22, 24
Ford, Gerald 127, 137, 141, 143, 152, 153, 160, 167, 168
Francisco, Jerry 163
"Frankie and Johnny" 73
Franklin, Benjamin 12
Frees, Paul 89, 92
From Elvis in Memphis (LP) 79
From Elvis Presley Boulevard (LP) 152

Index

Frost, David 160, 161
Gannon, Frank 144
Geissler, Harry 164
Geller, Larry 85, 103, 110, 146, 147, 157, 163; family history 85; rejection by Elvis's group 86
G.I. Blues (LP) 64
G.I. Blues (movie) 64, 66, 73
Giant (movie) 82
Gingrich, Newt 13
Girls! Girls! Girls! (movie) 66
Godfrey, Arthur 47
Goldwater, Barry 74, 75, 76, 120, 134
"Good Rockin' Tonight" 39
"Good Time Charlie's Got the Blues" 138
Good Times (LP) 138
Goodbye Mister Chips (movie) 82
Graceland 60, 63, 80, 90, 93, 102, 103, 108, 110, 125, 128, 143, 150, 151, 152, 156, 160, 161, 162, 163, 164, 171; history of 60
Graham, Billy (Reverend) 76, 167
Graham, Katherine 166
Grand Ole Opry 38, 39, 46
Grateful Dead 82
Gray, Patrick 116, 117, 122
Great Society 76, 81
Grimes, Mrs. J.C. (Presley's teacher) 19, 20, 21, 43
Grob, Dick 163

Haldeman, H.R. 91, 94, 99, 114, 115, 116, 117, 121, 122, 124, 125, 129, 143
Hank Snow Jamboree 49
"Harbor Lights" 37
Harrison, George 104
"Heartbreak Hotel" 49, 65, 66, 79
Hebler, Dave 133, 153, 154, 162
Hello Dolly (movie) 82
"Helter Skelter" 83
Hendrix, Jimi 82
High Noon Round-Up 24
Hill and Range 47, 67, 68
His Hand in Mine (LP) 74
Hiss, Alexander 33, 34, 51, 72
Ho Chi Minh 80
Hodge, Charlie 157, 158
Hoffer, Eric 1
Holden, William 64
Hollies 66

Hollywood Ten 33, 82, 101
Honolulu International Center Arena 123
Hoover, J. Edgar 91, 92, 94, 95, 96, 97, 99, 102, 116; death 116; history of 96; sends note to Elvis 94
Hopkins, Jerry 89, 90, 162
Hopper, Dennis 82
Horack, Claude 16
Hotel Grunewald 62
"Hound Dog" 79, 123
House of Un-American Activities 32, 33
How Great Thou Art (LP) 74
Howes, Arthur 145
Hughes, Howard 149
Humphrey, Hubert 77, 78, 81
Hunt, Howard 102, 115, 116, 117, 122, 124
Huston, Tom 97
Huston Plan 97, 124

"I Love You Because" 37
"I Wanna Hold Your Hand" 73
"If I Can Dream" 78, 85
"I'll Never Stand in Your Way" 27
"I'm Leavin'" 138
"I'm Left, You're Right, She's Gone" 25
In the Arena 8, 9, 167
"In the Ghetto" 79, 85
Ingersoll, John 89, 91
International Hotel 79
International Narcotics Enforcement Officers Association 87, 88
"It Wouldn't Be the Same Without You" 27
"It's Midnight" 138
"It's Now or Never" 64

Jackson State 84
"Jailhouse Rock" 79
Jailhouse Rock (movie) 59
Jamboree Productions 42, 46
Jaworski, Leon 129, 132, 133, 134
Jenkins, Mary (Presley' cook) 128, 143
Jenner, Bruce 157
Johnson, Lyndon 70, 75, 76, 77, 80, 81, 96, 97, 99, 101, 120, 121, 130, 170; death 121; views on Civil Rights 75
Johnson, Samuel 98
Johnson, Susie (Presley's teacher) 22
Jordanaires 45

Keisker, Marion 25, 26, 27, 45
Kennedy, Edward 13, 115
Kennedy, John Fitzgerald 31, 64, 69, 70, 71, 72, 74, 75, 76, 77, 80, 82, 170; death 74; family history 69; freshman congressman 31; 1960 debates with Nixon 71
Kennedy, Robert 77, 78, 81; death 78
Kent State University 83, 84
Khachigian, Ken 144
Khrushchev, Nikita 69, 70, 113
Kid Galahad (movie) 59, 66
King, Martin Luther, Jr. 77, 78, 85; assassination 85
King Creole (movie) 59, 65
"Kissin' Cousins" 68
Kissinger, Henry 99, 101, 111, 120, 121, 126, 127, 137, 167, 168
Klein, George 27, 63, 93, 106, 109, 157
Krogh, Bud 91, 92, 93, 94, 95, 102, 119, 121

LaBianca, Leno 82
LaBianca, Rosemary 82
Lacker, Marty 110
Laos 83
Lauderdale Courts 22, 23, 24, 37, 40
Lawford, Peter 64
"Lay Lady Lay" 82
Leaders 166
Led Zeppelin 95, 152
Leiber, Jerry 65
Lennon, John 61, 63, 65, 68, 73, 83, 170
Lewinsky, Monica 171
Lewis, Jerry Lee 58, 104
Liddy, Gordon 102, 115, 116, 117, 122
Life with Elvis 86, 133
Lisa Marie (airplane) 149, 158
Locke, Dixie 40, 48
Lodge, Henry Cabot 69, 70, 75
Louisiana Hayride 39, 47
"Love Me Do" 65
"Love Me Tender" 64
Love Me Tender (movie) 59
Loving You (movie) 59

M. B. Parker Machinists 25
McCarthy, Eugene 77, 78, 81
McCarthy, Joe 51, 52, 53
McCartney, Paul 65, 68, 73, 83

McCord, James 115, 117, 122
McGovern, George 113, 114, 120
Magruder, Jeb 114, 115, 117, 122
Mansfield, Rex 40
Manson, Charles 82
Mao Tse-Tung 153
Marshall Plan 32
Martin, George 68
Martin, Joe 32
Memphis Press-Scimitar 26, 156
MGM Grand Hotel 152
Miami Herald 115
Midnight Cowboy (movie) 82
Mississippi-Alabama Fair 19
Mississippi Slim 18, 19, 21, 22, 23, 24, 43
Mitchell, John 99, 101, 113, 114, 116, 117, 118, 121, 122, 143
Mitchell, Joni 73
Mitchell, Martha 113
Monroe, Bill 38
Moody Blue (LP) 161
Moore, Grace 60
Moore, Scotty 28, 37, 38, 39, 40, 44, 45, 47, 64, 65, 78
Morris, William 94
Moynihan, Pat 83
Murphy, George 91, 94
Muskie, Edmund 81
"My Happiness" 26

National Archives 130, 167, 171
National Citizens Political Action Committee 31
National Guard 83, 84
National Security Council 97, 99
NBC 74, 78, 79, 123, 167
Neal, Bob 24, 39, 41, 45, 47, 48, 49
Nelson, Ricky 58
New York Times 101, 166, 168
Newman, (Chief) Wallace 15, 43
Newsweek 54, 79, 84, 166
Nicholson, Jack 82
Nichopoulos, Dean (Dr. Nick) 114, 118, 128, 133, 151, 162, 163
1999 Victory Without War 166
Nixon, Alexander 74
Nixon, Arthur (Nixon's brother) 5, 6, 47, 108, 145
Nixon, Don (Nixon's brother) 9, 76, 130, 162
Nixon, Francis (Nixon's father) 4, 5, 7,

Index

9, 10, 12, 13, 55, 60, 77, 108, 132, 142, 169; death 55; employment 4
Nixon, Guthrie 74
Nixon, Hannah (Nixon's mother) 4, 5, 6, 7, 8, 9, 10, 12, 13, 18, 76, 77, 108, 132, 142, 169; death 76; employment 5; expressing affection 7, 8
Nixon, Harold (Nixon's brother) 5, 6, 9, 12, 108
Nixon, Mudge 74
Nixon, Pat (Nixon's wife) 17, 30, 36, 39, 40, 48, 67, 71, 72, 107, 112, 130, 137, 138, 143, 155, 166, 171; death 171; family history 17; suffers stroke 155
Nixon, Richard: accepts nomination for President (1968) 78; addresses American Newspaper Publishers Association 166; addresses students at Lincoln Memorial 83; announces end to Vietnam war 121; brother Arthur's death 5; brother Harold's death 5; Checkers Speech 35, 36, 37, 43; confrontation with Khrushchev 69; converation of June 23, 1972 ("smoking gun" tape) 117; death 168; decides to resign 136; disbarred 143; early debates 13; employment at OPA 17; expressing emotion 6, 13, 31, 37, 54, 55, 72, 76, 93, 107, 108, 136, 137, 138, 155, 161; feelings on Ford's pardon 141; "final" press conference 72; financial troubles 143, 160; fires John Dean 122; first job out of law school 16; Frost interviews 160, 161; funeral 168; handling of Middle East crisis 127; Hiss Case 33; hospitalized 125, 142; "I am not a crook" speech 129; impressions of JFK 31; installs tape recorders in Oval Office 97; learns of Watergate break-in 115; loses bid for governor (1962) 72; loses first presidential bid (1960) 71; marriage 17; music 10, 56, 82; navy years 18; 1960 debates with Kennedy 71; phlebitis 134, 141, 142, 150; playing sports 14; post–Watergate exhile in California 143; reaction to mother's death 76; reelection (1972) 120; relationship with father 13, 55, 60; religion 10, 18, 35; requests resignations of Haldeman and Ehrlichman 122; resignation speech 137; Senate election (1950) 34; signs ABM treaty with Soviets 113; silent majority 84, 132; *Six Crises* 142; South American trip as VP (1958) 68; speech at Oxford Union 165; success as author 165, 166, 167; trip to China 112; trips abroad as VP 68; troop withdrawals 83; Watergate 57, 99, 114, 115, 116, 117, 118, 120, 121, 122, 123, 124, 125, 126, 127, 129, 130, 131, 132, 133, 134, 136, 138, 141, 142, 143, 144, 150, 151, 152, 153, 154, 156, 160, 161, 167, 169, 170, 171; wins first congressional seat 31; wins VP renomination 55; years at Duke University 16; years at Whittier College 15
Nixon, Rose 74
No More Vietnams 166
Nobel Peace Prize 111

O'Brien, Jim 46
Office of Price Administration (OPA) 17, 18, 30
O'Grady, John 87, 89
O'Keefe, Danny 138
"Old Shep" 19, 20, 22, 150
"One Sided Love Affair" 157
Overton Park, 24, 38, 44

Paget, Debra 59
Parker, Colonel Tom 42, 45, 46, 47, 48, 49, 50, 51, 53, 54, 58, 59, 61, 63, 64, 65, 66, 67, 68, 69, 72, 73, 74, 76, 78, 79, 86, 90, 95, 102, 106, 107, 119, 120, 123, 144, 145, 146, 147, 148, 149, 151, 152, 153, 154, 159, 162, 164, 170; control of Presley's recording material 67; history 45; influence on Presley's marriage 73; influence on '68 special 78; negotiates deal with RCA 49; reaction to Elvis's death 164, 170
Parker, Ed 103, 105, 106, 109, 110, 114, 120, 135, 144, 145, 147, 153, 156, 159; history of 105
Pentagon Papers 101, 115
Penthouse 83
Perdue, Bill 16
Phillips, Dewey 37, 38
Phillips, Sam 25, 26, 27, 28, 37, 38, 39, 40, 43, 44, 45, 47, 49, 53, 58, 63, 79, 104, 159; sells Elvis's contract to RCA 49

Pieper, Frau 62
"Please Please Me" 65
Plumbers 102, 111, 124
Precision Tool 23, 25
Presley, Dee Stanley (stepmother) 62, 63, 66, 148, 156
Presley, Elvis: academics 11; attitude on movies 67; birth 3; break-up with Dixie 48; break-up with Linda 156; church attendance 10, 20; criticism of 38, 41, 50, 59, 64, 79, 94, 126, 155, 156, 163, 170; death 163; divorce 109, 128, 139, 143; drafted by army 59; drugs 40, 86, 95, 114, 116, 118, 119, 124, 126, 128, 133, 135, 140, 148, 151, 162; early movies 59; early musical training 10, 18, 21; engagement to Ginger 157; expressing emotion 7, 79, 85, 92, 108, 155; failing health 118, 124, 128, 134, 148, 150, 159, 161; family moves to Memphis 21; feelings on touring outside U.S. 144; films 59, 64, 66, 73, 120; fires bodyguards 154; first guitar 19; first session with Scotty and Bill at Sun Studios 37; first visit to Sun Studios 26; friends' and family members' dependancy on 23, 27, 39, 50, 67, 103, 104, 105, 114, 116, 159; gains stepbrothers 63; girlfriends 40, 62, 109, 143, 157; guns 86, 87, 88, 92; Hawaiian vacation March 1977 159; hires Colonel Parker 49; hospitalized 128, 150, 159; jam session with Beatles 68; karate 103, 105, 106, 108, 135, 136, 147, 148, 169; Las Vegas 87, 102, 106, 138, 141, 143, 145, 147, 148, 150, 151, 153, 157; life in Germany 62; live performances 19, 38, 39, 45, 47, 63, 66, 78, 126, 135, 138, 139, 141, 148, 149, 150, 152, 153, 155, 156, 157, 159; loyalty toward foreign fans 119; marriage to Priscilla 73; meeting with Nixon 92, 93, 96; meets Linda Thompson 109; meets Priscilla 62; 1968 television special 74, 78; obtains narcotic's badge 93; patriotism 84, 85, 88, 92, 118, 123, 146; playing football 6, 24, 135; police badges 86, 89, 92; post-army image 64; reaction to mother's death 60, 61; reasons for Nixon meeting 90; recording sessions 26, 37, 38, 64, 79, 148, 152, 158; relationship with fans 66, 68, 73, 87, 116, 119, 124, 126, 135, 136, 140, 150, 159, 160, 161, 169; religious studies 85, 86, 161, 162; signs will 159; sings at Mississippi-Alabama fair 20; sings for classmates 19, 23; television appearances 49, 63, 123; tours F.B.I headquarters 94; unrealized projects 144, 147, 148; world's reaction to death 163, 164; years at Humes high school 22, 23, 24
Presley, Gladys (Presley's mother) 3, 4, 5, 6, 7, 8, 10, 19, 22, 23, 26, 27, 38, 40, 41, 43, 44, 48, 49, 50, 59, 60, 61, 62, 64, 76, 77, 84, 104, 109, 116, 157, 164, 169; alcohol 61; death 60; employment 4, 23, 26; house on Audubon Drive 50; miscarriage 5; protectiveness toward Elvis 6; reaction to Elvis's fame 41
Presley, Jesse Garon (Presley's twin) 3, 5, 6, 7, 61, 86, 104
Presley, Lisa Marie (Presley's daughter) 74, 103, 108, 125, 128, 139, 142, 147, 151, 158, 159, 161, 162
Presley, Minnie Mae "Dodger" (Presley's grandmother) 62, 159, 161
Presley, Priscilla Beaulieu (Presley's wife) 62, 67, 73, 74, 86, 87, 90, 103, 104, 107, 108, 109, 112, 118, 124, 125, 128, 139, 142, 143, 147, 148, 156, 157, 161, 162; history of 104; moves in with Elvis 67; moves out of Graceland with Lisa 108; relationship with Mike Stone 108
Presley, Vernon (Presley's father) 3, 4, 6, 7, 8, 10, 19, 20, 21, 22, 23, 26, 40, 41, 44, 48, 49, 60, 61, 62, 63, 66, 104, 105, 146, 147, 148, 149, 153, 154, 156, 157, 159, 163, 164; education 4; employment 3, 7, 21, 22; marries Dee 63; suffers heart attack 148
Presley, Vester (Presley's uncle) 19
Prisonaires 26
"Promised Land" 138
Pumpkin Papers 33

Quarry Men *see* Beatles

Randall, Bill 47
RCA 46, 47, 49, 61, 63, 64, 67, 73, 78, 120, 146, 148, 152, 156, 161, 163, 164

Index

Reagan, Ronald 76, 77, 166, 167, 168
Real Peace 166
Real War 166
Rebel Without a Cause (movie) 82
Rebozo, Charles ("Bebe") 99, 100, 106, 107, 129, 130, 136, 143; history 100
"Revolution" 82
Rhee, Kang 135
Richard Nixon Library and Birthplace 92, 167, 171
Richardson, Elliot 127
Rivers, Johnny 106
RN: The Memoirs of Richard Nixon 17, 32, 51, 55, 68, 70, 71, 74, 77, 80, 81, 83, 97, 99, 108, 114, 115, 117, 130, 133, 134, 165
Robinson, Curtis 24, 25
Rockefeller, Nelson 69, 70, 74, 77, 99
Rogers, Bill 99
Rogers, Jimmie 10
Rolling Stones 66
Ross, Bill 13
Ruckelshaus, William 127
Ryan, Pat *see* Nixon, Pat
Ryan, Sheila 143

Sadat, Anwar 127
Safire, William 167
Sahara Hotel 141
Saturday Evening Post 83
"Saturday Night Massacre" 127
Saturday Night Roundup 39
Sawyer, Diane 144
Scheff, Jerry 105
Schilling, Jerry 90, 91, 93
Scientific Search for the Face of Jesus 163
Seamon, Kathy 151
secret fund 35, 36
Seize the Moment: America's Challenge in a One-Superpower World 167
Shakespeare, William 89
Shaw, George Bernard 58
Sinatra, Frank 59, 63, 64, 159
Sirica, John 121, 122, 126
Six Crisis 16
Smith, Dana 35
Smith, Frank 19
Smith, Gene (Presley's cousin) 25
Smith, Lillian (Presley's aunt) 49, 60, 61
Smothers Brothers 85, 90
Snow, Hank 25, 38, 46, 47, 60

Snow, Jimmie Rogers 60
Speedway (LP) 73, 74
Stamps Quartet 152
Stanley, Billy (Presley's stepbrother) 63, 73, 85, 87, 90, 109, 110, 125, 131, 135, 143, 158
Stanley, David (Presley's stepbrother) 63, 86, 87, 133
Stanley, Rick (Presley's stepbrother) 63
Stanley, William 62, 63
A Star Is Born (movie) 147
Starr, Ringo 65
Stassen, Harold 55
Steve Miller Band 95
Stevenson, Adlai 37, 53, 56
Stoller, Mike 65
Stone, Mike 108, 109, 124, 128
Streisand, Barbra 147
"Stuck on You" 64
Studio B 64
Sullivan, Ed *see* Ed Sullivan Show
Summit II 125
Summit III 134, 136
Sumner, J.D. 152
Sun Records 25, 27, 38, 44, 45, 47, 49, 64
"Suspicious Minds" 66, 87
Sweet Inspirations 149

Taft, Robert 34
Tate, Sharon 82
Thatcher, Margaret 165
"That's All Right (Mama)" 37, 38, 39, 40, 66
That's the Way It Is (movie) 73, 120
"That's When Your Heartaches Begin" 26
Thieu, Nguyen Van 120, 121
Thomas, Rufus 25
Thompson, Linda 109, 110, 114, 128, 131, 143, 148, 151, 152, 156, 157, 158
"Till I Waltz Again" 24
Truman, Harry 32, 34
Tupelo, Mississippi 3, 4, 6, 7, 18, 19, 20, 21, 22, 23, 24, 38, 48, 67, 102, 140
Tutt, Ronnie 139

United States v. Nixon 136

van Kuijk, Andreas Cornelius *see* Parker, Colonel Tom
Vee, Bobby 58

Vellenga, Dirk 45
"Victory at Sea" 82
Vietnam 66, 75, 76, 77, 78, 80, 81, 83, 85, 97, 99, 101, 111, 113, 114, 116, 120, 121, 125, 170
Vincent, Gene 58
Vinton, Bobby 64
von Schlegel, Friedrich 9
Voorhis, Jerry 30, 31, 34

"Walkin' in the Rain" 26
Wallace, George 77, 81, 82
Wallis, Hal 59
Washington Hotel 90, 91
Washington Post 94, 115, 166
Washington Times 167
Wayne, John 152
Weathermen 96
Welcome Home Elvis (Frank Sinatra television special) 63
West, Red 7, 46, 62, 88, 89, 91, 94, 96, 153, 154, 156, 158, 159, 161, 162
West, Sonny 88, 89, 91, 94, 96, 153, 154, 156, 158, 159, 161, 162
Westmoreland, Kathy 149
White Album (LP) 82, 83
Whitman, Slim 49
Whittier College 15
"Why Don't We Do It in the Road" 82
Wicker, Tom 35
Wild in the Country (movie) 59, 64
Wilkinson, John 133, 152, 161
Williams, Andy 95
Williams, Hank 18
Wingert & Bewley 16, 17, 18, 27, 29, 34, 71
"Witchcraft" 64
Woods, Rose 126, 127, 129, 137
Woodstock 82
Woodward, Bob 155

Yeltsin, Boris 167
Young, Faron 49
"Young and Beautiful" 150

www.ingramcontent.com/pod-product-compliance
Ingram Content Group UK Ltd.
Pitfield, Milton Keynes, MK11 3LW, UK
UKHW041949140426
5217IPUK00014B/723